Scary Monsters and Super Creeps

Also by Dom Joly

The Dark Tourist

Scary Monsters and Super Creeps

In Search of the World's Most Hideous Beasts

by Dom Joly

**SIMON &
SCHUSTER**

London · New York · Sydney · Toronto · New Delhi

A CBS COMPANY

First published in Great Britain in 2012 by Simon & Schuster UK Ltd
A CBS COMPANY

Copyright © 2012 by Dom Joly

1 3 5 7 9 10 8 6 4 2

Simon & Schuster UK Ltd
1st Floor
222 Gray's Inn Road
London
WC1X 8HB

www.simonandschuster.co.uk

Simon & Schuster Australia
Sydney

Simon & Schuster India
New Delhi

All pictures provided courtesy of the author

A CIP catalogue copy for this book is available
from the British Library.

ISBN: 978-0-85720-764-7

Typeset by Hewer Text UK Ltd, Edinburgh
Printed and bound in Great Britain by CPI Group (UK) Ltd,
Croydon, CR0 4YY

'Scary monsters, super creeps, keep me running, running scared'

David Bowie

For Toast (12 November 1924–2 July 2011):

'The joys of parents are secret; and so are their griefs and fears'

Francis Bacon

Contents

Foreword

Before we start . . . A little admission. This book is not really about monsters at all. Don't get me wrong – I did set off on various adventures around the world to places where 'monsters' were reputed to roam, in the vain hope that I might bump into one. It's just that both you and I know that this was very unlikely to happen – and, even if it did, I was probably the worst person in the world for it to happen to.

In the UK I'm famous for being a practical joker and an accomplished liar. In my first show, *Trigger Happy TV*, I used loads of furry costumes – including a Yeti outfit, in which I scared skiers on a Swiss ski-slope. So if I suddenly announced, in a much-hyped press conference broadcast live around the world, that I had found a 'monster', and then showed footage of said encounter, I might face some incredulity.

Done right I could probably still get away with it, though. Experience has shown that there is little our rapacious news outlets like more than a 'monster' story. Such scoops give them the excuse to endlessly replay blurry, shaky footage (does nobody own a tripod?) and get weird hairy men into the studio to talk about new discoveries of wild weird hairy men.

The former kind of hairy men often profess to be crypto-zoologists. This is a posh scientific name for people who are interested in 'monsters'. A lot of cryptozoologists decide to write books on the subject. Most of these books are incredibly dull. This is because these guys are writing about something that serious scientists don't really take very seriously. So, to show how serious they are, cryptozoologists tend to write long, boring, pseudoscientific books in which they try desperately to prove to a disbelieving world that they are not nutters but actually distinguished men of science.

This is not a book like that. This is a book documenting my year spent travelling the world looking for 'monsters' and getting into all sorts of trouble with the 'super creeps'.

Why do you keep putting the word 'monsters' in quotation marks?

Thank you for asking. It's because I think it would be unfair to describe the creatures I've been after as 'monsters'. The dictionary definition of the word is: 'An imaginary creature that is typically large, ugly and frightening.'

This sounds more like some of my least-favourite British towns than it does anything I was going in search of.

Before I set off on my adventures I wasn't convinced that they were all imaginary. Most were definitely supposed to be quite large. 'Ugly' is a subjective term anyway and certainly not one I'm prepared to throw at an eight-foot missing link. And these creatures are frightening only because we don't know anything about them.

So far they have defeated science and managed to keep hidden(ish) from our modern world. Besides one kind of Yeti none of them are supposed to attack humans. As I set out, it seemed to me that they just want to be left alone to do whatever it is they like to do . . . If they exist at all. Confused? Welcome to my world.

Well, we didn't start this – you called the book *Scary Monsters and Super Creeps*!

Yes . . . I know. I couldn't resist. I'm a huge David Bowie fan and it was just perfect for the title. It sounded cool and I went with it – sorry. But from now on I won't put the word 'monsters' in quotation marks. It would start getting really annoying, wouldn't it?

Why monsters?

I love to travel – it's my obsession – but I always need a purpose. For my last book, *The Dark Tourist*, I went on holiday to the sort of places that most people wouldn't: Chernobyl, North Korea, ski slopes in Iran, etc. For this book I needed something new.

Some people travel the world birdwatching. (Costa Rica, for example, is a place where such nerds go to holiday – it's full of twitcher couples all off to find some specific bird.) Big-game fishermen sail the Seven Seas trying to catch some special fish. I just decided to do the same: to try to find out as much as I could about the Big Six monsters of cryptozoology.

The 'Big Six'?

OK – I don't know why it had to be six. I guess that I was just thinking along the lines of the Big Six when you go on safari.

Some were obvious: Bigfoot and the Yeti were a given; the Loch Ness Monster was another obvious contender, though I was initially loath to choose it as this would hardly be the most exciting of foreign trips.

This left me with three others. I found some stuff about the Mokèlé-mbèmbé in the Congo. This sounded like a proper adventure and, since the big lure of my Yeti-expedition research was reading *Tintin in Tibet*, I thought that the theme could be continued with a *Tintin in the Congo*-type adventure (minus the hideous racism and the murdering of hundreds of animals).

Further googling – sorry, *research* – revealed a story about a monster that lives in the hills around Hiroshima. It's called the Hibagon and one theory is that it's a man who was irradiated in the Hiroshima explosion. This at first seemed the most tenuous of stories but I've always wanted to visit Japan and it's a country with an enormous monster culture – after all, it's the home of Godzilla.

This left me with a spare. I'm married to a Canadian, love Canada and have always wanted to write something about my semi-adopted country, so I chucked Ogopogo into the mix. Thus are adventures decided.

I think my initial interest in monsters came from a book I was given for my birthday as a kid. It was called *Arthur C. Clarke's Mysterious World* and was a companion piece to the 1980 series on UK telly. I loved this book. I read it from cover to cover, over and over again, and longed to go and find out more about the weird Yeti footprints found in the Himalayas and to find the spot where the infamous Super 8 footage of Bigfoot was filmed.

At about the same time a man came to my prep school and gave us a lecture about the Loch Ness Monster. I was transfixed. He showed us footage and photographs of 'Nessie'. Once day, I vowed, I'd go and look for her.

So that's how this book got going. I set off on all my trips with an open mind. I'd really love to think that there was a Bigfoot or a Yeti or even a Big Cat of Cirencester out there. My local newspaper in the Cotswolds loves to run a 'Big Cat Spotted' story every slow news day (there is quite a fat Siamese that sits in the window of a house on Blackjack Street but I don't think that's the one causing the commotion). Once, I . . .

Get on with it!
Oh great: first you ask questions and now you're actually heckling my Foreword . . .

I hate forewords.

Actually, so do I. I groan when I see a big, long foreword before a book. It's just padding. If a book is any good then it doesn't need a foreword. They are usually random, wistful musings from an author desperate for anything to delay him having to face that terrifying moment of actually starting to write the book. If anybody really does have any questions, then ask me on Twitter . . .

So stop writing and get on with it.

Alright. Here it is. I hope you enjoy the adventures.

Dom Joly, Cotswolds, 2012

Ogopogo

'What would an ocean be without a monster lurking in the dark? It would be like sleep without dreams.'

Werner Herzog

I woke up in my bed in my house in the Cotswolds. It should have just been another normal day – but it wasn't. Today was my first day of being a monster-hunter. I woke up the kids and kissed them goodbye in a slightly formal manner, like some Victorian explorer off to deepest, darkest Africa for three years.

'Where are you going, Daddy?' one of them asked sleepily.

'I'm going monster-hunting,' I replied casually.

'What kind of monster?' they asked, slightly more awake.

'It's a lake monster in Canada . . . Sort of like a dinosaur-type thing . . .' I didn't sound very clear on the matter.

'Is it dangerous?' asked Jackson, my seven-year-old son.

'No, I don't think so,' I replied in a manner intended to convey that danger was not really something that bothered me.

'Then it's not a monster.' He seemed very sure of himself on this fact.

'Well . . . Yes, actually, it is . . . But anyway . . . Bye . . .' I wandered downstairs feeling slightly deflated and made myself a very strong coffee from the Nespresso machine that has turned my wife Stacey and me into caffeine junkies. We have terrible cold-turkey days when we run out of the little coffee capsules and hang around looking out of the window, waiting for the man. (The Nespresso man, who'll deliver our next box of coffee crack.) I sipped my perfectly frothed macchiato and started to worry a little. For someone who was off monster-hunting I felt distinctly spoilt and unprepared. Should I have gone to Millets? What did a monster-hunter need? A knife would have been good but I was flying to Canada so it wouldn't be allowed on the plane. What about a long stick? They probably wouldn't let that on board either. What did a monster-hunter wear? I quite fancied having some sort of uniform – something a touch Indiana-Jones-ish – but I'd just packed my usual Carhartt gear, the uniform of the overgrown London media wanker who refuses to grow old gracefully. Someone on Twitter once said that they thought men like me dress in the same manner as we did at our sexual peak. I'm not sure I've ever had a sexual peak but I knew what she was saying.

It was exciting: this was the first of six trips around the world in pursuit of six legendary creatures. I had decided to go to British Columbia first. It was probably the most civilized of all my destinations and I still wasn't entirely sure what the form was for monster-hunting. I was looking at this trip as a bit of a trainer mission before I hit the more difficult ones.

My destination was the Okanagan Valley in British Columbia – a popular summer-vacation destination for West Coast Canadians. Lake Okanagan, an eighty-mile-long glacial lake that runs the length of the whole valley, is supposedly the home of Ogopogo: a monster that has been chronicled and talked about for more than 200 years. Ogopogo is pretty big news in Canada – every bit as famous as Nessie.

I said goodbye to Stacey in the manner of a hunter-gatherer off to collect meat for the family: I hit her over the head with a large club and had my way with her. Actually, no, I didn't. I kissed her and told her I'd be back in two weeks . . .

At Heathrow I readied myself to face the worst part of any journey: airport security. Obviously I don't want to be blown out of the sky but you can't help but look at the 'security specialists' screening you in international airports and immediately think, *Failed traffic wardens.*

I'd tried to think ahead and had bought a couple of see-thru washbags so that I didn't have to put all my liquids into the see-thru bags that are always too tight and that BAA now try to sell you for £1 a go. I shouldn't have bothered. A fourteen-year-old boy with acne and an ill-fitting uniform demanded that I take all the liquids out of my see-thru washbag and put them all into one of their see-thru bags. How this might prevent terrorism was beyond both him and me.

'We are just here to help you stay safe . . .' is the repetitive mantra of airport security staff. They're not, however, there to explain anything. I'd be concerned leaving a sandwich assembly in their hands yet this is the first line of defence against global terrorism. God help us all.

Once I was through the X-ray machine a twelve-year-old Indian woman told me that I could put the liquids back in my own see-thru bag. Again, there was no explanation.

I was then free to set about my preferred, slightly OCD departure routine. First I went to buy *Vanity Fair*. As usual, I couldn't find it. As usual, I eventually checked the Women's Lifestyle section and, sure enough, there it was. *It's not a women's lifestyle magazine!* It's a fabulously aspirational monthly fix of American snobbery, travel and good journalism. I gave up complaining about this kind of misrepresentation long ago, though. The people manning checkout counters are the younger, idiot brothers of the 'security specialists'.

I now headed for the ludicrously overpriced seafood bar to have my usual prawn cocktail and half-bottle of house champagne. This has become a ritual. If a meal could be my last on earth then I want it to be good and hang the eye-watering cost.

I was slightly tipsy as I boarded the plane to Vancouver. It wasn't very full so I ignored my assigned seat number and grabbed one in the front row with loads of legroom. This is always a tense time, waiting for the doors to close and the certainty that the row's yours. Now, at the very last minute, a bald man bustled on board and plonked himself down right next to me. I suspected that he was doing the same as me, and this wasn't his assigned seat, but I was in a fairly weak negotiating position. My new neighbour started reading Lionel Shriver's *We Need to Talk About Kevin* while subtly trying to gain control of our mutual armrest. Unfortunately for him, he had little idea that he was taking on a hardened veteran of elbow wars. For a good twenty minutes or so we jockeyed for position while studiously 'ignoring' each other. I could feel his growing hatred of me and realized that this was my first of what I was sure would be many encounters with a super creep.

'Excuse me – has there been some mistake? Have you paid for two seats?' I lifted my elbow in mock-exasperation. This caught him totally off-guard. He wasn't prepared for direct confrontation and backed off fast. His elbow disappeared down by his side and victory was mine. I spread my arm out triumphantly over the whole of the armrest.

He attempted to disguise the defeat by pulling out his laptop (a PC, not a Mac: total confirmation that he was a super creep). I checked out his screensaver. This was a photograph of a red Rolls-Royce parked on a street in Knightsbridge. I hate Rolls-Royces – I just don't see the point of them. If this vehicle was his he was definitely a super creep. But if he'd just taken a photo of one and then used it as his screensaver he was a *sad* super creep.

I was flying economy. Not only that but on Air Canada – and their economy is very far from the best. I loathe airline seats. We can put men on the moon but can't make a comfortable seat for international travel? Let's get our priorities right. It's physically impossible to sleep in the weird half-back position that an airline seat forces you into. I'm convinced that they use them in Guantánamo for sleep-deprivation experiments.

I'd scrounged this flight off the Canadian Tourism Commission. Canada suffers from an image problem: people tend to think it's incredibly boring. Bill Bryson once wrote that publishers went quite pale when he'd announced that he wanted to write something about the place. The Canadian Tourism Commission had high hopes that I was going to change all that . . .

I watched *Super 8*, a Spielberg homage recommended by Mark Kermode, my all-time favourite movie critic. It was good, but not great. (Curiously, given the subject of this book, I've never really been that into monster movies. *Jaws* was good, but that's about it.) The movie over, I was bored; so I started snooping on my neighbour's emails. He was Danish and something to with paediatrics. I watched in fasciation as he spent more than an hour perfecting the dullest email I have ever read.

To all area coordinators:

A. Get idea of timelines so that inputs can be planned
B. Get an idea of how inputs should be provided
C. Get a timeline for when inputs should be provided
D. Get provision for extra input on timeline

I checked twice to see if he'd spotted that I was reading his email and was now taking the piss. Surely nobody could write an email that dull without seriously reassessing their life choices? At that moment I was *so* glad that I was a monster-hunter. *My* emails would never be like the dull Dane's. They would be like this:

Dear Tony,

I need that underwater sonic device as soon as you can make it. Were my designs clear enough? Gotta go – I'm picking up some infrared-camera stuff and a really big net and want to get to Millets before it closes.

Dom (Monster-Hunter)

It was just as we started our descent into Vancouver that I realized I'd left my beloved Leica camera at home. This wasn't the greatest start to my first monster-hunting trip. Now if I did actually see Ogopogo I was going to have to draw the bastard.

The stewardess offered me a glass of Dasani. It appeared nobody had yet told the North Americans that we ran this bottled water out of the country when it was revealed that the contents were simply filtered tap water.

I had to go through Canadian Immigration before catching a little turbo-prop plane to Kelowna. A smiling, friendly official looked at my passport and asked me my reasons for coming to Canada. I couldn't help myself.

'I'm here to look for Ogopogo,' I said, smiling back a little too hard and aware that I might look a bit unstable.

The official's friendly smile disappeared and was replaced with a world-weary version.

'Best of luck with that, eh? Now, what is your real reason for visiting Canada?' She had a hint of steeliness about her.

I smiled again. 'I'm here to look for Ogopogo . . .' There was quite a long pause as she sized me up, wondering whether to call security for a cavity search. Then she seemed to remember that she was Canadian and not American.

'And is that for business or pleasure?'

I thought hard for a second and then replied truthfully.

'It's purely for pleasure, ma'am.'

She stamped my passport and waved me through. I was in. I was in a foreign country hunting monsters. This was turning out to be rather Tintin-esque. Unlike Tintin, however, I have a family – not a loose, shady cabal of homoerotic acquaintances plus a white dog.

Vancouver's internal departure lounge didn't have a seafood bar so I had to change my pre-flight order to a doughnut. This made me nervous. The twin-prop was, like most twin-props, rather unsettling to the passenger. On normal planes you can't really see where the power's coming from. On a twin prop, like in a helicopter, you spend your whole time staring at the rotors imagining what would happen if they suddenly stopped turning.

An hour into the flight and I got my first view of Lake Okanagan. It's an ominous-looking thing: a long, dark stretch of water, dwarfed on both sides by steeply rising earth – a physical reminder of the immense glacial forces that once shaped it.

The first time I'd seen this lake was on *Arthur C. Clarke's Mysterious World*. Here Clarke had investigated the innumerable sightings of a 'creature' in the lake. These sightings went way back into the nineteenth century among settlers. The beast was supposed to be not unlike the Loch Ness Monster – there were reports of 'humps', long black shapes in the water and stories of a dinosaur-type creature. There were also several intriguing snippets of footage and a multitude of blurred photographs. There was definitely something in this lake that was attracting attention. Legend had it that whatever it was lived in a cave under a place called Rattlesnake Island in the middle of the lake. I decided that this would have to be my first destination.

I picked up my car from Budget. Unlike her UK counterparts, the woman behind the desk was friendly, apparently well-travelled and very helpful. I'm banned from most major car-rental outlets in Central London because I constantly get into altercations with the staff. In the UK the car-rental business seems to be designed to test just how determined you are to rent said vehicles: they'll do anything they can to prevent you leaving in a rental car. In North America it's always a joy; they even seem slightly apologetic that you actually have to pay for marching straight out into their car park and driving off in any car with the keys in the ignition.

I'd decided to stay at the south of the lake and work my way up the valley, ending up in the main town of Kelowna. My first bed for the night was in Summerland. I wondered what Summerland was going to be like in October. Not that summery, I imagined. The busy holiday season was long over and the weather was starting to get pretty cold. There was zero boat traffic on the lake, not a single vessel. As I drove south along the lakeshore I realized that I genuinely didn't have the first clue as to how to monster-hunt. I kept half an eye on the water hoping that maybe I'd get a sighting of Ogopogo immediately but I was intensely aware that this was very unlikely.

I turned on the local talk-radio station – always the best way to get under the skin of a community when in North America. The big news story of the day was about a man who had repelled an intruder to his trailer by using a screwdriver and 'bear spray'. I wondered what was in bear spray. It definitely sounded like something a monster-hunter should have in his backpack.

I kept driving and put the Kermode/Mayo movie podcast on. This has been my constant companion on so many road trips, my little slice of normality in weird surroundings. A wind had picked up and the lake was choppy and rather mean-looking. Okanagan reminded me a lot of Loch Ness. It's on roughly the same latitude and is the same sort of shape, although a lot bigger. If I'm honest, lakes have always creeped me out a bit. There's something rather ominous about their stillness and murky depths. I don't like swimming in them.

In Summerland I checked into my hotel, a rather posh beach resort that was totally deserted. Summer had indeed left Summerland, seemingly taking all the inhabitants with it.

This was the limbo season – after the summer hordes but before the ski season started in nearby resorts like Big White. I wandered the empty *Shining*-like corridors until I got to my room. This was satisfyingly huge. As the only resident in the hotel I'd been given a suite overlooking the lake. Just below my balcony, on the lakeshore, was a hot tub. Now this was my kind of monster-hunting. I was tired from the long day travelling and slipped off my smeggy clothes and hopped into the tub. I lay back and sighed. This was the life, lounging in a hot tub while keeping half an eye on the lake for monster action . . .

I must have dozed off because I awoke with someone shaking me and shouting, 'Sir! Sir, are you OK?'

It was a security guard, probably freaked out enough to see a guest let alone a naked one passed out in the hot tub. Or maybe he just thought I was a trespasser. I tried to look authoritative but I'd been dribbling down my face and the whole thing was not a good look. I retreated to my room with as much dignity as I could muster and fell asleep. I slept like a log and woke up twelve hours later feeling a whole lot better about things. The weather had turned and it was a beautiful autumn day. I spent a cursory ten minutes staring out at the water looking for monsters until hunger took over.

I drove into Summerland proper but there wasn't anything there so I headed down to Penticton, a larger town right at the southern end of the lake. This too was like a ghost town. My spirits dropped. I rather hoped that Ogopogo hadn't also left the area for the winter.

I wandered the empty streets before opting for a place called Fibonacci on Main Street where the coffee smelt good. It tasted good as well: I had a monster latte as I surfed the Net for information about Ogopogo and Penticton. There'd been a famous sighting here back in 1941. A bunch of kids swimming off the beach saw a huge, thirty-foot-long object that looked like a snake. It was swimming just beyond the wooden-log buoys about fifty feet offshore. They all ran to get an adult but the thing was gone when they got back.

I rang the local Ogopogo expert, Arlene Gaal. She'd been on the original Arthur C. Clarke programme and had written a couple of books on Ogopogo so I hoped that she could maybe point out areas of the lake where there had been more sightings than elsewhere. I had a quick chat with her and we agreed to meet on Saturday, the day after tomorrow, at her home in Kelowna.

With no plans for the day, I decided to explore Penticton. This took about five minutes. It was like the beginning of *28 Days Later*.

I wandered down to the beach where the kids had seen Ogopogo. A man in blue overalls was at the top of a ladder, putting a fresh coat of vivid-orange paint on an enormous metal peach. The peach was about twenty feet tall and looked quite cool. The Okanagan Valley has a very curious weather system. The areas to the north end of the valley get more rain and record far colder temperatures than the areas to the south, which are almost desert-like. For years the area's main agricultural business was fruit production – hence the big metal peach. Recently, however, locals have realized that the climate's perfect for wine production and this has become a boom industry, superseding the fruit business.

On the shore was a sign warning bathers of potential hazards: 'Check depth. Check weather forecast. Don't trust inflatable devices . . .' and, my personal favourite: 'Learn to swim.'

There was no mention of Ogopogo danger. Indeed, so far I hadn't come across much mention of the creature anywhere. I think I'd expected the whole area to be teeming with Ogopogo stuff and paraphernalia. I'd thought it would be the big thing around there, like Nessie is at Loch Ness. Okanagans, however, appeared to be pretty uninterested in their local monster.

I spent a futile five minutes staring at the lake hoping that Ogopogo would show up. I then wandered along the shoreline past a gargantuan old steamboat, beached like a dead whale. Before the arrival of the bridge that now spans the lake at Kelowna, vessels like these were incredibly popular with both day-trippers and locals as a means to get round the lake. In 1926, seven years before the first recorded Nessie sightings (archival records of Ogopogo sightings go back to 1872) the British Columbian government announced the commencement of a ferry service between Kelowna and Westbank. They also declared that the vessel would be equipped with 'devices designed to repel attacks from Ogopogo'.

I checked the beached steamship for signs of any such devices but could see none. I imagined some guy perched on the prow of the ship atop a terrifying harpoon scanning the dirty grey waters for monsters. I walked round a corner and finally came across my first sighting of Ogopogo – sadly this was only in the form of a badly painted depiction on a sign advertising the Ogopogo Motel.

I wandered into the reception only to be accosted by a large lady at least as scary as the legendary beast itself. She looked at me suspiciously and asked me what I wanted. Slightly caught off-guard and embarrassed, I didn't identify myself as one of the world's foremost monster-hunters. Instead, I found myself telling her that I needed a room.

'A room?' she barked in surprise, as though I'd just asked her to bare her breasts.

'How long for?'

My pointless web of deceit started to unravel. 'A week – I'm in town for a . . . convention.'

She looked at me suspiciously. 'A convention? What convention? There ain't no convention in town.'

I replied that it was the 'ZGB Inc.' convention, hoping to confuse her with the initials.

'Well, why aren't you staying at the Convention Centre, then?'

Clearly you had to be very much on the ball if you wanted a room at the Ogopogo Motel. I imagined that guests were as frequent as sightings of the creature itself.

I wanted to leave, just run out of the door screaming, but instead I continued my fantasy.

'Because I'm a . . . recovering addict and can't be near a casino or . . . I go mental.'

She looked at me funny. There was a long silence. Finally she announced that the motel was 'completely full' as all the 'orchard workers' were there. I felt like a relieved blond trucker who'd just been turned away from the Bates Motel because there was no room.

I walked quickly back to the safety of my car. The weather had turned and ominous black clouds hung low over the lake. I drove to Summerland in driving rain.

It was eleven in the morning when I got back into my lakeside suite. The rain had stopped and the lake was flat calm, like a mirror. It was seven in the evening back home in the UK so I thought I'd Skype them. By means of the kind of modern technology that Tintin would never have been able to enjoy, even if he'd had a family, I was soon looking at my sitting room back in the Cotswolds. Stacey started telling me a long story about something that happened to the kids at school but I wasn't listening. My attention had been drawn to some weird movement in the lake about 100 yards away from my window. Two shapes, like twin heads, were making very fast figure-of-eight motions in the water.

'Are you listening?' said Stacey, but I ignored her and jumped up, grabbed my iPhone and rushed to the window to start filming. In the background Stacey was still talking to me but couldn't see where I'd gone. With my iPhone rolling I shouted at the laptop to tell them what was going on. I backed away from the window a touch and turned the computer round so that they could see what I was seeing. The zoom on the iPhone wasn't great but I could see close enough to know that whatever was making the disturbance was not a bird. It looked like a pair of three-foot bumps sticking out of the water and whatever it was was thrashing about, as though feeding or chasing something. I couldn't quite believe it and Stacey was sure that I was joking. Below my suite, to the left of the hot tub, was a dock that stuck out very near to the disturbance. I shouted to Stacey that I was going to run down to the end to try to get some closer footage. By the time I'd got there, though, whatever it was had disappeared. But it had disappeared underwater: nothing flew up or swam away in sight.

This genuinely was a puzzling moment. As I walked back along the dock I spotted the same security man who'd found me asleep in the hot tub the day before. He'd obviously seen me screaming and running down the dock and probably assumed that I was about to do weird naked shit again. As I walked past him he nodded at me hesitantly.

'Everything OK, sir?' he asked, keeping a safe distance.

I told him about what I'd seen and showed him the iPhone footage. He looked at it for quite a while and then asked to see it again.

When it finished he looked at me seriously and said, 'Looks like you've just had your first sighting of Ogopogo . . .' He had no idea that I was the world's most famous monster-hunter or that I was looking for the very creature he was now saying I'd captured on film. I couldn't believe it. Had I really got a bona fide sighting, on film, of a monster on my very first full day of monster-hunting? Surely it couldn't be that easy? I walked back to my room and immediately posted the footage on my Facebook page. I'd just told everyone that I was off on this trip and now I was posting a sighting. Nobody was going to believe me but I swear this is exactly what happened.

Rather adrenalized by events, I drove up to Kelowna to find the main bookstore and buy Arlene Gaal's book *In Search of Ogopogo*. I wanted to do a bit of flattery research before meeting her. As I looked for it in the store I couldn't get my Ogopogo sighting out of my mind. I'd set off to find a monster and had an 'encounter' on my very first day. I was slightly buzzing but also worried that nobody would believe me. I wondered if this was what happened to other people who spotted things in the water but were worried about public ridicule.

I found the book with some difficulty and the woman behind the counter seemed surprised to be selling it. I kept the news of my sighting to myself. It was now very sunny again. I had never been anywhere where the weather changed so rapidly. I headed for the waterside park to read on a bench. There, to my delight, I spotted a statue of Ogopogo. It was green and white with humps rising in and out of the concrete ending in a slightly dopey-looking horned head with a big red tongue flapping around. It rather reminded me of Puff the Magic Dragon. I sat on a bench right beside it and started reading the book in between watching Japanese tourists drape themselves all over Puff for hour-long photo sessions. I so admire the Japanese race's dedication to having their photos taken while striking curious fictional 'gangsta-san' poses. They will think nothing of taking more than 500 photographs of a woman in an oversized sun visor giving the camera the peace sign while gurning. It must have been the sheer amount of holiday footage needing to be developed in Japan that turned their inventors towards thinking about a digital camera.

I found the Gaal book quite a difficult read. She was not the most gifted of writers and it became more of a long list of sightings. A great part of the text seemed to comprise the numbers of TV crews she'd worked with. After a while I became a little bored and nodded off on the sun-drenched bench.

On Friday I got up at the crack of dawn as I was still on UK time. I headed off into Penticton again. I wasn't quite sure how this was possible but, if anything, it was even more deserted. Back at Fibonacci I had the strongest coffee of my life so far. I'd sent an email to a man who'd promised that he could rent me a boat even though the season was over. We'd arranged to meet behind the waterfront casino at half past nine. The weather had turned again and it was unbelievably cold and very overcast. The lake looked choppy and rather foreboding.

I hadn't really brought any warm boating clothes with me. I looked around but there was only one clothes shop open, and that was in the foyer of the casino. I was surprised that the place was already open. It turned out to be the busiest place in Penticton, with about seven sad-looking individuals sitting life-lessly in front of one-arm bandits robotically feeding the voracious machine with quarters. If there is anything more depressing than a casino at nine in the morning then I haven't yet come across it.

I bought the only warm thing available: a short-sleeved fleece with the words 'Canadian Lover Man' embossed in big red letters on the back. I was sartorially mortified but had very little choice. Even the shop assistant looked at me in a weird way.

'It's getting cold . . .' I said to her almost apologetically.

'*Yeah . . . But not* that *cold . . .*' I sensed her thoughts.

My boat guy was all sensibly wrapped up against the cold. He didn't say anything about my outfit but you could feel a touch of slight tension once he'd spotted it. Fortunately, because of my regular summer vacationing in Ontario, I have a Canadian Pleasure-Craft Licence; this seemed to relax him a touch. We started going over what I needed to know about the boat and he asked me where I was intending to go. I told him that I was headed north, towards Peachland. I didn't mention Rattlesnake Island. I'd been told that locals were rather superstitious about the place and didn't like people going there. This guy didn't seem to be concerned about anything but payment.

I gave him my damage deposit and asked him, 'What happens if I hit Ogopogo and sink the boat?'

'Then you won't be getting this deposit back,' he said without hesitation.

'But if Ogopogo attacks me then it's not my fault . . . Do you have a special clause for that?'

He looked at me as though I was a lunatic and I didn't want to push the issue as I wanted to get on the boat. I bade him farewell and put-putted out of the marina.

The lake was rough – very rough – and my little boat and I started to be tossed about quite violently. I looked around. Mine was the only boat on the whole lake. Was this a wise thing to be doing? I looked up at the steep sides of the valley that towered high up above the dark water and I felt very, very tiny in my little vessel. I gunned the engine and the boat speeded up, bumping fast across endless advancing walls of enemy waves.

About ten minutes in and the lake got even rougher. Huge waves battered the front of the boat and I was forced to slow right down. The clouds above me darkened and the boat started to be chucked about like a piece of driftwood. I suddenly got nervous. What was I doing here? There was nobody about to help me if I got tipped over, and the water was ice-cold. It would definitely get me before Ogopogo did.

I remembered a story that I'd read in Arlene Gaal's book, about the local Indian tribe. They would always take a small animal out with them in a canoe so that, should the monster they called the N'ha-a-itk whip up a storm, they could throw the poor thing overboard as an appeasing sacrifice. I'd brought nothing with me, not even a sandwich. There'd been a McDonald's on the edge of Penticton: maybe I could have could have sacrificed some chicken nuggets. (The added problem here being that I'm not convinced those are actually made from real birds.)

To my right, the landscape looked rather nightmarish. Back in 2003 a huge fire laid waste to the forest. Now the stark grey rock is littered with the burnt skeletons of dead trees. It was crazy but I was starting to get very spooked. I put the radio on to try and calm myself down a bit but I couldn't get anything except white noise that only increased my self-imposed paranoia. The lake was crazy rough now and I tried to hug the barren, burnt shoreline to get some calmer water. The cliffs loomed over me like predatory giants and I got really freaked out by a weird noise. It sounded like howling – evil howling. Then I realized that it was just one of the ropes holding my canopy. It had snapped at the attachment and was now juddering in the wind and making an odd sound – odd, but not howling and certainly not evil. I looked down into the water: my depth finder told me that it was 600 feet deep. I tried to man up and carried on rounding Squally Point, where the lake turned right. As I did so, I spotted my goal: Rattlesnake Island was dead ahead.

I approached it gingerly. It was ridiculous but I was actually quite scared. My heart was racing and my mouth had gone completely dry. Obviously my own sighting yesterday wasn't helping. I got close and cut the engine. The waves had abated a little and I took a good look at the island. This appeared to be a barren piece of terrain, no more than a rock, really, with a lone scraggly tree clinging to it. There were no signs of either rattle-snakes or Ogopogo. I pulled out my iPhone and started filming. This was mainly so I could speak and break the silence that was starting to become a little oppressive.

Ogopogo is (or are) rumoured to live in a cave that leads into a series of tunnels starting just below the island. Sonar scans have shown a large hole down there. Ogopogo enthusiasts claim that this is why no bodies of these creatures are ever found: because they retreat inside to die. I say 'creatures' because there would have to be several. For something to exist for so long in this lake it would have to breed, start a family, get a mortgage . . .

I kept filming and started shouting, 'Hello, Ogopogo!' at the top of my voice. I had now clearly lost my mind. I gunned the motor and decided to try to navigate the very narrow channel between the island and the black, burnt mainland. This was a really stupid thing to do, as I had no charts on board and the depth finder would tell me about jutting rocks only when it was too late. I went for it anyway and an invisible current immedi-ately caught the vessel and powered me through. I held my breath. I really didn't want to hit anything. The idea of having to get into the dark, cold water beneath me was not pleasant. I was immensely relieved when I got through and was back in safe waters. I felt like I was in some weird episode of *Scooby Doo*. I laughed out loud but it sounded a little hollow on my own. I suddenly longed for human company and started to head back to Penticton. As I rounded Squally Point the lake suddenly calmed itself. I zoomed away fast from Rattlesnake Island and kept to the western shoreline on the way back, which is populated and felt safer than the barren eastern shore. Finally I spotted the two tall buildings behind the casino on Penticton Beach and breathed a sigh of relief. I had survived my first ill-prepared expedition on Lake Okanagan. I tied the boat to the dock and called the boat guy on his mobile. He was down to meet me about fifteen minutes later. We had a little chat as he checked the boat for damage. He told me about the divers who worked on the new bridge that replaced the old floating one between West Kelowna and Kelowna itself.

'A lot of them quit. They said it was scary and that there were some seriously big things swimming around down there. Some say it's a sturgeon but nobody has ever caught one. The visibility is limited but these guys are not spooked easily. At least three I knew quit as they were so freaked out.'

I nodded and laughed as though they were weak idiots. I didn't tell him about just how freaked out I'd been about an hour ago just floating on top of the water. The idea of getting under the dark water (and I love scuba diving) was pretty unthinkable to me.

I said my goodbyes and got in the car. As I drove my phone rang. It was the aunt of an acquaintance back in London who had grown up in the Okanagan. I'd emailed her saying I couldn't find a boat to rent and she'd contacted her family. Now they were offering to take me to Rattlesnake Island on their family boat. I was too embarrassed to tell them I'd found a rental guy and had just been. So I agreed to meet them at Peachland marina at three-thirty that afternoon – I was going back out there . . .

Peachland is a pretty little community right on the lake directly opposite Rattlesnake Island. There are actually two marinas, one rather grandly calling itself a 'yacht club' and the other seemingly a little less exclusive. I parked my car and sat waiting. At almost exactly three-thirty I saw an old speedboat with two men in it zoom towards the locked marina. Since there were no other boats on the lake I presumed these had to be my guys. I peered at them through the fence and one shouted, 'You from London?' I nodded and they told me to come down. I indicated that I couldn't and so they told me to walk down the road towards the beach where they'd pick me up.

As I clambered aboard the old speedboat I noticed it was covered from front to back in weird blue carpeting. Sort of the nautical equivalent of the avocado bathroom set. The guys introduced themselves: Al and Kevin. They were both in their mid-fifties and very friendly. Al had been born in the valley and Kevin had moved there in 1985.

They had absolutely no idea why I was in the Okanagan. Al had received an email from London asking if they could help me out, so here they were. I filled them in on my mission and they both started laughing – in a good way.

Another dramatic change in the weather meant it was now a beautiful sunny day. The sun glinted off the water and the lake was almost enticing.

I asked Al and Kevin whether either of them had seen Ogopogo.

'No, but I've seen the Sasquatch. Me and my son saw one on a hunting trip only an hour and a half from here.' Kevin looked serious for a second. I asked him what the Bigfoot looked like.

'He looked like a big drunken Irishman – about eight feet tall, covered in red hair with a fast lolloping walk. He just stared right at us for a good twenty seconds and then made off into the trees . . .' This was promising: I felt these guys wouldn't think I was mad.

I asked them about Ogopogo again. Did they know anybody who had seen anything? They'd both seen big wakes in the lake but not 'the humps' – though both of them knew people who had. Kevin started talking again.

'Anyone local believes in Ogopogo. It's the fucking Albertans coming here who all poo-poo it. The thing is, nobody's scared of Ogopogo. It's not a monster; monsters kill people. It's a creature, a USO [unidentified swimming object], but not a monster.'

I nodded and looked at the fast-approaching Rattlesnake Island. It was unbelievable. In the bright sunlight it looked like a totally different place. The water lapping around it was crystal blue and sparkling. It was lovely. We motored around it, just as I had that morning.

'Do you want to see the pyramid?' asked Kevin.

'The what?' I said.

'Wait and see.'

We beached the boat in a perfect little harbour hidden behind two protruding rocks. I hadn't noticed it earlier. We hopped off the boat and clambered up the steep slope towards the island's summit. As we climbed I spotted the remains of something man-made. It almost looked like an overgrown crazy-golf course. It couldn't be, of course. This was the forbidden place, the sacred home of the monster. How could there be a crazy-golf course here? We got to the top of the island and Al was standing on a big stone pedestal. This was clearly man-made. I asked him what it was.

'It was the pyramid,' replied Al. 'Eddy Haymour's pyramid . . .' He was smiling at me.

'Sorry, I'm being thick, but I don't understand what you mean. Who's Eddy Haymour and why are there the remains of a pyramid and a crazy-golf course here?'

It turned out that back in the early 1970s a Lebanese man, Eddy Haymour, moved to the Okanagan Valley. He had emigrated to Canada and had done rather well setting up a chain of barber shops in Edmonton. He'd caused quite a stir, however, in the white-bread Okanagan community because he was, to say the least, quite a character. After a little while living in the valley Eddy noticed Rattlesnake Island and decided to buy it and turn it into a Middle Eastern theme park. Al started to tell me about the things that Eddy had either planned or actually built for the park and I just didn't believe him. He suggested that I try to find a copy of Eddy Haymour's life story, *From Nut House to Castle*.

I later managed to get a copy from a second-hand bookstore in town. Here is Eddy's description of what he wanted for the island:

On the four-point-five acre island would be great landscaping with beautiful gardens. There was to be a forty-six-feet long, twenty-six-feet high concrete structure in the form of a camel with a hollow stomach where thirty-nine flavors of ice cream would be served. You could peek out of the windows of the camel's eyes, music would come from his mouth and the garbage from his tail. The washroom would be in the legs. All the cultures of the Middle East would be represented; India by a miniature Taj Mahal; Kuwait by fountains; minarets would depict Saudi Arabia; and there would be a large pyramid for Egypt. In a huge tent Middle Eastern films and other entertainment would be presented. Kids could go around the island on ponies led by Arab storytellers, or in a chariot pulled by a white horse. There would be a toddlers swimming pool with babysitters and lifeguards. I figured I needed something familiar to Canadians so I designed a unique miniature golf course, all landscaped and each hole relating to an Arab landmark. I wanted to have a small submarine to take kids down to the underwater cave, home of Ogopogo . . .

'Did it actually open?' I asked Al.

Al laughed and said that the story got even weirder. The theme park did half open – for one day. The pyramid and the camel and various other bits were built, and locals came over for the grand opening, but the local British Columbian government then stepped in and closed Eddy's island down. He had clearly rubbed some important local people up the wrong way. They tried to change the zoning for the island, refused him ferry permits to take people over there and then challenged his plans for sanitation facilities. Eddy was left with a lot of debts and no way to pay them off as it became clear that officialdom was never going to let him open the island properly. Things spiralled out of control. Eddy's wife left him and then the government inserted an agent provocateur to make friends with Eddy and get him to make threats against the government. Eddy was thrown into a nut house and the government forced him to sell them back the island at a tiny percentage of its actual value.

I couldn't believe this kind of thing went on in straight-laced, well-behaved Canada.

'It gets even worse . . .' said Al.

It was eventually agreed that Eddy Haymour would be released if he left Canada. He went back to Lebanon where, clearly, his resentment at the way he had been treated by the country he'd been so proud to make his home – and become a citizen of – boiled over. Lebanon was just starting the slide into civil war and there were armed factions all over the country. Eddy got together a couple of his cousins and forcibly took over the Canadian Embassy in Beirut, holding thirty hostages for three days. Following slightly panicky negotiations, Eddy released the hostages and, unbelievably, was allowed back into Canada, where he spent ten years fighting his case through the courts. He eventually won; Eddy was awarded damages and it was admitted that the government had behaved appallingly towards him. Eddy never got Rattlesnake Island back, though. He built a 'castle' on the shore opposite the island, which he turned into a hotel. However, he never forgot his island and eventually had a thirty-foot statue of himself built and placed outside his castle pointing at it.

I longed to know what had happened to Eddy's statue when he died but neither Al nor Kevin knew its whereabouts.

Back on the boat we cruised around Rattlesnake Island again and checked Squally Point. This was the place where the local Indians claimed Ogopogo was most often sighted. We saw nothing.

Later Kevin and Al dropped me off at the little beach. Back at my hotel I sat on my balcony with a bottle of Sumac Ridge and stared at the lake. I gave up when the bottle was empty and it started to get dark.

The following morning I checked out and drove to the big city: Kelowna. My appointment with Arlene Gaal was at two-thirty that afternoon. I wasn't quite sure what to expect but she definitely believed in the beast and was sure to have something to say.

With the morning to kill in Kelowna, I decided to wander around and get my bearings. I ambled down the main street and ended up at the lakeside park where the statue of Ogopogo was. On an adjacent patch of grass, facing a raised concrete step, was gathered a small crowd of people I don't think it would be unfair to describe as shabby. They were all listening to a black man wearing a long leather trenchcoat and dirty dreadlocks who was shouting into a microphone. Intrigued, I approached the scene. Several people were carrying placards. One of these read, 'Marx said there'd be days like this'; another said, 'Decolonize the vallley'.

For some reason it really irritated me that the word 'valley' was misspelt. I wandered up to the man in a gasmask who was carrying it and pointed to the sign.

'It's spelt wrong,' I said, smiling.

'What is?' came the slightly Darth Vader-esque voice behind the mask.

'"Valley" . . . You've spelt it with three *l*s and it should be just two.'

'Go fuck yourself,' said the gasmask.

'Only trying to help,' I replied, edging away.

About twenty yards away was another gentleman in a gasmask. His sign read, 'Capitalism – stop that sh*t'. However angry he was, the Canadian in him had forced him to asterisk the *i* in shit.

I listened to the speeches for a while. It was only after about ten minutes that I worked out what this was all about. It was an Occupy Kelowna demonstration, taking its lead from the Occupy Wall Street demos in New York that were being reproduced all over the world. There seemed to be a general dislike of plutocracy, the rich, CEOs, bankers . . . Basically the usual suspects.

Some guy stood up to talk about some new miracle energy that could power his home. Another guy got up and started going on about the postal service and how they should all go on strike. Thankfully the stench of patchouli oil in the air was thick enough to mask the omnipresent BO.

The Rasta, who seemed to be the MC of the event, was back up speaking.

'Guys, anybody who wants to speak – anybody – please don't be shy, just get up here and say your piece. This is what it's all about.'

Nobody moved and I couldn't resist. I found myself walking past a huge earth mother who was clutching a Mega Slushy as though her firstborn. I got up on the stage and grabbed the microphone. I raised my right fist and shouted: 'Greetings, comrades . . . !' Everyone shouted greetings back. This was fun.

'This isn't exactly my bag . . .' (I tried to sound like someone at Woodstock and was briefly tempted to warn the motley assembly that there was some bad acid going round.)

'I'm over here from the UK to look for Ogopogo and . . . I was wondering what you guys thought? Anybody here seen the monster? Can I see by a show of hands who thinks he exists?'

The crowd turned in a second. They started booing and one guy shouted, 'Fuck off, you stupid asshole!' It seemed that asterisks applied only to written profanities. A small Asian postal worker grabbed the mike and told me to get lost . . .

I left the stage and felt the disapproving stares of everyone around me. I even got half shoulder-barged by a man holding a sign saying, 'Eat the rich'. I decided to move on.

After walking around town for a while I had lunch in a Japanese restaurant opposite the demo so that I could people watch from safety. A woman in a Beatles cap was now on stage playing a guitar and screeching loudly. Her song seemed interminable and even the protestors seemed relieved when it was over. She, however, was nothing compared to the man in wheelchair who followed. He couldn't get up on the stage so the Rasta brought him the microphone and then told everyone to gather closer so that they could all see him. There were about 200 draft dodgers littered around the park. I reckoned if the police swooped now they could end crime in the valley in one go.

The wheelchair man was a very spiritual fellow. Rarely had I heard more bollocks spoken. He urged the surrounding crusties to close their eyes and imagine themselves to be in a happy place. Then he started chanting some mantra in cod Tibetan. It was embarrassing. To try to drown him out I asked my Japanese waitress whether she had heard of the Hibagon. Sadly, her English wasn't that great and she thought I was ordering something off the menu. It all became quite confusing.

After lunch I drove north, away from the lake and towards the mountains where, so my sat-nav promised me, Arlene Gaal lived. As I drove further and further inland it dawned on me that I'd rather expected her to be on the lakeshore with cameras trained on the waters. When I eventually got to her place I realized you couldn't even see the lake from there.

She greeted me at the door to her home, a little white puppy yapping at her feet. She was a sweet little old lady and had set up a table on which loads of photos were laid out. Some of the snaps were from strangers who'd sent them to her; others were ones she'd taken. She had become a focus for Ogopogo sightings. People who didn't know what to do with them were always directed to her. I really wanted to tell her about my sighting but thought I should be polite and wait a bit. I looked through the photos. A lot of them could easily have been freak big waves on a calm lake but there were several that were not so explainable. To me what was convincing was the sheer number of unexplained sightings, especially by people who did not want their names released for fear of ridicule. I'd assumed most people would be publicity seekers using the opportunity to get on the television. Far from it: Arlene said a lot of people were very reticent to discuss their sightings because they didn't want to be laughed at.

This was my first meeting with a cryptozoologist and she didn't seem that strange – but I noticed that whenever we talked about Ogopogo a steely determination appeared in her eyes. The 'Folden film' in 1968 had been what started it all for her. Sawmill worker Art Folden was driving along the lakeshore when he noticed something strange in the water. He pointed it out to his wife and they stopped the car and Art got out his 8mm cine camera and started filming. The object was diving in and out of the water so Folden, being aware that he didn't have much film, started to shoot every time the thing reappeared. Eventually it swam away from its initial position quite near the shore and disappeared into the deeper waters in the middle of the lake. According to Arlene this was still the best footage ever taken. She said that on the lakeshore road just near where Folden took his footage there used to be an official sign that read:

OGOPOGO'S HOME

Before the unimaginative, practical, white man came the fearsome lake monster n'aavit was well known to the primitive, superstitious Indian. His home was believed to be a cave at Squally Point and small animals were carried in their canoes to appease the serpent.

Ogopogo is still seen each year – but now by white men.

It seemed quite a patronizing sign and the government who originally put it up clearly felt the same, as it had now been removed.

I told her that I'd assumed the locals would have really used the Ogopogo story to attract tourists, but there was almost nothing visible in the valley except for the statue in the port.

She said that she loathed the statue because it was 'stupid and Disneyesque'.

I told her what hotel I was staying at and she said that there had been a great sighting from there. She advised me to sit on my balcony and watch the lake. If it hadn't been for my sighting the other morning using this 'method' I might have been more dissatisfied by her suggestion.

I'd been hoping that she might have more scientific methods for me to try. I suppose I'd always thought of monster-hunting as being a bit more exciting than just sitting staring at a lake. I wanted underwater cameras, sonars, submarine trips . . .

With my sighting in the bag, however, I was very happy just to show her the footage on my iPhone and wallow in the glory. She watched it without saying a word but her eyes were sharp and focused on my little screen. When it finished she looked up at me and smiled.

'Looks like you've got yourself a sighting . . .'

I secretly wondered whether I'd make it into her next book. I sat back, hoping for something to now happen. Maybe the international news media would start swarming in? Possibly I would be asked to tell my story to packed amphitheatres? Whatever, I was sure that Arlene would know what to do. She did nothing. After some polite conversation she offered me some tea and biscuits. It was all a bit of a let-down.

I said goodbye to Arlene and drove away a little disappointed. I wasn't sure quite what I'd expected . . . But I hadn't got it. Once back at my hotel I sat on my new balcony and watched the lake.

I watched the lake for quite some time until I started to get bored of watching the lake and wandered downstairs to have a meal. I ate some duck with a bottle of local wine. It was exceptionally good wine. I asked the waitress where the winery was and she told me that it was fairly nearby, on a hill 'with an amazing view of the lake'. I figured if I was going to have to stare at the lake then I should do it from a winery rather than my hotel balcony. I thanked her and said, 'I saw Ogopogo yesterday.' She looked at me blankly and I didn't pursue the matter.

Therefore, the following morning, I found myself driving through the plush Mission quarter of Kelowna until the road started to climb out of town. Soon I was high above the lake in front of the Summerhill Pyramid Winery. To my right as I drove in was a gargantuan grey pyramid overlooking the lake. What was it with this valley and bloody pyramids?

It was an absolutely gorgeous day and I stood on the terrace overlooking a vast expanse of the lake. I could clearly see the bridge the scuba divers had resigned from working on after spotting 'large objects' down there. It was a curious design: solid, flat concrete blocks were set in the water from both banks. In the centre two arches in the shape of humps rose into the air; these allowed boat traffic through. It basically created a narrow funnel in the middle of the lake. For Ogopogo to travel from north to south, or vice versa, he'd have to swim beneath these two arches. Surely science was at a stage where two motion-sensor cameras could be placed underwater? I supposed it was money: who would pay for something like that? A monster-hunter, that's who, so technically me . . . I sat on the terrace of the winery and gorged myself on the beautiful view and a Mimosa.

I got chatting to the waitress and asked whether she'd seen Ogopogo. She said no, but she had a friend who'd seen it – although he wouldn't talk to media because everyone would laugh at him. She said she tried not to think about Ogopogo when she was swimming in the lake. A manager approached my table and asked me where I was from and whether I would like a tour of the winery. Why not?

Two minutes into the tour I remembered why not. I'd already promised myself I'd never go on another winery tour ever again. They're all identical and incredibly dull. Nobody cares how the stuff's made – just pour some into a glass and get on with it. I've always found myself trying to ask intelligent-sounding questions that I couldn't really give a shit about. It's weird: people don't go on tours of biscuit factories or tuna canneries (although both would be more interesting), so why do we go to wineries? The answer is that we all think we're going to get free wine under the auspices of 'tasting' – but so what? Are we really that cheap?

All this was going through my mind as I was shown a *kylini*, an old Indian-style home like a huge underground yurt. We descended some steps into the cavernous room with a chimney in the centre for the smoke from the fire to escape through.

There were a couple of teens with dreads cleaning up after an event the previous night.

'Was it a wine-tasting?' I asked.

'No,' replied my guide, 'a witchcraft healing session . . .'

I nodded like this should have been obvious but started to wonder whether I had stumbled into some New-Age vacation retreat by mistake. As we climbed up towards the pyramid my guide told me that it was exactly an eighth the size of the Great Pyramid of Giza. I've been to the Pyramids and, looking at this edifice, I privately doubted her claim but I kept schtum. My guide told me (though it was rapidly becoming obvious anyway) that the owners of this winery were hippies and very spiritually inclined. All the wine made on the property had to be stored for a certain time in the pyramid as 'history suggests that pyramids have magical powers over liquids'. The owner claimed to have blind-tested people on two versions of the same wine, one that had been 'pyramided' and one that hadn't. Ninety per cent supposedly preferred the pyramided wine. I didn't really know what to say. I just did my nodding thing and wondered how long it would be until I could get some free wine.

'I believe this is the only winery in the world where the wine is stored in a pyramid . . .' said my guide.

I wasn't going to argue but . . . So fucking what? I tried to steer the subject away from New-Age bollocks to something a lot more real: Ogopogo. I asked my guide if she had ever seen it. She said that she hadn't but her dad was a firm believer. He'd been out on his boat as an eighteen-year-old when Ogopogo surfaced right in front of him. He saw two huge humps and massive water displacement. It lasted for about thirty seconds and then it was gone. She said that he was loath to talk about it with strangers but all the family had heard the story many times.

We left the pyramid and got to the tasting room. I knocked

back about seven glasses of sparkling wine in quick succession and started waffling on about how pyramidic it all tasted. She could tell I was taking the piss and it soon became clear that both the tour and the free wine were at an end.

All this fizzy stuff had gone to my head a touch so I decided to go for a short walk. I headed off down a quiet little road that snaked south just above the lake. There was hardly anybody about and I thought I could find a spot to sit and watch the lake for a while. After about five minutes I spotted a narrow turn-off towards a viewpoint, the edge of a tall cliff with a perfect panorama of the lake. There was nobody about except for one man, sat alone on the edge of the cliff on a collapsible camping chair. He had a flask of something by his side and was scanning the lake with a medium-sized pair of binoculars. I sensed a kindred spirit. I wandered up to the edge of the cliff and looked out as well. He noticed me and we nodded politely at each other. Emboldened, I approached him.

'Looking for Ogopogo?'

I tried to stop the moment I started saying it, realizing that, should he happen not to be familiar with the legend, this would sound very much like an offer of some rather specialist gay sex.

He wasn't familiar with the legend and suddenly looked very panicky. He replied defensively.

'No, I don't want anything like that . . . Please go away.'

Mortified, I tried to explain that I was talking about a lake monster and that I wasn't some cliff-top cruiser but this just made things worse. I eventually slipped away after forcing myself to stay and survey the lake for a couple of faux-nonchalant beats while trying to look really relaxed. He watched me walk away while shaking his head in clear disgust.

As I walked on downhill I laughed to myself at the absurdity of the situation. A bit further down the road there was a sign for a car park: 'Cedar Creek Beach'. Just beyond it was a little pebble peach and the water actually looked quite inviting – the sun sparkled off it and there was nobody around. The water was reasonably shallow but I could see where it dropped away about 100 yards offshore. The guys who'd taken me out to Rattlesnake Island had mentioned that Kelowna was actually built on a rock shelf that jutted out into the lake. I had a strong urge to swim. I was a little freaked out about swimming in these waters but something inside me wanted to try to conquer my fears. Also it was really quite hot and I knew I could do with a cool down. I could see the bottom and it was a mixture of seaweedy-type stuff and big round pebbles. I decided to go for it. I didn't have any swimming trunks or towel with me but a 'what the fuck' feeling enveloped me and I felt adventurous. I looked around: both the car park and the beach were totally deserted. I stripped off naked, took one last look around and headed off towards the water holding my left hand over my privates. I gingerly stepped on to the beach and started walking into the lake until I was about knee-deep. It was crazily cold and I realized that this was going to be a very quick dip in and out but I was determined to at least submerge myself once in Ogopogo's home. I stepped forward again and suddenly felt a searing pain in my left foot. I'd stepped on something incredibly sharp – I don't know if it was a piece of broken glass, a can, or whatever, but it had made a huge cut in my foot and I was in incredible pain. I screamed blue murder: 'Fuck . . . ! Fuckity fuck . . . Fuck fuckity shitting fuck!' Screaming obscenities made me feel a little better.

My hand had come off my freezing privates and I was now dancing about in the shallow waters with my hands on the side of my head trying to somehow compress the pain away. The sound of my screaming echoed around the beach and bounced off the tall cliffs around me. It was only after about twenty seconds that I happened to look up. The man on the chair who'd presumed I'd offered him specialist gay sex was now standing on the edge of the cliff looking right down at my naked form hopping and screaming in the shallow waters of Lake Okanagan.

Our eyes met for a second and, even at that distance, I could sense a mixture of withering pity and disgust. It was useless trying to explain.

I bolted back to the car park, grabbed my clothes and legged it. I eventually found cover in a little copse of trees, got dressed and tried to wrap my T-shirt round my bleeding foot.

This was turning into a stressful Sunday. I was bored of hotel food so decided to head into town for dinner. Sunday nights in Kelowna were *not* rocking and there wasn't that much open. Eventually I opted for a chain place called the Keg. It was semi-buzzing and did obese portions of steak and seafood. At the back of my mind I was worried that I might bump into my cliff-top friend – and if I did, I wanted to look as manly as possible, downing pints, eating raw meat and talking to loggers . . . Actually, talking to loggers sounded a bit weird as well.

So, I was sitting at the bar nursing a pint and watching Canadian football. For some unfathomable reason this is slightly different from the American version so they can't play each other. The Canadian version has twelve players on the pitch, as opposed to the American eleven, and they have only three downs per possession whereas the American game has four.

Not that this really matters: Canadians are all about ice hockey anyway. Kelowna's ice-hockey team is the Rockets and they have Ogopogo as their mascot. The team was originally from Tacoma, just below Seattle, but they were surrounded by big cities so they moved to Kelowna for more fans. They kept the name Rockets because Tacoma was where Boeing made rockets but they adopted Ogopogo as a mascot to incorporate some local colour.

But I digress. I was at the bar in the Keg when a face suddenly came right up to mine.

'Guess who?'

It was a girl and I genuinely had absolutely no idea who she was.

'Hey, how are you?' I said, desperately trying to work out who she might be.

'How weird is this? You doing the rounds about town?'

Suddenly I clicked: this was the waitress from the winery and it looked like news of my anal cruising hadn't yet spread too far.

She moved on to join a table of friends for dinner and I returned to my pint. Then Krist Novoselic walked in. I first noticed him because he was freakishly tall – around six feet seven, maybe eight? He had put on some serious poundage since his skinny youth noodling on the bass in Nirvana but it was him all right. I was certain. He was with a girl much younger than him. She was pretty and blonde with a weird name like Skylar. I know this because the barman went a little gushy and asked Krist how he was doing. Krist nodded and introduced Skylar. The barman totally ignored me from then on and just talked to Krist. He asked Krist if he was playing at the moment. Krist nodded and mentioned a couple of gigs. Did Krist want something to eat, wondered the wide-eyed barman? No he didn't; he and Skylar were just having a drink and then going to see a friend in a band. I liked Krist. Krist seemed nice.

I moved into major eavesdropping mode. I love listening to other people's conversations, especially when those people used to be in Nirvana. It made total sense that he should be here. Seattle is only an hour or so away from Kelowna and lots of famous people have houses here on the lake: Arnold Schwarzenegger, Wayne Gretzky . . . And, clearly, Krist Novoselic from Nirvana. I pretended to play with my iPad while I listened in. Krist was telling Skylar, clearly a musician herself, that he was really impressed with her playing.

'You know the chords,' he said, smiling at her, 'but now you need anticipation.'

Skylar looked at him adoringly and Krist continued with his master class. Krist told her that when he saw a hand move over a fretboard he instinctively knew what was going to be played, allowing him to kick in bang on time, not a millisecond late.

'But that only comes with years of playing,' he said.

Skylar lapped it all up. I tried to think about what I knew of him – I thought he was Croatian in origin and he started the band with Kurt; he fought with Courtney Love over the Nirvana legacy and he was pretty political . . . Oh and he once hit me over the head with his bass guitar.

This is a true story, I swear. When I was at SOAS in London for my university years I used to help organize bands to play at the union. We once got an offer of a band I loved, Mudhoney, but we also had to take the band supporting them on their mini Sub Pop tour. We weren't happy but said yes, as we really wanted Mudhoney. That support band was, of course, Nirvana, who'd just finished their first album, *Bleach*, and were relatively unknown. Come the day of the gig, I told them that they had five songs and then they were off so Mudhoney could come on. They ignored me and played on into a sixth song so I pulled the plug on their PA. The band went mental and Krist swung his bass guitar at me, and it glanced off my head. Never mind, though – my job was done: we wanted Mudhoney on, not these grungy losers . . . Whatever happened to Mudhoney?

I looked over at Krist again wondering if I should just bring this up. We'd all laugh about it and he'd invite me along to the gig tonight? But Krist was now busy tongue-sandwiching Skylar so conversation was difficult. Whatever, I needed proof of this encounter. I waited until they came up for air and then brought out my iPhone. It was in a casing designed to look like an old cassette tape so it was quite subtle. I turned the camera on and manoeuvred the thing so that it was pointing to my left – right at Krist. I paused then pressed the button. To my horror the flash went off. I'd turned it on to get a photo of Arlene Gaal in her dark house. Krist and Skylar both looked up with a start and stared at me. I went into panic mode and started fiddling with the phone as though it was faulty. I made the flash go off a couple more times in my face to make it look like I was just an idiot trying to get the camera to work. There was no way I could talk to him now but at least I had proof. I surreptitiously checked the shot and the photo was clear. I wolfed down a New York striploin and then left about the same time as Krist, who towered over Skylar as they walked off arm in arm. I briefly considered following them to their gig but realized this might be a tad creepy. I'd once done this when I spotted Mick Jones from the Clash in my local Tesco in Portobello Road. I followed him all the way to Holland Park and watched him browse through the paperback section in a charity store. I thought I was being subtle but, years later, when *Trigger Happy TV* was at its height, I ended up at his house with a group of people that, weirdly, also included Kate Moss and Sadie Frost (I know – clang, clang – who dropped those names? But it was just a weird night). Anyway, I'd got talking to Mick Jones and he was bit pissed and he ended up saying, 'You followed me once all the way home from Portobello – I thought you were doing some hidden-camera stunt on me.' I was mortified and slipped out soon after.

I drove back to my hotel and immediately googled a recent photo of Krist. It definitely wasn't my guy. I couldn't believe it. I was angry. What was this fraudulent bastard doing swanning around pretending to be Krist Novoselic? Then I remembered that he'd never claimed to be him. It had been me who'd made that supposition and, not for the first time in my life, I felt a bit of an arse.

The next morning I awoke early and snuck up to the curtains, whipping them open with some force as though I was going to somehow surprise Ogopogo and catch him mid-feed with a red face staring up at me. But there was only a lone duck who proceeded to 'duck' down leaving only his feathered ass wiggling insultingly in my direction.

It was my final day in the Okanagan and I'd agreed to go on a little road trip with Al, one of the two guys who'd taken me out on the boat. He was going to collect me in his enormo-pickup truck and we were going up to Myra Canyon to check out the old railway line. There was little chance of lake monsters in the mountains but Al said it was something that I had to see – and, besides, there was a chance to see cougars, bears and wolverines. I wasn't quite sure what a wolverine was. I thought they were fictional creatures? (In the eighties Brat Pack flick *Red Dawn*, the Russians invade the USA and the kids from the high school run to the hills and become resistance fighters – calling themselves 'Wolverines'.) Al didn't know how to describe a wolverine but he settled on ROUS (Rodent of Unusual Size). He said it was like a huge chipmunk, the size of a goat with big teeth and long sharp claws. 'They are mean sons of bitches,' said Al.

At the entrance to the trail was a large handwritten sign warning that a bear had been spotted with cubs. 'Under no circumstance should you run away from a bear unless you have somewhere to go . . .' was the very curious advice here.

I'd seen other signs in the valley that suggested you take a bell with you on hikes and ring it frantically should a bear approach. I decided that, should we be faced with this predicament, I'd stand directly behind Al and cower.

The old railway line spanned the entire canyon and used to be used to transport gold from mines in the hills. It was a spectacular feat of engineering that had burnt down in the huge forest fire of 2003. The bridges had been restored and now comprised part of a cycling and hiking trail. We walked and walked and walked. I had no idea how far Al intended to go but I didn't want to look like a wimp. This was a big day for my left foot. In 2011 I broke three metatarsals on a TV show in Argentina and this would be the first big test of my recovery. At the sixth mile I couldn't walk much more and had to sit down and take my boot off. I think Al was secretly quite chuffed that he'd 'broken' me and went a bit easier on me as I hobbled back towards his pickup.

Sadly there were no signs of bears, cougars or wolverines. The Okanagan Valley is not one to easily give up her fierce creatures – real or fictional.

We drove back down to Kelowna, where Al left me to a final spot of monster-hunting. Just along the shoreline from my hotel I'd bumped into a guy who had a boat he could rent me for the afternoon. It had a depth finder *and* a fish finder. This kind of sonar device could possibly help me spot an unusually large creature in the water beneath me.

Having left a hefty deposit, I roared off over the lake. It was like a mirror: 'perfect Ogopogo conditions', the renter had said just before I set off. Once again mine was the only boat on the entire eighty-mile expanse. I wanted to head north this time and this meant going under the new bridge. I put-putted under the left-hand arch and looked down into the black water. The fish finder was not seeing anything. I headed out into the very centre of the lake. The depth finder told me that it was 356 feet deep. Not bad, but there are areas near Squally Point that supposedly go down to 800 feet.

I turned the engine off and all was silent. I floated quietly on Lake Okanagan, all alone save for a solitary loon staring at this loony cockily. I peered earnestly at the fish finder but it could find no fish let alone a monster. I could see how an obsession with something in this lake could drive a man insane after a while. The more you told people about your obsession the more determined you'd become to prove it so they'd stop referring to you as 'that monster guy', the loony who believed in Ogopogo. Now *I* was a loony who thought he'd seen Ogopogo, endlessly propping up bars showing people the footage as they attempted to shuffle a couple of stools away. After an hour or so, I gave up. I switched on the engine and turned for home. As I docked the boat I wondered what had happened to Eddy Haymour's statue after his death. Here was an inhabitant of the Okanagan who'd been driven crazy by a different obsession. There was no record of Eddy ever having seen Ogopogo; he'd simply used the story to help him with his brilliantly crazy project. It was funny, two people – Eddy and myself – both born in Lebanon, both fixated by something in this curious stretch of water so very far away from the distant cedars of our homeland. I turned towards the lake for the last time and gave a little nod to both Ogopogo and Eddy Haymour. Things and people like these are what make life so interesting.

Hibagon

'Godzilla is the son of the atomic bomb. He is a nightmare created out of the darkness of the human soul.
He is the sacred beast of the apocalypse.'

Tomoyuki Tanaka

I remember asking my dad whether he'd ever killed a man.
Obviously I was asking about the war, and not hoping that
he'd suddenly buckle under my interrogation and admit to a
string of grisly murders. He flew in the Fleet Air Arm against
the Japanese in the Pacific in the last two years of the Second
World War. Like many of his generation, he wouldn't talk
about that kind of stuff very much; but one night, after a
couple of drinks, he let on that he'd shot down a Zero. He
hadn't seen a parachute.

At Heathrow Airport, about to fly off to Japan, I felt slightly
odd knowing this. My father had passed away just four months

previously and to me this trip was something of a connector mission with him.

The departure lounge was, unsurprisingly, stuffed with Japanese, all uber-trendy, some reading cartoon books and most wearing those curious surgical masks. Until recently I'd always thought this demonstrated some sort of national OCD, a Wacko Jacko fear of germs. But then I'd read that this is all a cultural misunderstanding. They're actually worn in politeness: so as not to spread germs. I had a feeling that I would come across a lot of misunderstandings like this over the next ten days. I'd never been to Japan before and already had that heady feeling I get when I'm about to visit a new country.

Having wangled my way into Virgin Upper Class, I slept most of the way – and there is little that makes a traveller much happier than this. I did, however, make the mistake of watching the Steven Soderbergh film *Contagion*, about a pandemic spreading round the world. The moment the film was over I felt desperately keen to join the Japanese and purchase a job-lot of surgical facemasks. I listened to the latest Kermode/Mayo movie podcast. There was a great interview with the film director John Landis, of *Thriller* and *An American Werewolf in London* fame. He had just written a book about 100 years of movie monsters. He talked about how Godzilla was such an obvious metaphor for the atomic attacks on Japan when it was first written, in the early 1950s. The father of the guy who wrote it had actually survived one of the explosions. Monsters feature heavily in Japanese life. Their mythology is chock-a-block with them and a quick trawl through the Internet revealed a veritable cornucopia. Here are some of my favourites:

Aka Manto: a malicious spirit who haunts bathrooms and
   asks the cubicle occupants if they want red or blue paper
Akaname: a spirit that licks untidy bathrooms
Mujina: a shape-shifting badger

Hikiko: the ghost of a girl who was treated badly by her
   parents and bullied by her classmates
Ittan-momem: a possessed roll of cotton that attempts to
   smother people by wrapping itself around their faces
Kasa-obake: a paper-umbrella monster
Sazae-oni: a turban snail that turns into a woman
Zorigami: a possessed clock

I could carry on with a list of more than 200 but you get my
drift.

There are a couple of internationally famous monsters that
initially seemed perfect for my quest. The best-known of these
is Issie, a lake monster who apparently resides in Lake Ikeda at
the far southern end of Kyushu Island. However, I found a
much more interesting prey. I'd read about the Hibagon, a creature that is supposed to roam the mountains around Hiroshima.
A lot of people refer to it as the 'Japanese Bigfoot'. Others,
though, say it's some sort of mutant man who survived the
atomic bomb dropped there in 1945 by the Americans. This
really intrigued me. The Hibagon seemed to be a very Japanese
type of monster and the bonus was that I'd also have an excuse
to visit Hiroshima itself. My father had flown over the city a day
after the bomb was dropped and the experience had affected
him deeply. So it was decided like that. I was off to Japan to find
the Hibagon.

As the plane started its descent into Tokyo I spotted in the
inflight magazine the worrying suggestion that an International
Driving Permit is required when renting a car in Japan. I hoped
this was bollocks because I'd stupidly left mine at home.

My landing card asked me to give my reason for visiting
Japan. 'Monster-hunting', I wrote proudly.

The very first thing I noticed after we'd landed was that the
machines that registered your fingerprints and took your photo
at the passport desk were framed in an almost childish, Hello

Kitty-type cartoon design. This made a nice change from the usual stern-looking welcome.

Once through I caught a train going to Shibuya, the area of Tokyo famed for its crazily populated intersection and where my hotel was. On the train I noticed built-in combination locks so that you could attach your suitcase to the luggage rack. This is a genius idea. Why don't *we* have that, so I don't have to spend the whole time on the Worst Great Western's Kemble-to-Paddington ride hoping some chav hasn't pinched my bag?

Also, despite the Japanese famously being half our size, there was a lot of legroom, maybe double what you get on the Worst Great Western. All in all, this was a supremely civilized experience. The only slight problem was quite a pungent smell of BO, but this couldn't be blamed on my hosts. Two nearby Spaniards had clearly just spent fifteen hours in economy and were not looking well on the experience.

The train flashed past a mish-mash of bamboo and electricity pylons as we entered the outskirts of Tokyo. I arrived at Shibuya Station feeling very smug. Everyone had told me that getting round Tokyo was a nightmare. Obviously not one of them was an experienced traveller like me. I walked outside and hopped into a cab. I showed the driver my hotel name and he nodded enthusiastically. Strangely, however, my door suddenly opened automatically in a very *Total Recall* manner. The cabbie indicated that I should get out. I did as he asked and he pointed vaguely in a direction in which I started walking. I had zero idea of where I was going and there were no English street signs. I got to the Shibuya Crossing. I guess if Tokyo has a 'sight' then this is it: Piccadilly Circus times ten with supersized neon. I wandered lost as a lost person in Lostland. I tried to ask a couple of people but each one sent me in a different direction. This was not a good start.

I walked down what looked like Carnaby Street on acid. Alien noise was coming from everywhere. A giant video screen showed a band called the Funky Monkey Babys, while the warblings of what sounded a little like George Michael emanated from behind a window displaying rubber clothing.

I felt big, dwarfing the pedestrians around me, as I trudged through the streets, already Lost in Translation. I spent a good hour and half wandering aimlessly about, hopelessly lost. Every time I returned to Shibuya I could see where I was on my map but I'd then head off in the wrong direction again. Finally, in complete despair, I tried another cab. I hopped in and attempted to pronounce the street address in my best Japanese. Amazingly the electric door stayed shut and we set off. He seemed to know where I was going. Ten minutes later we got back to Shibuya Station, where the first cabbie had refused me entry. We continued on in the exact opposite direction to the one the first guy had pointed me in. The hotel was about three minutes' walk from the station up a narrow lane. I stumbled into reception, deliriously happy. To my great relief the receptionist spoke a little English.

'Mr Jory. Your woom is weady. It is larger than one you weserve – no extwa charge . . .'

I thanked him profusely and got the key.

I got into a lift that was pitch-black but I managed to find the button for the third floor. The corridors were also barely lit and it took me some time to find my room. When I opened the door I assumed there had been some mix-up in the reservations for a hamster and me, as the room was so small I could barely get in it. I rather longed to see the smaller one from which I'd been upgraded. There was about half a foot between the tiny bed and the wall and I edged myself down to the window and dumped my bag. I then edged back and squeezed into the bathroom, which resembled something I'd seen in a doll's house. I needed the loo but this was not simple. I had to keep the glass door open so that I could sit on it and push my legs into the room. There was a frankly terrifying control panel to my side that appeared to show the various methods in which this contraption could give you an enema. I left the panel alone, did my business and then pressed a button from the safety of the bedroom. A jet-like spray fired up from inside the bowl and I thanked the Lord I hadn't been sitting on it at the time: it looked like this process could remove skin. I closed the glass door and decided to deal with all this later.

Downstairs in the restaurant the menu comprised a simple list of sentences in Japanese. It was giving very little away. I took pot luck and pointed at one for the waitress. Three minutes later a basket of goodies was placed before me. Among the various little bowls of stuff I immediately recognized tofu and possibly some cabbage, but the rest – besides an extremely fishy fish in the middle – amounted to total wild cards. I tucked in anyway. It was all quite edible and I felt pleased with myself for being so 'local'. I sat back and looked around the restaurant. The Japanese family next to me were chowing down on bowls of spaghetti Bolognese onto which they were shaking Kraft 100% Parmesan. Opposite me a spotty fat woman was also devouring some spaghetti Bolognese. It looked rather good.

I headed out of the hotel and back towards Shibuya Station. Now I had my bearings I was very happy: I have a pretty good internal compass, which was now set to magnetic north. Outside the station hundreds of people were crammed in to the outdoor smoking area, puffing away like it was going out of fashion. Here also stands a statue of Hachiko: the dog who sat and waited every day for his master to return, not understanding that he had died. I think Richard Gere made a film about it . . . (Or was that a gerbil? I forget.).

I crossed the Shibuya Crossing again and spotted a Starbucks with a perfect view over the pedestrian maelstrom. Upstairs the window seats were all jam-packed apart from one section that was curiously empty save for one woman. I sat down and started snapping away at the crowd below. It really was a ringside seat for people-watching. Then I realized why the section was empty. The lone woman next to me was scribbling furiously in a book in red ink (always a giveaway). She looked up, spotted me looking at her, and let loose a stream of furious invective. Froth and spittle appeared around her lips. I had no idea what she was saying but it was clearly not 'Welcome to Japan, stranger!'

She started to get quite violent and mock-punched me a couple of times while screaming at a new level. I held my ground and pretended to ignore her, which was exceedingly tricky as the whole place was now ignoring the people river on Shibuya Crossing and watching the loon and me.

I wondered whether I'd maybe broken some social code, committed an awful cultural faux pas. I took a quick look at the loon. She was quite attractive but now dribbling all down her face, which somewhat offset the look. In the end I gave in and moved to a vacated spot in a more peaceful area. I was then free to watch a young American approach the crazy woman and ask her if the seat next to her was free. I sat back and enjoyed the fireworks . . .

Below me a camera crew was filming four pretty young girls, all clad in leopard-skin and, on cue, sauntering across the crossing trying to look carefree yet sassy. They had the look of a band. Maybe they were the female equivalent of the magnificently named Sexy Zone, a boy band whose huge poster looked down on the crossing? Curiously, it appeared that – unlike anywhere else in the world – the Japanese give photography a miss at home: the only people snapping away here were tourists.

I walked out through a music shop where I discovered some more great names for groups. I was particularly pleased to see that Bump of Chicken had a new album out. So did Heartful Voice with Tackey and Tsubasa. I had a listen; *Hurt*ful Voice would have been more apt. Sadly I was unable to find any of Bump of Chicken's work but I googled them later and found out that they were on their seventh album, so no flash in the pan.

Once back in my matchbox, I googled the Hibagon to see where I could start. There was very little information available. The epicentre of Hibagon sightings seemed to be based around Mount Hiba, 125 miles from Hiroshima in the north of the prefecture. I needed to get to Hiroshima and then get a car. I also realized that I would definitely need an interpreter. I turned to Twitter for help. I asked my followers, a random bunch, for help finding a good, interesting interpreter in the Hiroshima area for five days. Within about five minutes someone had Tweeted me that his friend ran 'Get Hiroshima' and could definitely help. I Tweeted them and they gave me the name of a lady called Koizumi who would be available. I emailed Koizumi with my requirements and hoped she wouldn't think I was a nutter.

I lay scrunched up on my bed and watched *Lost in Translation*, one of my favourite films anyway and absolutely perfect to watch on your first day in Tokyo.

I left the hotel at dusk and went to look at the Shibuya Crossing lit by neon. Tokyo is a city best seen at night, when it gets seriously *Blade Runner*. I entered a lively looking counter-service place. The food was spectacular: pork and noodle ramen with a gratifying excess of chili. Through the window I watched the neon city fizz with energy and loud, bad pop music.

Back at the hotel I checked my emails. There was one from Koizumi, who was very up for being my interpreter and extremely excited about hunting the Hibagon. She wrote that she had contacts in the Hiroshima prefecture with whom she was going to set up interviews. This was very good news. I was asleep before my head hit the midget pillow. The room was incredibly hot and I kept waking up and thinking I was in some weird washing machine. Come the morning I packed fast while standing on the bed before going downstairs for breakfast.

A waitress doing what seemed to be a pitch-perfect impression of Minnie Mouse served me with a bowl of soup and some cold meats. Ryuichi Sakamoto's soundtrack for *Merry Christmas, Mr. Lawrence* floated hauntingly in the ether.

I had to get to Shinagawa Station to catch a Shinkansen (Bullet Train) to Hiroshima. I looked at the Tokyo subway map. At first it looked as though I might need an Enigma machine to crack it but I toughened up and worked out that I needed the green line to Shinagawa. I was pretty sure that the numbers by each station corresponded to the amount I needed to pay. I pressed 160 yen and put in the money. A ticket was spat out and I was off. On the platform a mass of humanity awaited the train. This was a whole different ball game from the peaceful airport shuttle. For a moment I worried that I might be on some private penal line. The cars were full and I mean *really* full. Little faces sporting white facemasks were squashed right up against the door glass and it looked very tricky to breathe. As the door opened a tsunami of people swept on to the platform, all elbows and shoves, the usual Japanese politeness totally abandoned. I valiantly fought my way in and blockaded myself into a corner using my suitcase as a perimeter wall. An official in white gloves was physically pushing people into the carriage until nobody could move either arms or legs.

I was fortunate in being a good foot taller than anybody else so I could see over the chaos. On the walls of the train ads were playing on a multitude of screens. The first one was of a smiling woman sitting on the loo. She had what appeared to be a mini-basketball net positioned in the sink and she was bouncing a ball and trying to get it into the net. When she succeeded, she went totally mental and seemed to forget that she was on the loo. Next up: what appeared to be an ad for an erotic barbershop. Western men were portrayed having their faces massaged by very beautiful women wearing barbers' smocks. No haircutting seemed to take place and the camera lingered over the girls' bodies as they floated just above the man's submissive face. At the end, the man walked out looking very happy and a beautiful blonde in the street stopped and stared at him lustfully.

It reminded me of being in Moscow filming a scene in which a naked woman gave me a haircut. The entire crew was so British and awkward about the whole situation. It soon became clear that we were in a brothel and girls lined up outside waiting for the filming to finish. When it did, we all skulked out giggling like schoolboys. I don't think we did the sexual reputation of the British any good.

The final ad was brilliant. It was for a new Nintendo game called *Monster Hunter*. The Japanese voiceover kept shouting 'Mooonster Hunttter' over and over. I looked around but it was clear that nobody knew that they were in the presence of the world's greatest monster-hunter.

At Shinagawa I fought my way on to the platform and joined yet another tide of humanity cascading into the main station. I found the Shinkansen counter: I needed a Nozomi Shinkansen as this was the super-express. Amazingly I seemed to be able to purchase a return, with reserved window seat, mainly through the art of drawing. My artistic skills being on a par with those of my cat, Colonel Mustard, I hoped that I was OK. Twenty minutes later and I was standing confidently on platform 21. Every car had its own gate and I was at the far end, car number 16. I filmed a Bullet Train coming in. They really are beautiful: sleek, impressive pieces of engineering, probably one of the most iconic sights in Japan. I had to admit to being quite chuffed with how easy it had all been. Again, I'd been warned that it was infernally complicated – but not for me. Maybe I could become a sort of unofficial Shinkansen expert? Shinkansen-San, they would call me. My train arrived and I got on, taking my reserved place by the window next to two Japanese businessmen in Wacko Jacko masks.

We were back in the world of massive legroom and comfort.

I was very happy. I was on my way to monster-hunt in Hiroshima, somewhere I'd wanted to visit since I was a boy. It was all too perfect. The train stopped and everyone got out. This was even better. I had the whole carriage to myself. I sat and waited. Three women in pink uniforms got on and started cleaning. One of them shouted at me and indicated the platform in the very same fashion as the Tokyo cabbie had done.

'Hiroshima?' I asked.

'*No!*' she screamed.

I got my bags and got off – mortified. I'd got on the wrong train and was now at Tokyo Central, the world's most confusing train station. What a bloody idiot.

Fortunately the Shinkansen system is infinitely more efficient than both Worst Great Western and me and I was quickly able to get on one heading the right way at the speed of a bullet.

Twenty minutes out of Tokyo and I spotted Mount Fuji. It was a crisp, sunny day and the summit was absolutely clear, which is apparently rare. I saw this as a good omen. I was going to get a second monster spot: first Ogopogo and now the Hibagon. I was feeling confident.

The ticket inspector entered the carriage. As she did so she bowed to everyone inside. The woman with the food and drinks carriage did the same. Could you even imagine this on Worst Great Western? In between every carriage was a little tiny glass capsule in which you could go and smoke. It was like a scene I'd done for *World Shut Your Mouth* when I'd had people in glass cases full of smoke in the middle of a park.

Outside, Japan flashed past my window. For some reason there seemed to be an extraordinary amount of graveyards by the track. Fortunately the Shinkansen had a 0 per cent accident rate, which is pretty impressive. After three hours of silent, ground-level flight we pulled into Hiroshima. As I stepped on to the platform birdsong was being piped through hidden speakers, which was rather eerie. It was almost as though the city wanted you to know that there was still life there. The Lonely Planet, in its infinite wisdom and clearly used to dealing with idiots, wisely warned visitors that the place was not 'rubble' but 'a thriving city'. No shit . . .

As I walked through the station building I saw a big 'Welcome to Hiroshima' sign, behind which was a garishly vulgar McDonald's sign. It looked like the American occupation was still ongoing. I caught a cab and, fabulously, the driver knew where my hotel was. I checked in and got a room on the four-teenth floor in which I could actually swing a cat. I liked Hiroshima already.

The hotel rented out bikes so I grabbed one and used it to pedal about town. Despite Hiroshima being almost flat the bike was motor assisted, which made cycling a dream. I was careful in the traffic, though – the irony of being killed in a bicycle acci-dent in Hiroshima was not lost on me. I felt pretty certain that the Japanese must have a 'possessed-bicycle' monster – they definitely have one for everything else. Like a two-wheeled version of Christine it would have a mind of its own and propel the hapless rider over the nearest cliff at the first opportunity.

I cycled down Peace Boulevard until I got to a bridge spanning a river and saw the Atomic Dome on my right. This is the remains of a factory built by a Czech architect in 1915. The bomb exploded 600 metres above it and the walls and dome partially survived – unlike 70 per cent of the rest of the city, much of which was made of wood. Eighty thousand people were killed instantly.

I pedalled around the building and then cycled on through the Peace Park and up and down lively alleyways. As in Tokyo, when the sun set and the lights came on, the city really came alive. Everywhere I looked was blazing neon and gaudy lights. Old Japan built architecture of exquisite, intricate beauty. New Japan builds with neon and chutzpah. What looks drab and unexciting in the day becomes an exhilarating assault on the senses by night.

I headed for Okonomi Mura, a three-storey building filled with dozens of little places solely cooking the local speciality: *okonomiyaki*. Although sounding like a name for yet another type of monster, this is a kind of Japanese pancake filled with cabbage, meat, egg and noodles. I chose a spot run by a wizened old lady who looked like she knew exactly what she was doing. She cooked it on a hot steel counter right in front of me. It was phenomenal. I waddled away sated and content in the direction of my hotel. I was still jet-lagged and buzzing from the excitement of possibly 'bagging' another monster. The following morning I would meet my guide, Koizumi, and my hunt could begin.

I awoke at four in the morning and couldn't get back to sleep. I watched a very good Scorsese documentary on George Harrison before going downstairs to find some breakfast.

I really wanted to attempt the numerous Japanese options but most were squidgy, oily-looking things in cubes and my heart wasn't in it. I opted for scrambled eggs but had a green tea instead of coffee to 'keep it real'.

I sat down and looked at my watch. It was 8.15 a.m., the exact time that this city was wiped off the map on 6 August 1945. So far there was not a hint of this traumatic event in the air. The psyche – the 'feel' of this city – was entirely positive. I was curious to find out how a city dealt with being defined by its destruction. The only other place I'd come across like this was Halifax, Nova Scotia: a city that was totally flattened when a French munitions ship exploded in the harbour in 1917. Up until then it had been the largest explosion in history. I'd had the misfortune to be snowed in at Halifax once and, believe me, Hiroshima has way more going for it.

After breakfast I met my guide, Koizumi. She was a lady of about my age and bubbling with energy and smiles. She was very excited about the Hibagon hunt. She said that the locals of Mount Hiba had worried that everyone had forgotten their story so were honoured to have one of the world's foremost monster-hunters visiting them. She had organized a trip there for the following day. Today, however, she wanted to show me round her home city. I was a little disappointed: I was perfectly capable of exploring the town myself and was itching to go monster-hunting, for which I needed her help. There was little I could do, though, and I didn't want to cause offence. So off we went.

Minutes later we were on Peace Boulevard again, where I'd cycled the previous afternoon. Koizumi stopped by a clump of trees. They all had little yellow signs attached to them, indicating that they'd survived the atomic bomb. I would never have noticed these natural 'survivors' had Koizumi not pointed them out to me. Maybe having a guide wasn't too bad?

We crossed the bridge and went into the Peace Park, a large area with various statues and memorials as well as a museum all dedicated to the atomic explosion. The museum was utterly fascinating. What particularly grabbed me was the information about how and which cities were targeted. Four large cities had been chosen. The Americans had wanted the drop-site to be cloud-free so that they could analyse what happened. The selected cities were Hiroshima, Kokura, Niigata and Kyoto. However, the then Secretary of War, Henry Stimson, had honeymooned at Kyoto many years before, and had been captivated by its beauty, so when he saw that it was one of the targets he had it removed from the list. Nagasaki was chosen instead. Such are lives changed.

Hiroshima was an important port city and therefore the target for the first raid. Unluckily for the city and its inhabitants, the skies were clear on the chosen morning: the bomb was dropped and exploded 1,900 feet above the city. In addition to the 80,000 people killed instantly, 70,000 more suffered appalling injuries. Whatever my views on what the Japanese did in the Second World War – and the fact that the dropping of the bombs may have shortened the war, and possibly saved my father's life – this is a shocking event to consider. We looked at burnt items of clothing, molten metal and an extraordinary exhibit of the stone steps of a bank with a stone wall behind it. Someone had clearly been sitting on the steps when the bomb went off, because his shadow was burnt into the wall behind him.

I looked at a map that showed the area where the atomic 'black rain' fell. This stretches way out into Hiroshima province. As I've mentioned, one theory about the Hibagon suggests that it's a human who was transformed by the radiation following the explosion. The radiation produced by the bomb here was not long-lasting. Unlike the stuff unleashed by Chernobyl, which has a half-life of about thirty years, almost all radiation in Hiroshima dissipated within six days. Was it possible that in those six days something had somehow been so heavily irradiated that it had mutated into the Hibagon? This kind of story is very common in Japan (Godzilla was 'created' in much the same way) but it seemed pretty unlikely. Maybe it was less spectacular than some glowing green radiation monster? Maybe it was some form of deformed beast, a bastard product of some radiated animal? I had no idea but it was intriguing and I could find out a lot more the following day.

We left the museum and walked around the park. In its centre was a huge bell that you could ring using a pole suspended on ropes. This was a memorial bell for all the victims of the bomb. I pulled back the pole and gave the bell a hefty thwack. The peal resonated deep and long around the park. I stood there for a second absorbing the shock waves and thinking about my father. I wished he'd been a proper dad. Moving on, we reached the Atomic Dome that I'd cycled round the day before. It was right by the T-shaped bridge that had been the precise mark for the bomb, though wind had pushed it slightly off target and therefore the hypocentre was about 200 yards away directly over a hospital. Our atomic tourism over, we hopped on a boat to Miyajima, an island in Hiroshima Bay and home to one of the most famous shrines in Japan. As we put-putted through the city Koizumi told me that I should call her Naoko, as Koizumi was her surname.

It was a gorgeous day so we stood on deck to have a look at the oyster-shucking machines on the bank. In hindsight this was probably a mistake as we went under four or five very low bridges and Naoko had a mini-heart attack every time, thinking we were going to hit them. As we approached each bridge she'd scream, 'Dom-San, get down!' and then pull me to the floor in a slightly hysterical manner. If bridges freaked her out, I wasn't sure she was of the right temperament to go monster-hunting with me.

As we left the river and entered the bay proper the boat roared across the delta to the island. Once docked, we meandered through the streets of the tiny town in the direction of the shrine. The builders had sunk the posts of a huge red gate deep into the seabed so it appeared to be floating. It was rather soothing to see something old and cultural after the shock of the new of my first couple of days in Japan. Naoko wanted to show me the temple. You had to give a financial donation to do so and the first thing we saw when we entered was an entire corridor of colourfully decorated sake barrels. Life is good if you're a monk. We climbed up through exquisite ornamental gardens on the way to the cable car. I wanted to get right to the top of the mountain for a view over Hiroshima. Naoko kept trying to put me off and eventually admitted that she prayed for bad weather when bringing clients here as the climb after the cable car was quite arduous and she was lazy.

Once off the cable car we started to walk. As we did so, Naoko filled me in on what she'd done so far to organize a Hibagon hunt. She told me that she'd contacted the Mount Hiba district council and that they were very excited about our visit as there hadn't been much press interest lately.

'The whole Hibagon office is at our disposal,' said Naoko

laughing. 'We will meet with the man responsible for the Hibagon and he will take us to the places where there have been sightings. He is happy to answer all questions and he is very knowledgeable. I am very happy we are going to hunt for a monster, Dom-San. This is a big adventure.' She paused for a second with glorious comic timing. 'This, however . . . We don't have to do this . . .' she continued, puffing and looking up the path. I teased her and suggested that she should advertise herself as a 'lazy' guide. Eventually we got to the top. I felt good. It was from this very spot that an incredible photo was taken of the mushroom cloud six minutes after the bomb went off. I'd seen it in the museum. What must the photographer have thought as he raised his camera? It must have seemed like the end of the world. Had the Hibagon, whatever it might be, been created at that very moment? Had it maybe gazed too long at the fiery skies over the city, transfixed, as so many were, by the sheer enormity of what was happening around it?

We were very happy on our summit and stayed there for quite a while. Eventually Naoko took me a down different way because there were several holes in the rock that supposedly had certain powers. One hole, for example, cured 'itchy body' – unless you were 'bad', in which case it actually *gave* you 'itchy body'.

Back at the bottom, we stopped in a Shinto shrine while Naoko prayed for a while. I stood on an outside platform, smelling the incense and gazing down at my feet – ever the awkward atheist. I have to admit to feeling very calm there. These sorts of places seem to work better the older you get.

We caught the boat back to Hiroshima. I'd done enough 'normal' tourism. It was time to crack on with some monster-hunting.

The next morning I was up early and ready to bag me a Hibagon. But first, breakfast: monster-hunting is always more productive on a sated belly. The dining-room walls were wallpapered with black-and-white photographs of New York. Some of them showed New Yorkers flying the Stars and Stripes and cheering in a ticker-tape parade. I rather hoped it wasn't a war-related celebration and marvelled at the insouciance shown by Hiroshimites towards their destructors.

I met Naoko and we set off to rent a car. Having been told that I needed an International Driving Permit I was rather worried but I needn't have been. Renting a car in Japan was akin to being greeted on a royal visit. Every production of a form or a credit card was met with much bowing and smiling and we were soon sitting in a tiny little Toyota Box (not the real name but it would be apt) while the entire staff of the rental agency lined up to bow as we drove out of the garage. We were headed for Saijo, seventy-five miles north-east of Hiroshima. Naoko had arranged for us to meet a Mr Maeda, who was head of the town's tourist association and also ran the 'Hibagon office'. As with the low-bridge experience, Naoko was a very nervous passenger and I worried for her fingers as she gripped the door handle for dear life. Not that we could do much speed in the Box. I managed to get it up to about sixty miles an hour but that was it.

Saijo is an unremarkable little town at the foot of a small range of mountains, the highest being Mount Hiba. We parked up outside a building in the centre of town and were met by Mr Maeda, an unassuming man who seemed incredibly pleased to see us. He invited us into his messy office where he handed me his business card. It had a cartoon drawing of a rather cuddly-looking creature that Mr Maeda confirmed was the Hibagon. It turned out that he had designed this endearing image to make the Hibagon more tourist-friendly, as the original UMA (uniden-tified mysterious animal) was not quite so sweet.

We sat around a table and I asked Mr Maeda to tell me the history of the Hibagon. He produced a map that marked every sighting of the beast as well as a photograph of a footprint, taken about seven miles from where we were sitting. As I looked at these he told me the story, with Naoko translating:

On 20 July 1970, very near Mount Hiba, a farmer reported seeing a big ape wandering through his field. The ape measured about two metres seventy centimetres, had dark reddish-brown hair, a big head like a cone and was walking on two feet. They had small monkeys in the area but nothing remotely like this. After the farmer's original sighting there followed about ten more sightings within a month – all fitting the same description. A local newspaper wrote the story and coined the name 'Hibagon' after the nearby mountain. Things then got a bit hysterical, with schoolchildren having to be accompanied to school by the police and a lot of locals becoming incredibly nervous about going out. The story exploded all over Japan and all sorts of weirdoes came from all over the country to hunt the creature. Universities set up Hibagon student-exploration clubs and groups would come and roam the mountains for weekends. The initial panic lasted for about a month but then things started to calm down a little. Journalists came from everywhere and the locals started getting a bit annoyed because Japanese magazines and newspapers started making fun of them.

The local government set up a special 'Anthropoid Section' and they got a budget to deal with press and inquiries.

Then, in August 1974, a local, a Mr Mitani, took a photo of the Hibagon. He had stopped his car on a road in the mountains when he spotted the beast in foliage at the side of the road. This was the only photograph that had ever been taken of the Hibagon and it kicked off the story again. More sightings were reported and then started to dry up.

The Anthropoid Section was eventually closed in 1975 and the town declared the 'end of the Hibagon', as they'd had enough of all the attention. Despite these protestations, though, soon products as varied as noodles, washing powder and sweets appeared bearing the Hibagon name. Mr Maeda was very much still a believer in the beast but recognized that it was a scary thing that might not really attract too many tourists. This was when he came up with the cartoon version of the animal. This logo was now used on everything related to the town, from the Forest Commission to tourist literature and hiking guides.

I was just going to ask more about a movie called *Dear Hinagon* that had been shot in the town when the door opened and a very fat man waddled in. He was a journalist from the local paper in Chugoku and he'd been tipped off that one of the world's most eminent monster-hunters was in town. He asked if I'd mind doing an interview and then have him follow my investigations. I agreed and we all decided that we should set off in Mr Maeda's car to check out some of the places where the Hibagon had been spotted.

We drove to the place where a rice farmer spotted the Hibagon. He'd been driving up a remote road when he saw the beast crossing the road in front of him. When it heard the car, it ran off up into the woods above the road. The farmer's description of the beast broadly matched that of the first sighting, but he also said the creature had a vaguely human face.

I got out of the car and looked around, not exactly sure what I was supposed to do about something that had happened forty years previously. It was very unlikely that the Hibagon was still hiding in the bushes above. I was mindful that the local journalist was watching me intently and taking loads of pictures, however, so I felt that I needed to act out the part. I knelt down beside the road and ran my hand through the earth in a questioning manner. I then went and smelt the bark on a nearby tree for quite a long time before nodding and writing stuff on my iPhone. This seemed to satisfy the journalist, who took more photos.

We got back in the car and drove on up a river valley until we got to the farm where the original sighting had taken place. We got out and trudged over a ploughed field until we reached a particular spot in between the farmhouse and some woods.

Mr Maeda told us that the farmer had been working in this field and had been just about to stop for the day as it was getting dark when he saw a figure approaching him. He said that the first thing he'd noticed was that there was a terrible smell. At first the farmer thought it was his elderly neighbour and shouted out a greeting. (I thought this didn't say much for either the looks or the personal hygiene of his elderly neighbour, but I kept quiet.)

When the farmer shouted out the figure stopped moving and the farmer walked towards it. He said the smell became even worse and he saw that the creature was not his elderly neighbour but a tall, hairy man 'like a caveman ape'. As he approached, the creature bolted back into the woods at the same time as the farmer ran to his neighbour's house.

Presumably when he knocked on the neighbour's door in panic he left out some of the details, and didn't just blurt out, 'I just saw a really ugly, hairy beast in the field; it stank to high heaven and I presumed it was you but it wasn't . . .' Whatever, the farmer was absolutely terrified, in quite a state of shock, and refused to go back to his house.

I wanted to speak to the farmer but he had since died. Mr Maeda had spoken to all these witnesses at length, though, and saw absolutely no reason to disbelieve them. Mr Maeda said that Mount Hiba was a 'holy' mountain and had been sort of off limits to people before 1970. At that time, there had been talks of developing the area for tourism and it was then that the initial sightings happened. Some said the Hibagon was angry about this invasion of his territory and this was why he was coming closer to humans.

Hungry from all this monster-hunting, we stopped at a mountain lodge to have lunch. The local reporter started to interview me. It turned out that he was something of a monster aficionado himself and had been to the home of another of Japan's big monsters, Issie, at Lake Ikeda. I told him that I intended to try to go there and check it out for myself. He was quite encouraging and said that there were boats that took people out to search for the beast and that he had spoken to several local fishermen who had all seen peculiar things.

We all headed back off down the mountain to the city, where Mr Maeda showed us the roadside signs that he'd had erected. These all featured the cuddly Hibagon welcoming people to the town. He then took us to a local bakery where they made Hibagon sweets. It was all a little desperate and I was quite glad when it was time to finally say our goodbyes and head off back to Hiroshima. There was something a bit depressing about the whole Hibagon affair. It felt like the creature had left town a long time ago. I'd sort of hoped for more of the irradiated-man angle but Mr Maeda didn't even seem to factor this in as a possibility. The journalist told me that foreign journalists had heard about the Hibagon, noticed it was in Hiroshima prefecture and put two and two together to make five. I tried to look bewildered at how people could be so stupid while subtly emphasizing that I was not one of those idiots. I'm not sure that I was entirely successful.

Mr Maeda waved at us sadly as we disappeared down the road. I drove back towards Hiroshima while Naoko chatted away about her travels to Europe. She told me that she'd been terrified while on the sleeper train from Venice to Nice because someone had told her that people gassed sleepers and stole their stuff. She and her husband had barricaded their compartment and refused to let the ticket inspector in because they were sure he was a baddie.

As we re-entered Hiroshima I glanced at our little rented car's incomprehensibly complicated sat-nav system. I noticed a plethora of swastikas dotted all around the city. For a moment I worried that these might denote secret Nazi bases in town but Naoko laughed and told me that they represented Buddhist temples – the swastika being an old Buddhist symbol before the Nazis swiped it for their own nefarious purposes.

Back at the hotel, I said goodbye to Naoko and gave her a copy of my last book. She promised to find the article by the local journalist when it appeared in the newspaper and to send me a translation.

'Soon you will be famous in Hiroshima, Dom-San,' she joked. I loved her calling me Dom-San – I don't know why – and I wondered whether I could persuade Stacey to start doing so too. It being a mark of respect, I somehow doubted it. Naoko and I bowed to each other and she wandered off smiling to the end.

Despite the appealing prospect of my forthcoming celebrity status in Hiroshima, I had decided to leave the city the following day. The Hibagon had not been as exciting a prey as I'd hoped. I'd had an actual sighting of Ogopogo in Lake Okanagan whereas here so far I hadn't even spotted a shape-shifting badger. I decided that I was going to take a Shinkansen and get down to the very bottom of Kyushu Island to see if I could learn anything about Issie the lake monster.

That evening I headed out to a Yakitori joint that Naoko had recommended. When we'd been wandering round town she'd popped in and introduced me to the owner. Had she not done this, I think I'd have been too nervous to walk in on my own – it was a low-ceilinged room packed with Japanese patrons. My entrance through the sliding door caused some raised eyebrows until the owner waved at me and beckoned me to sit down at the lone remaining seat. I was immediately given a plate piled high with raw cabbage covered in soy sauce and tons of pureed garlic. An enormous glass of chilled Sapporo was plonked in front of me. I didn't order anything. Every time the owner cooked a round of skewers he'd walk up and down the bar placing one on each plate. When you finished a skewer you put it in a cup opposite you and this was how you were charged at the end of the meal. Life was good. I ordered some cold sake and the owner suggested I have some from a beautiful-looking bottle. Some rice wine can be slightly vomit-inducing but this was perfect – and incredibly strong. Within half an hour I was showing the whole bar photographs of my wife, kids, dogs, cats, mother. The reserve was down on both sides.

On the way back to the hotel I stopped at a portrait painter's and had him paint me. When he'd finished, he handed me a portrait of an elderly drunken Irishman. I presume that it was supposed to be me but nobody who has seen it has ever yet guessed this fact.

The following morning I had a sore head and found the lift ride down particularly tricky. There was some sort of convention happening in the hotel and it was even fuller than the Tokyo metro. However calm and 'Zen-like' the Japanese character is supposed to be, there's always one man hammering away at the 'close' button in every lift. Should he get out at a certain floor, then another man just steps up to take his place. At breakfast I checked my emails. There was one from Naoko. The fat journo's story was in the paper and she had translated it for me.

Dom Joly, 44, an English comedian, visited Saijo Town, Shobara, to write in his book about Hibagon, which was seen there in around 1970. He is writing a travel book on six UMAs in the world, including the Nessie and Yeti. Hibagon has been included in the six.

He energetically reported the area where Hibagon was first seen and the vegetable field where the local resident met Hibagon at a very close distance. He said that the nature and the atmosphere in Saijo is similar to that of the forest in California where Bigfoot roams.

Mr Tadanori Maeda, 44, Secretary General of the Saijo Town Tourist Association, said, 'It is our honour that Hibagon has been included in the top six UMAs in the world. I'm glad to know that, even today, Hibagon has been paid attention to.'

Mr Joly will soon go to look for a dinosaur in a deep forest in Africa in January, and Yeti in the Himalayas.

There was a photograph of me, Naoko and Mr Maeda. I was in the middle and pretending to be inspecting something. Naoko wrote, 'You are very famous now in Hiroshima, Dom-San; all my friends have seen this.'

Monster-hunters like myself, however, do not do this for fame or women or free food: we do it for science.

I caught the Shinkansen and, an hour out of Hiroshima, we pulled into Kokura. I gazed out of the window at the city. This was the 'B' target on the day of the Hiroshima bombing. It survived purely because of clement weather over Hiroshima. The train flew on, like a silent projectile (a bullet, if you will), through Japan. An overly helpful man insisted that I get off at Hakata.

'You need to change here for sure.' He smiled, almost tugging on my sleeve.

'Are you sure? I thought the Shinkansen went all the way to the bottom of Kyushu?'

'No . . . You change here one hundred per cent. I go where you go.'

'To Lake Ikeda? I want to see Issie.' I tried to make what I considered to be the international sign for 'lake monster' but was not convinced it worked.

'Yes, yes, we must hully, please . . .' he smiled and I followed him off the train meekly. I had to admit that my Japanese train-getting had not been brilliant so far. The man took me through some barriers and we entered what looked like a distinctly less-salubrious train platform.

'Shinkansen?' I asked, looking concerned.

'No Shinkansen . . . Local train.' The man seemed absolutely convinced and the signs were now in Japanese so I relinquished all control and got on a smaller train. I sat down and the man sat opposite me. I sort of wanted to be alone but he seemed to have taken me under his wing. I hoped that I wouldn't end up in some gimp basement and surreptitiously got my penknife out from my bag, just in case. The train rolled along the coast and the scenery became rather beautiful. Occasionally my new friend would point out of the window and say something like 'Sea . . .' while pointing at the sea.

I would nod and say 'Yes, sea . . .' back to him and then stare intently at the sea as though I had just noticed it.

'Tree . . .' he said, pointing at a rather nondescript tree.

'Yes, tree . . .' I said, now longing for an escape route.

The train rolled on for a good two hours. We stopped at several places but I didn't have a map so I had no idea how far we had gone or how long it would take. The train started to slow down and the tannoy lady was very vocal for a while.

'We are here,' said my friend. 'Velly good.' He smiled at me and I smiled back. He had been very helpful and didn't seem to have any hidden weapons or chloroform at the ready. As the train pulled into the station, I thanked him.

'Thank you,' I said.

'Welcome to Nagasaki,' he said.

I'm still not sure how my 'friend' ever got it into his head that I was going to Nagasaki. Certainly I never mentioned it. All I could think was that he assumed every foreigner on a train was bound for his hometown. Maybe they had a very proactive visitor programme? Whatever, there was very little I could do. I checked the map and I was way off course. Nagasaki is on a peninsula on the westernmost part of Kyushu and it would take an age to get back to a line that would take me down to near Lake Ikeda. I had limited time left in Japan so I decided to go with the flow and visit Nagasaki. To my knowledge it has no monsters – but it *was* the site of the dropping of the second atomic bomb in the Second World War and so, in a Dark Touristic way, it sort of made sense that I be here.

I was joking about my friend on the train thinking that all foreigners must be going to Nagasaki but this actually used to be the case. The city was 'opened' to the world by the Portuguese in 1571. It was a flourishing trading port and the centre for all Christian missionaries in Japan. In 1641, however, Christianity was banned and the Portuguese were chucked out of the country. Japan's only connection to the outside world was the Chinese settlement in Nagasaki and some Dutch merchants who were quarantined on Dejima Island in Nagasaki Bay. This alienation from the outside world lasted for 200 years and made Nagasaki far more liberal and cosmopolitan than the rest of medieval Japan. I was expecting great things from the place and hoped that I might stumble on a monster story or two.

I found a hotel called the Monterey. A whole section of the city was built in a European style by the foreigners who lived there after being released from their island exile. I dropped my bag off and immediately set off for some more atomic tourism. Surprisingly the museum and hypocentre aren't in the centre of the city but are in Urakami, a little suburb to the north. Cabs in Japan are eye-wateringly expensive and my experiences in them so far hadn't been wonderful, so I opted for the tram. We headed through Chinatown and started trundling up towards Urakami, where the bomb exploded at 11.02 a.m. on 9 August 1945 – three days after Hiroshima.

I remembered the terrible story of a man who had been on business in Hiroshima when the bomb was dropped. He was wounded but survived and managed to make his escape from the devastated city. He headed for home – you guessed it: Nagasaki. He arrived there just in time to be hit by the second bomb, which he also survived. He'd only recently died.

So, I was off to my second atomic memorial site in a day. I hopped off the tram, crossed a big road and entered a park – and within seconds was standing at the spot above which the bomb went off.

The 'A' target city had been Kokura. Lucky old Kokura, however, had been too cloudy so, after making a couple of circles, the plane headed for the secondary target, Nagasaki. The drop site was supposed to be the centre of town, near my hotel, but there was more cloud here and the pilots were by now very low on fuel. Then they spotted the Mitsubishi factory that was situated in this industrial suburb and dropped the bomb there instead. Because Urakami lies in a valley, the centre of the city was spared the very worst effects of the bomb. That's why there's much more left of 'original' Nagasaki than there is of Hiroshima.

The hypocentre memorial features a big black column shooting up into the sky surrounded by a set of concentric rings spreading out like the ripples of a blast wave. Right next to it are the remains of the Catholic cathedral that was completed in 1925 and had, until it was vaporized, been the largest in the Orient. I looked up into the sky above and tried to imagine that moment. There would have been no sirens wailing: this was a lone plane and wouldn't have been seen as a threat. The city would have gone from total normality to an inferno of hell in a millisecond.

I climbed the nearby steps to the Nagasaki Atomic Bomb Museum. As I entered the foyer a woman approached me and asked me if I needed a guide. I politely said no and tried to

move on but she seemed not to understand and started usher-
ing me towards a door on the right.

'Thank you, but I am happy to be alone,' I said, smiling and
half-bowing.

'I learn English and am honour to be my guide for your tour.'
She bowed back and almost pulled me towards the door.

'I really do not need a guide, but thank you for your most
kind offer.' I bowed again, slightly lower, smiled again and tried
to move in the other direction.

'Gratuities will of course be at your discretion; we am volun-
teer guide but we am also housewife . . .' She blocked my move.
There was no bow this time – just an iron will that would not
truck with dissent.

I gave in and followed her towards the door. What was it
with Nagasakians and their insistent dealings with visitors?

We set off on the 'tour'. Her initial pitch had been under-
standable but she now lapsed into virtual gibberish with an
almost comical Japanese over-accent. She reminded me of a
rather stern woman who had shown me round the Museum
Dedicated to the Evil Work of the Imperialist Pig-Nation,
America, in North Korea. (I don't think that was the actual name
but it was the gist of the place.) This tour was mind-blowingly
bad. My housewife guide just approached every exhibit and
read out the English blurb on the wall, but in a language that I
didn't recognize.

'Vis fologlaf dispray effect of ladiation on wesidnt of rbble
tin . . .'

If I tried to move too fast or look somewhere else, she would
scold me and I'd be pulled back hard on the leash. It was hell.

I remember very little of the tour, as I spent most of the time
trying to plot my escape. The one fact I did take in was that the
bombs' special antenna, which allowed them to register their
altitude and to explode at precisely 500 metres, were invented
by a Dr Yagi Hidetsugu, a Japanese scientist from Osaka.

My guide seemed to think that I would be fascinated by anything to do with Christianity. There was a little section of the museum – by far the least interesting, in my opinion – about a Japanese Christian who lived in the city at the time of the attack. There were moments when I felt that was where I was to spend the rest of my life, listening to a tiny, unintelligible woman waffle on about 'Jesus Clist'.

She also had a tendency to go on and on about 'enemy pranes'. While I accepted that they were the enemy to her, she was actually talking about my father and his friends and it started to really get on my nerves. I wandered off and read a notice informing me that, on the fiftieth anniversary of the bomb being dropped, the city of Nagasaki had bought the original colour footage of the bombing from the Hooper Institute in the US. Whatever the Japanese did in the war, I sort of thought that the Hooper Institute, whatever that might be, could have just given them the footage of their city being wiped off the map rather than selling it to them.

Eventually I couldn't take it any more and told my guide that I was feeling ill and needed to leave immediately. Unfortunately she got very concerned – too concerned.

'What is wong wiv you? Where is pain? I call doctor?'

'No, no . . . I just need to go back to my hotel and rest a while. Thank you so much for your tour, though; it was . . . good.'

'You sit down. I call doctor now.' She got on her mobile and started jabbering away while motioning me to a nearby chair. I started to panic. I was never going to lose this infernal woman. She wouldn't ever let me leave.

'I speak to doctor – what is sympton?' She held her hand over the speaker and kept the doctor hanging as she discussed my fate.

'Please, I just want to go back to my hotel.' I was almost shouting at this tiny woman, and several Japanese visitors to the museum wandered past tut-tutting.

'OK, I tell doctor to come now . . .' She started jabbering into the phone again. I looked around and saw some stairs just round the corner from where we were standing. The little lady was now deep in animated conversation with the doctor. I took my moment and bolted. I was up the stairs faster than Charlie Sheen out of rehab and I didn't look back. I came to a fire escape and pushed it open. Alarms started to ring and a curious wailing siren, remarkably like an air-raid siren, sounded out.

Once you make the decision to run you must commit. The last thing you want is to be caught or bump into the other party concerned. Otherwise you have to start pretending you've lost your mind or are on strong hallucinogenics and it all spirals ever further out of control.

'Oh, these tangled webs we weave . . .'

I could hear the siren wailing and could imagine my hyperactive little guide describing what was happening to a by now very confused doctor.

'He bleak thlough door; silens they wail rike clazy coyote . . . Now he lunnning away like clazy man! We leed sedative gun fast . . .'

At the bottom of the hill I spotted a taxi and jumped in and we roared away as fast as the little Japanese Box could roar.

Back at the Monterey hotel I lay on the tiny bed in my tiny room for a while. The tiny pillow had something very weird inside it. It felt like beans. Not beans as in a beanbag; beanbags are quite comfortable. These felt like actual beans: uncomfortable, hard beans that needed to soak for forty-eight hours. Why would anyone put beans in a pillow?

There's so much about Japan that I didn't get. It's a truly unfathomable place to the casual visitor. It's a country obsessed with modernity and cutting-edge gadgetry and yet still so steeped in tradition and mythology. I wondered whether their relentless surge towards the future has made the Japanese cling to beliefs about things like monsters more than people in most countries. The shock of the new, the 'Year Zero' effect of the Second World War and the subsequent rapid modernization might have left them with a need to hang on to old superstitions. When your country is set on fire, nuked and invaded by a civilization that you then aspire to you must need something to blame for stuff . . . And maybe to make uncomfortable pillows for visitors by way of subtle revenge.

I headed out into town to try to find a YO! Sushi type of place. I wanted somewhere I could sit and watch food go past me on a conveyor belt, choosing whatever took my fancy. I got the name of the best one off the Internet and tried to give this to a cab driver. He wasn't interested in my desired destination and dropped me off somewhere wholly wrong and quite insalubrious. I had learnt not to bother complaining to Japanese cabbies. I waited until he drove out of sight and then hailed another one and tried again. The new cab, driven by an elderly woman who seemed to have no idea how to change gears, took a look at the name of the place I wanted and took off. We drove for about twenty minutes and I soon knew that we were not going anywhere I wanted as we appeared to be leaving the centre of town. I decided to give up and simply go with the flow. Wherever this lady wished me to have supper would be where I did so. She eventually came to a stop down a tiny, smoky alley straight out of a kung-fu film. The electric door opened and she indicated that this was where I was going. It certainly wasn't but I was now committed. I got out and she screeched off, leaving me alone in the alley. I half-expected a large gang of martial-arts clichés to suddenly appear out of the smoke and say, 'So, Mr Jory, now we shall decide who is the master . . .'

The gang didn't appear and I looked around to get my bearings. Most of the buildings were unpromising, with the occasional fire escape and a lot of dustbins. One door looked to be vaguely inviting, however. It had a light over it as though it expected people to stand there. I knocked and a little hatch opened at eye level. A grumpy pair of eyes stared suspiciously back at me. The owner of the eyes said something in Japanese. I looked puzzled and pointed at my mouth. There was a long pause and then the door swung open to reveal a man in stained chef-type clothes. This was a start. At least I hadn't knocked on the door of some Yakuza heroin gang. Having said this, Chef, as I shall call him, looked very shifty, as though he had just been in the middle of doing something really terrible and had quickly hidden the evidence. The room was minuscule, like a cupboard (or a medium-sized Japanese hotel room). After a moment he indicated that I should enter. I hesitated but I spotted some beer under a table and I was thirsty and tired from my taxi adventures. I squeezed through the door and got past him. Between us there was not much room left for oxygen.

He stared at me for a very long time without doing anything. I wondered whether this might not be a terrible mistake. He pointed at a stool and I sat.

He produced a menu in Japanese. I looked at it helplessly.

'Biru,' I said in my fluent Japanese. He poured me a glass of beer and stared at me as I sipped it. It was very good beer. I raised my glass to him in a salute but he just stared at me as though sizing me up.

'Amewica?' he suddenly said in a very threatening manner.

Just what I needed: to be stuck in a cupboard down a back alley with a mad Japanese man who was going to blame me personally for the atomic destruction of his city.

'No . . . not Amewica . . . Boo to the USA . . . No, I am from . . . Brazil . . .' I've no idea why I plumped for Brazil. I suppose nobody dislikes the Brazilians. It did the trick, though.

'BRAZIILLL!!!' Chef was ecstatic. 'Brazil, Rio, goal, Ronaldo . . .' He had exhausted his whole Brazilian repertoire but he seemed happier than his homicidal appearance had started to suggest moments earlier.

'Goal, Pelé, Amazon, São Paulo, Ronnie Biggs!' I shouted, exhausting my own Brazilian knowledge and knowing as I said it that Ronnie Biggs wasn't going to cut the mustard.

I was right: he looked confused.

I stopped being Brazilian and studiously pretended to look at the menu. Chef jabbered at me in Japanese in a manner that made me fairly certain that he was asking me what I fancied. What I actually fancied was getting out of here but I was stuck now and determined to go through with whatever was to come. I pretended to look indecisive for a moment before pointing at two things on the menu decisively. He looked at my two chosen things and then at me quizzically. He asked me something in Japanese that sounded a little like, 'Are you sure, you flucking idyot?'

I nodded and indicated that, yes, this was definitely what I wanted – whatever it was. I then looked down and concentrated on my beer. I felt him continuing to look at me for quite a while before finally crouching down and starting to fiddle with stuff in a cupboard on his side.

After about five minutes he produced a bowl of what looked like raw cat sick and placed it in front of me. He then returned to his larder and fiddled a little bit more before producing a tiny bowl of slimy pickles. He then stood staring at me expectantly. Dinner was clearly served.

I looked at the meal and then up at Chef. Chef's eyes moved fast from the cat sick to me and back again. I stalled for a while but very soon I had to face the inevitable. I looked down. The cat sick had a putrid fishy smell and it was becoming quite overpowering in the cupboard. I gingerly lifted my chopsticks and tried a pickle. They were not terrible – revolting, but edible. I smiled at Chef but he didn't smile back. Chef looked at the cat sick again and then at me. I started to get hot and panicky. What if this actually *was* cat sick? Maybe that was what he was doing when I'd interrupted him? Forcing his fat fingers down some poor cat's throat.

Eventually I could stall no longer; I had to dig in. I picked up a small amount of cat sick and reticently put it in my mouth. Like uranium, you clearly needed only a tiny amount for an explosive reaction. This was a taste so awful, so utterly heinous that I genuinely have no words to describe it. I suffered an instant gag reflex and found it almost impossible not to projectile vomit. Thankfully some inner survival mechanism made me keep it in. Chef did not appear to be a man who appreciated being vomited on. This was the secret ingredient they needed on the Bush Tucker Trial on *I'm a Celeb* . . . It would be TV gold.

Eventually I swallowed this fiendish mouthful but weird things lingered in my teeth. I looked up at Chef, who had a big smile on his face. Was he laughing at me or just pleased that I was enjoying his cat sick? I hate to say this but he was inscrutable.

I downed an entire glass of beer. There was nothing on God's earth that would persuade me take another mouthful of that crap. I looked at him and did the *X Factor* sign with my arms to indicate that I was finished and wanted my bill. Chef looked at me in astonishment. He shook his head and pointed at the cat sick. I looked around subtly for any knives. There was a chopper lying on the counter about a foot away from him. I just wanted to get out of there and run away again.

Chef shouted something at me in a low guttural growl. I hated this situation. I didn't want to be here so why was I here? I was a grown man. I didn't have to do anything that I didn't want to – but how to get out? For the second time in the same day I feigned terrible illness. Having just consumed the cat sick, this was not tricky. I grabbed my stomach and started to make terrible noises. Chef looked startled. I pulled out a 1,000-yen note, dropped it on the counter and then stood up, pretending to stagger. I hit the door hard before sliding it open. I managed to get half into the alley but Chef grabbed me and was shouting stuff. This was becoming a terrible day. I pointed up to the sky and he let go for a second and I took my moment. I bolted, running as fast as I could, and I didn't stop running for five minutes. When I eventually did, I vomited all over the pavement. I was certain that this was the moment where my guide from the museum would walk by but fortunately I was alone. A hollow husk, I hailed a taxi that I had to direct myself to the Monterey hotel for a night battling the evil pillow monster.

My time in Japan was running out. I had to get back to Tokyo the following day to catch my flight home without a sniff of a monster.

The next morning, I caught a cab to the station and, to my surprise, the driver asked me in polite, stilted English whether I minded if he chatted to me. He'd learnt his English from the Internet and was keen to practise it on somebody.

'Sir, why are you visit Japan?'

'I am here to hunt the Hibagon.'

'Slow please . . . I no understand.'

'I . . . am here . . . to find the Hibagon . . .'

'Why are you in Japan? For tourist purpose?'

'No . . . To hunt the Hibagon . . . The Hibagon – the monster . . .'

'Slow please . . .'

'I'm a monster-hunter . . .'

'*Ghostbusters*?'

I looked out of the window and prayed for the cab ride to end soon. I'd really had it with Japanese taxis.

I didn't have long in Tokyo before flying out and I was seriously annoyed that I'd been unable to find a monster in the land of Godzilla. I wondered whether Japanese monsters were more subtle than others. The Hibagon had garnered international attention because it seemed to be more of a traditional 'Western' type of monster of the Bigfoot variety that we could understand.

Most Japanese monsters are more understated and can probably only really be understood or 'discovered' once you understand the Japanese psyche – something I was still a long way away from doing. I did a whistle-stop tour of the capital. I went to visit the weird manga kids in Harajuku who were all dressed up as zombies and scary nurses and freakazoid Goth characters. I found one who spoke English and asked her what she knew about the Hibagon.

'Hibagon he big hairy gorilla monsta in Hiroshima . . . He cool.'

I asked her whether there were any monsters in Tokyo.

'Monsta everywhere in Japan. Tree monsta, road monsta, shop monsta . . . Lot of monstas.' She gesticulated all around us and I nodded, trying to look like I understood.

I left her and her friends posing like the world's best tourist attraction while screaming at every tourist who tried to take their photo.

I headed for the Imperial Palace and spent ages wandering around the grounds trying to find the palace. It took me about an hour to realize that there isn't one. Nobody had bothered to mention this in any of the guides.

I ended up in 'Brand Street', a huge boulevard bursting with every big-brand store you can think of. The place was packed with rampant shoppers seemingly having a great day out. It was my idea of total hell and I was about to head back to my skyscraping hotel room when I spotted the Ginza Lion. On a whim I wandered in and discovered a complete gem. Slap in the middle of Tokyo, this is an extraordinary Munich-style bierkeller. It was warm and atmospheric and buzzing with people: a Gothic retreat from the Metropolis. It was teatime and the place was full of gossipy tables of Japanese ladies. Instead of tea, however, everyone was brandishing pints of beer. The Japanese customers were all impeccably turned out, the men in suits or tweed and the women looking smart and hip. It wasn't traditional dress but, as with much else, they had copied Western style but done it properly.

In the centre of the hall were a couple of tables of Westerners bedecked in sweat tops, hoodies and scruffy T-shirts. Had we moved on as a culture or had we lost something? I thought back to the cabbies in uniform, the smiling train conductors bowing to the carriage. I thought we'd lost something.

I sank my two-and-a-half-pint Sapporo with ease and ordered another one. I felt a lovely warm feeling come over me. Near the middle of the room I spotted a white-faced lady of about seventy. She was beautifully done up and in full traditional kimono garb. She had a healthy-looking glass of beer in front of her and was trying to eat beef and potato croquettes with chopsticks, a tricky task that she was accomplishing with much grace.

The following morning, and I was on the plane sitting on the runway at Narita airport nursing a rather splendid hangover. The stewardess was one of the same ones who'd been on the flight out.

'Did you have a nice time in Japan?' she asked.

'Yes, I did,' I replied.

'Business or pleasure?'

'A bit of both . . . I'm a monster-hunter.'

She gave me that look that people give to mental people who stagger up to them in the street, then moved on a little too fast to the next passenger. I looked out of the window and wondered whether she was right. Maybe I was a nutter and this was all a supremely pointless exercise? Then I remembered my Ogopogo spotting, the Super 8 footage of Bigfoot, the black-and-white photos of Nessie, the Yeti footprints in the Himalayan snow. Who knows what is right and what is wrong? I was on a great adventure and I was as likely to find something as anybody else. I took Robert Frost's words for encouragement:

Hibagon

Two roads diverged in a wood, and I—

I took the one less traveled by,
And that has made all the difference.

I was off to the Congo next and that was definitely a road less travelled. As we taxied off the ground crew were all lined up and waving goodbye to our plane. In Heathrow they'd be watching porn on the laptop they'd nicked from your luggage.

Mokèlé-mbèmbé

'"But what if the monsters come?'
"Fancy." Kit looked away from the drama to stare at her sister, surprised. "We are the monsters."'

Dia Reeves, Slice of Cherry

I sat on the rotating stool at the seafood bar in Terminal Four and tried to ignore the Russian couple sucking face right next to me.

I was heading to Brazzaville, capital of the Republic of Congo, by way of Nairobi. Stacey had been freaked out by the Congo. I'd tried to explain that I was going to the 'good' Congo as opposed to the 'bad' Congo. 'Good' Congo being the old French colony, the Republic of Congo. Yes, it had just had a civil war, but it was OK at the moment. 'Bad' Congo is the Democratic Republic of Congo, the old Belgian Congo. Experience has taught me that any country calling itself 'democratic' is always anything but (see East Germany and North Korea). The good and bad Congos face each other over the mighty river of the same name.

To make things worse there had been a Code Red terrorist alert in Nairobi on the eve of my departure. I had absolutely no idea what a Code Red was or what I should do about it. I'd tried to mouth some platitudes about this making the airport even safer but she was already in a tizz about the whole trip.

'You're going off on your own into the middle of bloody nowhere to look for a dinosaur? For fuck's sake, Dom, you've got responsibilities . . .'

She was right, of course: it was unnecessary. But then again, if you play by those rules then everything is unnecessary – and she had to remember that I was one of the world's foremost monster-hunters and knew no fear . . .

The more I looked into the Mokèlé-mbèmbé, the 'Blocker of Rivers', the more intrigued I became. In the vast swampy borderlands between Cameroon and the Congo is said to exist an aquatic creature that looks very much like a dinosaur. There have been reports of sightings going back to the very first Western explorers and local tribes have stories that go a lot further back in time. If there's something undiscovered in the world, this is the sort of place where it might reside. The area is almost inaccessible and very few Westerners have ever been there – the combination of war and remoteness has kept most people away. This was going to be a proper, middle-of-nowhere adventure: just a guide, porters and me heading off into the heart of darkness.

My two destinations were the village of Boha and then Lake Tele, where the creature is supposed to live. Information was scarce but it seemed to be a two-day walk after an EU-blacklisted flight, a seven-hour car ride and an indeterminate boat journey. This was it. I was an adventurer, an intrepid explorer . . .

'Excuse me . . .' A sixteen-year-old blonde girl interrupted my reveries. 'Were you on *I'm a Celebrity . . . Get Me Out of Here!*?' She looked at me enquiringly, having clearly been egged on by her pre-shaving companions in the queue for the plane to Nairobi . . .

'No . . . It wasn't me,' I muttered.

'Yeah, it was. Weren't you the one who pooed on the camp toilet seat and didn't clean it up?'

'That wasn't me. That was the stupid Playboy Bunny throwing false accusations about.'

'So it *is* you! What's your name? You were a comedian, weren't you?'

I started to almost run for the plane.

It turned out my neighbour on board was also on an adventure. He was an ex-army officer who now worked on pirate patrol. He spent eight weeks on, eight weeks off cargo vessels defending them against Somali pirate attacks.

We landed in Nairobi and as I got off the plane I felt the clammy wall of African heat. I made my way to my gate. The flight was going to Brazzaville and Kinshasa. It seemed that good and bad Congo shared a flight. There was a vast amount of people in the departure gate and they were a tough-looking bunch. There were three Westerners, a couple of Arabs, a handful of Chinese and the rest were Africans. It looked like the sort of plane that James Bond might hop on to and look around suspiciously.

Next to me sat an enormous Congolese man with a very annoying mobile-phone problem. Every two or three minutes his infernal ringtone would go off. It was a rather creepy voice whispering very loudly, 'Boss, you have received a text message.' To my right, a man was reading a local Nairobi newspaper – 'Moustachioed woman robs neighbourhood!!' screamed the rather wonderful headline.

The plane was an hour late and the general consensus seemed to be that this was rather better than usual. I went for a wander to get a cup of coffee. At the bar sat a Sloaney English girl yacking away on her iPhone.

'Yah, no, I'm in Kenya, on my way to Rwanda . . . I know . . . Totally weird . . . Absolutely . . . Yah . . . I'm meeting Milo . . .'

After an hour the packed room was explained: there were three delayed flights waiting – one for Zanzibar, one for Kigali and mine. I was secretly pleased that my lot looked decidedly rougher than the other two. The three Westerners were on other flights so I was the only non-African on mine apart from a lone Chinese man who looked decidedly shifty.

On the plane a surly African youth wearing the international costume of hip-hop twat was slouched in my seat. I explained the situation but Chocolate Ice just stared at me through dull, sullen eyes and didn't move. Fortunately he was only about fifteen so I was able to be slightly more assertive than I might have been with an adult. He moved to the middle seat and I sat down only to find myself in another elbow war. Fortunately, there was quite lot of turbulence and mini-gangsta almost shat his overly baggy pants. To show how unconcerned I was I fell asleep on the window. I woke up just as we were coming in to land in Brazzaville. Through my dribble I could see rows and rows of houses with rusty corrugated-iron roofs. An eerie, misty cloud hung over the city.

Once on the ground I walked through surprisingly clean corridors, with every Congolese I met welcoming me to Brazzaville. It all seemed very friendly and organized. Maybe I'd got the wrong end of the stick?

Then I got to passport control.

I handed over my passport and vaccination forms to an official staring at me in exactly the same way as the sullen youth had on the plane. He spoke to me in heavily accented French. This was to be the same throughout my journey in the Congo. Fortunately, having grown up in the Lebanon, I'm bilingual. (I have therefore translated all conversations into English for the purposes of this book.)

I gave the official my passport and he flicked through it rather contemptuously. He got to the page that had my visa.

'Where is your letter of invitation?' He looked at me accusingly as though I was hiding it in my pants.

Anyone applying for a visa to the Congo needs a letter of invitation from someone based in the country to support their application. I told Grumpy that mine was with the Congolese Embassy in London, as they'd needed me to send it to them so that they could issue the visa.

'So why don't you have it?' asked Grumpy.

I repeated that I had sent it to the Congolese Embassy in London and that that was how I'd got the visa that he could see in my passport. No letter, no visa.

'So can I see the letter?' Grumpy looked me straight in the eyes.

This was all starting to get a bit *Catch 22*. I repeated, slowly, that the letter was with the Congolese Embassy in London and added that I must have had one or I wouldn't have been issued the visa . . .

'But you do not have a letter of invitation. You need a letter of invitation.'

We stared at each other in silence for a while, neither of us backing down. Eventually I told him that someone outside was meeting me. Could I leave my passport with him, go and find the man who was meeting me and hopefully he could sort everything out? To my surprise Grumpy accepted this idea. I wandered past the luggage hall and several armed soldiers and into the morass of humanity waiting for passengers to come through. I looked around. I was supposed to meet a Cameroonian called Jean-Pierre. He'd come highly recommended and had travelled all over the Congo, although he'd never been to the area that we were off to. I scanned the crowd but there was nobody showing any interest. I tried to go back in to talk to Grumpy but an armed soldier placed his AK47 in front of me and shook his head.

'Nobody goes in: this is the exit.'

I explained that I had just come out and needed to go back in to get my passport but he was not interested.

'Nobody goes in through here.'

I was buggered. I was just wondering how I could deal with a trip to the Congo with no passport when a smiley face burst through the crowd.

'Monsieur Dom?' It was Jean-Pierre. I was saved. Jean-Pierre had a word with someone he knew and we both wandered back towards Grumpy un-hassled.

I introduced Grumpy to Jean-Pierre and told him that this was the man who had written my original letter of invitation. Grumpy looked at Jean-Pierre.

'Show me the letter . . .'

I groaned. We were back at square one.

Jean-Pierre started the same complicated set of explanations that I had attempted. He handed his passport over to Grumpy and explained our mission here. Grumpy looked at Jean-Pierre's Cameroonian passport.

'You are from Cameroon. You are not from the Congo.'

Jean-Pierre nodded in agreement at this statement.

'If you are from Cameroon you cannot invite someone to the Congo.'

This conversation went on for roughly half an hour. I believe money exchanged hands, though I never actually saw it happen – but, whatever, we were finally through and Jean-Pierre took me to the luggage hall.

'What does your luggage look like?' he asked.

'I don't have any more; it's on my back.' Jean-Pierre peered at my small, grey rucksack and then back at me with the look of a man who could not decide whether I was an idiot or an exceptionally talented packer.

We hopped into a cab and headed downtown to Mikhael's Hotel. I was dog-tired. During the Second World War, with his country under German occupation, General de Gaulle briefly made Brazzaville the capital of Free France. As we drove through it now the streets were awash with activity. Every time the car stopped people would shove useless things through the window, trying to make us purchase them. Fake-silver photo frames seemed to be a big favourite.

Jean-Pierre was very excited about our adventure. He told me that he had always wanted an excuse to travel to the part of the Congo we were going to and had been thrilled when my request came through. He warned me that we might not see the monster – 'but there are plenty of pythons and crocodiles'.

We drove on past a couple of markets, our little green taxi doing well negotiating the chaotic traffic. Suddenly we rounded a corner and there it was, the River Congo. It's enormous, far bigger than I'd expected. The water was dark and grey and I could see Kinshasa, capital of bad Congo, on the opposite bank, what looked like about half a mile away. Apparently this is the only place in the world where two capital cities are within sight of each other across a river (Buenos Aires and Montevideo on the Plate estuary are much, much further apart).

I gazed at this extraordinary expanse of muddy water that has both fascinated and thwarted so many explorers for so long. The Congo is a bit like Everest, one of those things that featured in so many stories of derring-do I remember reading as a schoolboy.

Kinshasa is huge, with a population of twelve million, whereas little Brazzaville is home to barely a million.

'It is crazy expensive here,' said Jean-Pierre as we arrived at the hotel that turned out to be run, like most of Brazzaville, by a Lebanese merchant class.

I tried to get some sleep but couldn't so I had a shower and then went to find the restaurant. I ordered the plat du jour – a uniquely Congolese dish (not) – Couscous Royale. It was delicious and I sat back contentedly and tried to eavesdrop on a tableful of five women whom I guessed to be Brazilian. The room was packed with Brazzaville's 'ladies who lunch'. They not only lunched but also smoked like it was going out of fashion and constantly showed each other videos on their laptops with the music turned up to the max.

There were still Christmas decorations hung up around the place despite it being late January. Christmas in the Congo: who'd have thunk it?

A man in an orange suit brighter than the sun, subtly offset with a fluorescent-blue shirt, wandered around the room permanently on his mobile. He was Belgian and was talking to someone on his phone about the fact that he was off to Moscow the following day for three days.

I ordered an Um Bongo to try to fit in. The waiter looked desperate to please but eventually returned to ask me to repeat my order.

'I'd like an Um Bongo please.'

He disappeared again but returned quickly, shaking his head in a disconsolate manner. He admitted that they had no such drink.

I wasn't going to let this go.

'I understand that you don't have any Um Bongo on the premises. Perhaps you have run out due to the high consumption rate? When will you be restocked?'

The waiter looked mortified to have to admit that he had never heard of Um Bongo.

'Are you a Congolese?' I asked him. He confirmed that he was born and bred in Brazzaville. 'And you have never heard of the soft drink Um Bongo?'

The waiter shook his head and slunk away. I was dumb-founded. All those years when I'd been taken in by the Um Bongo TV adverts with the catchy song: 'Um Bongo, Um Bongo, they drink it in the Congo . . .' It was all lies. The company responsible for the drink – the sinister-sounding

Gerber's Juice Company Ltd (known as Libby's, to make them sound friendly) had been lying to us all. Nobody drunk Um Bongo in the Congo. Nobody had even heard of Um Bongo in the bloody Congo. I smelt a lawsuit and ordered a beer instead.

I got an Ngok beer that had a very familiar crocodile on the label. Later, I asked Jean-Pierre what type of crocodile it was and he told me it was called a Lacoste. You couldn't make it up.

I sat on the terrace by the pool. For about the first time ever I was by a pool where swimmers weren't treated like retards. There were no signs anywhere telling you there was no life-guard around. Nobody was telling you that you couldn't heavy pet should you fancy it. There was not even an indication of depth or the almost compulsory 'No Diving' sign that seems to be on every public pool in the world. Not here. The Congo is a place that relies on you to make your own decisions. It's some-where that allows you to be a grown-up. It was hot – very hot – and the water looked inviting. I stripped off to my swimming trunks and dived into the cooling water. I hit my hands on the bottom of the pool so hard that it partially dislocated my right wrist. The pool was only three feet deep. It appeared that I had stupidly dived into the shallow end. I swam to the other end only to find, to my astonishment, that it was about a foot and a half deep. Had I dived in there (and it had been 50:50) I would have broken my neck for sure.

Three young and coquettishly beautiful African girls appeared and started swimming hesitantly. They had clearly been there before as they eased themselves in feet first. The only other people by the pool, an elderly Belgian couple, looked on rather disapprovingly. They were clearly locals and I couldn't help thinking that things must have certainly changed since the days when this area was the 'European district' and Africans swimming in their pools would have been punishable with the dreaded *chicotte*, a nasty leather whip.

Jean-Pierre came round and suggested a little tour of the capital. We grabbed a taxi and rented him for two hours. We drove slowly through Poto-Poto, the old 'native area' and now a bustling market full of life. Then Jean-Pierre showed me the Basilique – an extraordinarily modern church built by the French in 1943. The green malachite roof can be seen from most of the city and is a very useful landmark. We popped inside. I'm not a churchy person but this is a remarkable building: one vast, vaulted space with not a single column for support. Two Congolese choristers were practising and their haunting voices echoed beautifully around the space. It was an unexpected moment of serene calm in this most un-calm of countries.

Next we visited the artisans' market. I was after Tintin stuff for a souvenir but was unsure whether there would be any. *Tintin in the Congo* is now widely acknowledged as a very racist tome full of negative stereotyping, where every Congolese is represented in an overly caricatured manner as either evil or very dim and almost childlike, needing the wise assistance of their Belgian colonial overlords (not to mention that, in the spirit of the era, Tintin blasted away at about 200 animals, including a rhino he drilled a hole into then blew up with dynamite).

Hergé was simply of his time but I wondered what the actual Congolese made of it all. I presumed that Tintin had visited the Belgian Congo and not the French one but I was still curious to see what they might have. The moment I entered the little market I was faced with walls of scary tribal masks and figurines. Nestled in between these, however, were what I was after. In the same style as the masks and figurines were depictions of Tintin (almost always tied up) as well as Snowy and Professor Calculus. I spotted a particularly rubbish attempt at the moon rocket that I fell instantly in love with. The best, though, was yet to come. The ultimate Tintin/racist/tourist trophy was a gloriously bad version of the *Tintin in the Congo* book cover. The name Tintin had been left blank and the guy offered me the opportunity to own this artwork replete with my name on it instead of Tintin. I was hooked and haggled him half-heartedly down to about six quid. The deal done, he shuffled off to get the artist to do my name. I left thrilled with my booty.

Back in the car we went past the old president's house, the scene of much fighting. Cameras had to be put away as stern-looking soldiers with mirror shades and mean faces tracked us with their machine guns. They were used to trouble here. Here is my attempt at a potted history of the place:

The Republic of Congo used to be the French region of Middle Congo. King Leopold II of Belgium had been desperate for a colony for his little country and, by fooling the great explorer Henry Morton Stanley into helping him, he created a huge private fiefdom in 1877. Instead of this being the philanthropic exercise he had promised the world, however, Leopold turned the whole area into a horrific slaughterhouse. Estimates go up to ten million Congolese killed as they were forced to produce first ivory and then rubber for the coffers of the big-nosed Belgian king.

The reason that France got this part of the Congo was that the Italian-born French explorer Brazza claimed the northern bank of the Congo for his country from right under the nose of Stanley.

The Republic of Congo became the present-day country upon independence from France in 1960. There was a coup in 1968 and the country turned into a fully fledged Marxist experiment closely allied to the Soviet Union. The current leader, Denis Sassou Nguesso, took power in another coup in 1979. The country was oil rich, with the largest oilfields in Africa lying off her coast, and predatory foreign companies were quick to exploit this.

Under heavy pressure Nguesso finally introduced multiparty politics in 1990 and was subsequently defeated in the 1992 elections by Pascal Lissouba.

In 1997 things really came to a head when Lissouba's men (the Ninjas) engaged Nguesso's private militia (the Cobras). Lissouba accused Nguesso of trying to stage a coup. A devastating four-month civil war ensued, which tore Brazzaville apart. Finally, with the help of socialist Angolan troops, Lissouba was unseated and Nguesso reinstated. He has been in power ever since. Confused? Welcome to the 'good' Congo.

The local theories are that everything was about oil. Lissouba had done a deal with the American company Occidental Petroleum and the French oil companies that Nguesso was in bed with weren't happy about this.

Back on our tour of the city and we'd reached the banks of the Congo, where thin dugout canoes (pirogues) supported precariously balanced fishermen. Little unofficial ferries constantly crossed the river to and from Kinshasa. This was the city where, in 1974, Muhammad Ali fought George Foreman in the Rumble in the Jungle.

'*Ali, boumbaye! Ali, boumbaye!*' the little kids had chanted over and over while they ran next to Ali as he jogged along the banks of the Congo. In English: 'Ali, kill him!' They probably meant it literally.

Jean-Pierre got the car to stop at the edge of the city and we wandered down to the riverbank and on to a plastic-bag-strewn beach.

'*Plastique – c'est le nouveau SIDA* [AIDS] *d'Afrique,*' said Jean-Pierre sadly looking around us. We'd come there to see the rapids that turn this mighty river – beaten in tonnage of water only by the Amazon – into raging, angry foam. Most of the river is on an inland plateau but upon reaching Brazzaville it drops 1,000 feet to sea level in the space of about 200 miles. The water is forced through narrow canyons and more than thirty-two different 'cataracts' until it finally reaches the ocean, where its sheer force has carved out an enormous trench in the sea floor.

It was this final stretch of water that prevented early explorers from sailing up the river. The mouth of the Congo was discovered in 1482 but it was only in the middle of the nineteenth century that Stanley managed to navigate the whole length of the river, crossing the continent from East to West.

There are some islands just below the first rapids. One of them is called Devil's Island. My cab driver told me that couples used to take pirogues out there to make love. Unfortunately peeping toms started to do the same, to pry on the passionate couples. To counter this, pirogue pilots now only take couples out to the islands. These days if you want to be a peeping tom in Brazzaville you need to get organized and pair up with someone who shares your interest.

Beyond Devil's Island, across the river, is the Democratic Republic of Congo. We could just make out some figures on the other side.

'You would be stripped naked in two minutes over there,' laughed the cabbie.

'Two minutes? That's in the good areas . . .' laughed Jean-Pierre, a little too hard for my liking.

We drove back into town and changed some money, as this was probably the last place where we could do so. We were also taking food, drink . . . everything with us as we had no idea what was available where we were going. I started thinking about the fact that Jean-Pierre had never actually been to where we were going. This did seem to me to be a basic flaw in his role as a guide. He seemed pretty relaxed about the whole thing so I rolled with it. After all, as the guy who'd recommended him to me back in the UK had said: 'Listen, he has a satellite phone and with that you can get help wherever you are if it all goes tits-up.'

I asked Jean-Pierre how long the battery on his sat phone lasted and how he powered it up in the middle of nowhere.

He smiled ruefully. 'I have no sat phone any more – the humidity steams up the screen and I break three in three years – so now I just pray to God that all goes well.'

This was not the most comforting news to an awkward atheist but I tried to remember how I 'rolled' and attempted to laugh in what I took to be an overly manly fashion. In reality I felt a bit sick.

I'd been rather hoping that a shopping list for a monster-hunting trip into the African heartland might include:

A gun
A bigger gun
A big net of some sort
Machetes
A helicopter
A really stupidly big gun just to be sure

Sadly, none of these seemed to be on JP's list. It was more like water, corned beef and rice: slightly less glamorous.

We popped into a supermarket, the biggest in Brazzaville, to do our shopping. It was a Casino, like the ones in France. Well, sort of like the ones in France – if the ones in France had gone back to 1820. Just to be a 100 per cent certain, I scoured the shelves for any sign of Um Bongo but there was none. Jean-Pierre asked me what I was looking for but I was too embarrassed to explain.

What I definitely needed was sunblock. Casino didn't have any.

'There is not much call for it here,' laughed Jean-Pierre, pointing at his jet-black skin. 'Is too late . . .'

We walked through town trying to avoid being run over by the relentless stream of green and white taxis. I noticed a couple of signs on the walls: 'Il est interdit d'uriner ici.' I wondered whether there were pee police to enforce this rule.

Finally we got to a tiny chemist. I asked the chemist for sunblock and he appeared to be totally bemused. He looked around slightly randomly before pulling something off a shelf. It was a cream used to prevent brown blotches appearing on the skin. I looked around myself and finally found a cream that was to protect babies from the sun. I bought it and the chemist looked at me as though serving a paedophile.

I was now as ready as I could ever be. My only other problem was power. I'd bought a little folding solar panel with a USB outlet but it turned out not to be supported by either my iPhone or iPad. I'd also bought two USB-powered batteries that could recharge my iPhone. I plugged them into my laptop and charged them up as much as possible.

I headed for the hotel restaurant, where I joined a group of tables full of rather depressed-looking white men drinking beer way too early in the day. We all sat drinking Ngok beer and smoking cigarettes, each one of us quietly wondering what strange twist of fate had brought us here.

We had our last supper in Brazzaville on a terrace overlooking Kinshasa at Mami Water, a French-themed restaurant in a kind of marina.

'It's for the Brazzaville jet set,' said JP, pointing to various speedboats and jet skis lying around. We ate pizza served by a very grumpy waitress who brought a whole new meaning to the phrase 'couldn't give a shit'. Out on the river fishermen floated by in their pirogues as the lights of Kinshasa twinkled gently over the water.

JP told me about sitting where we were five years ago and watching tracer bullets arc over the river from fighting in Kinshasa. It made me think of Beirut.

We started talking about the trip and for the first time I realized that I was quite scared. The Congo is a creepy enough place, even in the capital. I had no sense of intuition in how to judge whether something was safe or not. I couldn't read people's faces as I could in more familiar surroundings. At first glance everybody looked rather intimidating and unfriendly. Also where we were going there are enough scientifically validated 'monsters' without worrying about a Mokèlé-mbèmbé: leopards, crocodiles, pythons, chimps, hippos, elephants, wild dogs, green mambas, black mambas, scorpions . . .

JP started talking about wading through waist-high swamps and all the things that could slip into various orifices but he ended on a positive note: there were no lions in the area.

I asked him what antidote he used for snakebites.

'Pray God,' he said in English.

Jean-Pierre was a most relaxed individual – a little too relaxed for my liking, but I didn't want to judge until we saw what happened up north. He went through our plan. We would fly to Impfondo and meet members of the WCS (the Wildlife Conservation Society), who had a base somewhere near the river we needed to go down. We would then find a boat and head off towards the village of Boha, whose inhabitants 'own' Lake Tele – the lake where the Mokèlé-mbèmbé is supposed to live. In the village we'd have to negotiate access, then get porters, a guide and then hike for two days to the lake. That was the plan. I was on a self-imposed tight timetable. I had exactly a week up north and had to be back to Impfondo in time to catch the weekly flight back to Brazzaville. This I needed to do because I had to be back in London for the most crucial meeting of my TV life. ITV would decide whether to go ahead with my new TV series or not. If they did, it was Saturday-night prime-time for me. If they didn't . . . Well, maybe I could apply for a job reading the news on Congolese TV? I was pretty sure that this was not the normal type of problem that international monster-hunters faced. They were probably more worried about having contracted some hideous disease or smuggling unusual skulls across borders.

JP and I shook hands outside the hotel and agreed to meet the following morning at seven. As I walked into the building I spotted a pack of wild dogs taking it in turns to pee into the hotel's main air-con vent . . . Which was nice.

The following morning, on the way to Maya-Maya, the airport from which our EU-blacklisted plane was to depart, the cab took us down a long wooded avenue bordered by desolate concrete buildings.

'This used to be the zoo but they shot all the animals and ate them during the civil war,' said JP ruefully.

The Chinese were building an extension at the airport but for the moment it looked like total chaos, despite JP assuring me that it was 'the best airport in Central Africa'.

Nevertheless, if you are of a nervous disposition then the domestic-departures area of Maya-Maya Airport is most definitely not for you. It was like a huge mosh-pit. People queue-barged from so many sides that the queue itself became non-existent. A lone Lebanese man who seemed to be nominally in charge hurled abuse at every passenger, flatly refusing their demands to have everything from huge fridges to flat-screen televisions, all wrapped in brown cardboard, allowed on board. One man ignored the Lebanese man and simply tried to hurl his cardboard box through the flap at the end of the conveyor belt. The Lebanese man did not hesitate: he punched the offender hard in the face and the guy went down like a sack of potatoes. The Lebanese man looked around triumphantly, as though daring anyone else to try something. The tide was stemmed for a minute or so but the battle was soon back on as the unconscious man was dragged away by a relative. To my great surprise we appeared to be flying 'Canadian Air'. I was pretty certain that Canada had very little to do with this outfit but what could I do?

The Lebanese man seemed almost shocked at how little luggage we were taking with us and he looked around suspiciously, as though smelling a rat. He gave me my boarding pass with some hesitancy and snarled at JP, who gave him one of his beaming smiles.

While waiting at the departure gate I started re-reading the notes I had on the Mokèlé-mbèmbé.

The earliest reference to the creature seemed to be in a book by the nearly appropriately named Abbé Bonaventure in 1776. Bonaventure was an early French missionary in the Congo and wrote about seeing 'huge footprints, about three feet in circumference'.

In 1909 the famous big-game hunter Carl Hagenbeck wrote in his autobiography, *Beasts and Men*, about hearing from several independent sources of a creature living in the Congo described as 'half elephant, half dragon'. Meanwhile the naturalist Joseph Menges told him about an animal that was 'some kind of dinosaur, akin to the brontosaurus'.

In 1913 German Captain Freiherr von Stein was asked to do a report on German colonies and wrote about what was now Cameroon, just on the other side of the border from where we were headed. He too described reports of a mysterious creature:

The animal is said to be of a brownish-gray color with a smooth skin, its size is approximately that of an <u>elephant</u>; at least that of a <u>hippopotamus</u>. It is said to have a long and very flexible neck and only one tooth but a very long one; some say it is a horn. A few spoke about a long, muscular tail like that of an <u>alligator</u>. Canoes coming near it are said to be doomed; the animal is said to attack the vessels at once and to kill the crews but without eating the bodies. The creature is said to live in the caves that have been washed out by the river in the clay of its shores at sharp bends. It is said to climb the shores even at daytime in search of food; its diet is said to be entirely vegetable. This feature disagrees with a possible explanation as a myth. The preferred plant was shown to me, it is a kind of liana with large white blossoms, with a milky sap and applelike fruits. At the Ssombo River I was shown a path said to have been made by this animal in order to get at its food. The path was fresh and there were plants of the described type nearby. But since there were too many tracks of elephants, hippos, and other large mammals it was impossible to make out a particular spoor with any amount of certainty.

In 1976 herpetologist James Powell went on an expedition during which he showed villagers illustrations of various animals both alive and extinct – the natives suggested that the diplodocus was the nearest match.

In 1979 Reverend Eugene Thomas claimed that the Bangombe tribe near Lake Tele had constructed a large spiked fence in the Tele tributary to keep Mokèlé-mbèmbé away from fishing. One broke through and was killed and the natives ate it and died from food poisoning. This was supposed to have happened in 1959.

In 1988 a Japanese TV crew flew above Lake Tele and filmed a large wake in the water . . .

I read these little nuggets of information over and over again. The truth is that nobody really knows much about the area we were going to and that was exciting enough in itself. It's a rare thing nowadays to find somewhere in the world that's still properly off the beaten track. If Canadian Air delivered then we would soon be heading off into just such a place. I had a very dry mouth. This normally happens when I'm nervous; it's a weird mix of excitement and nerves. I was excited about monster-hunting. I was nervous about the state of the plane, the flight, the landing, the insects, the animals, the heat, the cold, the unknown . . . It's the unknown that always scares us the most.

JP had been on his phone and announced that he had managed to get through to the WCS office in Impfondo. They knew we were coming and had confirmed that a car of some sort would take us to Epema, where we could get hold of a boat. They also confirmed that it would be possible to borrow two tents. This sounded fairly promising but JP just gave a fatalistic shrug. He'd travelled long enough in Africa to know that nothing was real until it happened.

We boarded the plane through a very narrow tunnel and the organization was clearly provided by the same people who'd dealt with the last helicopter off the roof of the US Embassy in Saigon. It was actual, physical fighting to get on board. At first I was a bit reticent. I was a visitor here and didn't want to behave badly. This was just taken as a sign of weakness by the other passengers and I was soon being shoved and elbowed to the back. It was sink or swim, so I thrashed and punched my way to the plane door in an almost hysterical manner. A woman was in a big argument with a soldier who was not letting her on board. He had drawn his handgun and was pointing it at the woman's chest but she seemed a lot less phased by this than I would have been. I was boiling hot and covered in sweat and starting to have a little panic attack. I wanted to tell JP that I didn't want to go to Lake Tele. I wanted to go back to my hotel in Brazzaville where there was CNN and the comfort of the Internet. Locals said that to go into the 'forest' was like going to war: you had to be prepared for anything to happen. I've never properly been to war – I've been in one but never actively gone towards one. I was really panicking badly and couldn't breathe. JP was looking at me and smiling and I tried to smile back, to mask my weakness. As ever, the mask worked.

The plane flew over dense, impenetrable forest for what seemed like hours. There was not a house, a hut, no sign of human life beneath us except for just occasionally a wisp of smoke escaping through the trees.

The plane landed in Impfondo, which seemed to suddenly appear out of nowhere beneath us. The landing was heavy and very fast. Both JP and I were sure that we were going to overshoot the runway and braced ourselves dramatically for impact. We survived and got off the plane into what seemed like complete wilderness. We immediately had a cigarette on the tarmac and watched as several passengers attempted to retrieve their luggage out of the cargo hold. One actually climbed into the plane's belly and was unceremoniously hurled out by a soldier. Another was grabbed and hit hard in the back of the head with a rifle butt. We decided to wait for due process. As we smoked, hundreds of bees swarmed around us forming a thick yellow cloud. I sprayed some Deet on to my arms and legs and wished I was back home.

We tried to enter the luggage hall and had our passports taken away by a man who disappeared into the crowd. There was very little we could do about this and we both hoped that he was some kind of official. We stood by the lone, broken carousel and waited for JP's luggage. I looked around. The room was packed with both the arrivals from our plane and the departing passengers waiting to get on it. I was the only white man in the building and felt that I was really sticking out. I could feel everyone staring at me and I buried my head in a book.

Finally JP's bags came through and we chucked everything on a trolley and tried to head out while looking for the man with our passports. The soldier at the gate took one look at me and directed us to a police room in the far corner of the terminal, where four men lounged about in virtual darkness. There's no electricity in Impfondo in the day and rarely any at night unless you have a generator.

The eldest of the four men stood up and shook my hand. He indicated that I should sit down in a chair opposite him. This I did while he perused my passport, which had suddenly appeared in front of him. He flicked through the pages for a while before looking at my visa.

'Where have you come from?' he asked.

'Brazzaville,' I replied. This being the only flight each week, the question seemed a touch unnecessary.

'How long have you been there?' he asked.

'Two days,' I replied.

'And what are you doing here?'

'I'm going to Lake Tele – I'm a tourist.'

His eyes suddenly lit up. 'A tourist? Your visa is a *visa ordinaire* not a *visa touristique*.'

I shrugged and told him that I had let the Congolese Embassy in London know what I was doing and this was the visa they had issued me with. The man smiled unpleasantly, as though talking to a thick worm.

'Monsieur, you have a *visa ordinaire* but you are here as a tourist – therefore you are here illegally.' I felt myself about to lose it. I was hot and tired and stressed and I hate bureaucracy more than anything else in the whole world. I started to argue in French and I could feel my voice rising. JP stepped in and started to explain in overly flowery French. He was charm incarnate. He gave me a glance to indicate that I should step away and I did what I was told. It was clear that these officials smelt money and were not going to let go. I sat on a chair just outside the room and watched two men scream at each other nonstop at a counter on the other side of the hall. One was trying to get a piece of luggage away from the other. The whole place was utterly chaotic. Normally I'd enjoy this sort of thing but I was really on edge. This didn't bode well.

Back in the little room where my passport was, the four officials were now arguing with each other while JP stepped out for a cigarette with me. It was all mind-blowingly pointless and not the best welcome to the Likouala Province. Eventually, after much negotiation, another man arrived, who was – judging by his puffed-up manner and arrogant swagger – a boss of some kind. He turned out to be the regional-tourism official for the local government and he took little time to inform us that we were in big trouble.

My visa allowed me into the Congo but, for me to do any-thing touristic, I should have got permission from the Tourism Ministry in Brazzaville. This we hadn't done, and we were now in the region illegally and could be arrested.

We were marched out of the airport by this new guy whom I shall call 'King' as he had that air of self-importance about him.

We were bundled into the back of a pickup truck and driven into town. We stopped at a wooden shack that revealed itself to be the Centre Pour Le Departement De Tourism Du Likouala. I'm guessing that this is probably one of the least busy build-ings in Africa.

King marched us into his office, which was like a sauna. An imposing photograph of Nguesso started down at us from the wall. King shouted at his secretary, who was sitting in an ante-room full of books, saying his office was a disgrace and asking why was it so untidy.

He was clearly trying to lay down the law and show that he was an important man. We nodded and looked suitably impressed. He picked up a mobile and rang his boss, the head of the prefecture, because (as he kept repeating to us like some demented mantra): '*On a un hiérarchie ici, et il faut le respecter.*' We nodded in agreement. With his boss on the line he informed him in puffed-up terms that he had two strangers here with no papers and that they were proposing to go to Lake Tele. He told his boss that the WCS had once again broken their agreement about being purely a scientific organization. They were now organizing tourist trips. He got off the phone and told us that we were to be taken to the prefecture. We nodded and smiled like this was the best news ever but JP looked worried. For about fifteen minutes we were marched through town, down dusty tracks and back alleys. The sun was burning hot and my rucksack was starting to cut into my shoulders.

Eventually we arrived at an unpainted concrete building with a terrace running around a little garden. Off this terrace were dozens of little offices full of official-looking people. We were ushered into the secretariat, a boiling-hot room in which sat three secretaries listening to music on a mobile phone. They were singing along and totally blanking JP and me.

We sat there for about twenty minutes with nobody saying anything to us. Eventually it got too hot and we escaped to the relative cool of the terrace. Half an hour later and King finally came out of an office looking a bit flustered and being a tad more friendly. He had clearly been given the brush-off.

'My boss is too busy to see you but he says we should go back to my office and we will do the necessary requirements . . .'

This sounded a bit more promising. We walked back down the sweltering dirt streets towards the shack with King's assistant, Noel. King had got a lift back in a car but we didn't mind as Noel was much friendlier. We started to talk about beer. Noel, it turned out, was a huge fan of Guinness. I pretended that I also was the world's biggest Guinness fan and we both made vague sounds of Guinness appreciation. When we got back to the shack King was still not there and Noel took us to the bar next door, where we had locally brewed Guinness and decided that no country with oil could ever be happy.

After a couple of resuscitative pints of the black stuff we returned to the shack to find King looking very miffed at Noel for slacking on authority. We sat back down in his sauna/office and watched as he spent ages filling out two official-looking forms replete with lots of rubber stamping and copies for various in and out trays that nobody would ever read. He'd occasionally look up and ask us a question, like how long we intended to be at Lake Tele. We took educated guesses but we really had no idea whatsoever and he knew it. Eventually he brought up the subject of money. Technically, he said, we should be paying a fine of 100,000 Congolese francs each but – and here he raised himself to his full pomposity – he did not operate that way and so we would only have to pay 50,000 Congolese francs (about €80) simply for the permit that we needed to be tourists. The whole charade was total nonsense but there had been hints of overnighting in a jail and we were both immensely relieved. JP paid the money, we got a receipt and we were allowed to go on our way.

There had been no sign of the WCS people and it was now too late to attempt to take the road to Epema, as it was getting dark. We asked around and found a guesthouse called Le Rosier where we could stay the night. It was fairly clean but had no electricity or water. We threw our stuff on our beds and I lay down for a rest.

JP's bank card had not worked in Brazzaville but he had got some money wired from Cameroon to the post office, so he headed straight off into town to try to get it. He was back pretty quickly because it turned out that the post office had closed at two in the afternoon. We were on a fairly tight schedule and this delay in Impfondo had already set us back, but JP had a plan. We could get to the WCS in Epema the following morning and set off straight away downriver. We hopped on to the back of two motorbikes ridden by local kids and found a restaurant called Tropicana right on the banks of the Oubangui River, a wide offshoot of the Congo.

As we were finishing up a man turned up at our table. He was Hermes, the driver from WCS, and he'd been looking for us all day. Hermes was with a friend who had actually been to Lake Tele. The friend told us that it was two days' walk from the village of Boha and that the water en route was not too deep at the moment. He said that it came up to your knees at the worst parts. This still sounded totally horrendous but it was better than what I'd read that we could expect. JP told them that we wanted to leave early the following morning after he had got his money from the post office. Hermes nodded in agreement. It looked like we were back on schedule.

We sat on the grass outside the Tropicana where a makeshift screen had been set up and a very dull French soft-porn film was showing. Our surly waitress was not happy with the choice of film and started shouting at the men watching. Someone changed the channel reluctantly. Suddenly we were watching Southampton vs Tottenham. God how I loathe football . . . But JP loved it. It turned out that he had been a very promising player in his native Cameroon but his father had disapproved and forbade him to play. JP had sneaked away and kept on playing. He eventually played in two international league matches but his father then heard his name on the radio and that was that. I told him that I loved cricket and he asked me who I support: India or South Africa?

We walked slowly back to Le Rosier through the town. It was pitch-black but we could hear sounds of life all around us. Occasionally a motorbike would appear out of the darkness and roar past us. JP and I talked about the Mokèlé-mbèmbé. His personal view was that it was more of a bogeyman-type thing that was used to keep order – i.e., 'behave or the Mokèlé-mbèmbé will get you'. I looked disappointed at this and he smiled at me.

'There is a thin line between reality and mystery in Africa, Dom.'

From somewhere nearby came the sound of a group of girls singing together. It was either a church or maybe a party. It was powerfully beautiful.

Back at Le Rosier I slept fitfully as it was hot and the bed was almost deliberately uncomfortable, but I was well aware that tomorrow this would feel like a Mandarin Oriental. At least there were no mosquitos. The rainy season had finished about two months before but I was still on hyper-alert, having been given a quick run-down of all the things I could catch from those buzzing plague-ridden bastards.

JP woke me up very early the next morning and we headed off through town for breakfast. I marvelled at how rapidly one adapted to places. Only yesterday we were under arrest and being marched through these streets by King and I'd wanted nothing more than to go home. This morning, however, I didn't want to go anywhere except off on our adventure.

JP and I shared a generous bowl of *ndongo* (chillies) with our breakfast omelette. He told me that I was the first Westerner he had ever travelled with who could pronounce words like *ndongo* and Impfondo correctly. I was incredibly chuffed.

After breakfast we sauntered down along the river towards what passed for a commercial district. I tried to walk slowly as it was already very hot. After ten minutes we got to the post office, which also served as the town bank and MoneyGram office. JP had been told that it opened at seven-thirty in the morning and he admitted that before I was awake he had already been and found it closed.

It was now nine-thirty and the place was finally open. We entered to find a lone woman sitting in a darkened room at a dirty wooden desk. JP told her that his assistant in Cameroon had paid in money at her end and he was here to pick it up. We needed the money to pay for boats and porters. No money, no trip. The woman gave JP a form to fill out. He completed it carefully and handed it back to her. She looked at it long and hard. JP was asking for 750,000 Congolese francs (about €1,100). After a long silence she looked up.

'The moneyman is not here. You must come back later.'

JP was annoyed by this and it showed. 'You are a bank. How can the moneyman not be here? This is your business!'

'You must come back later.' The lady was not for turning.

We asked her at what time the moneyman would be there.

'Two, maybe three hours,' she replied in a frustratingly non-committal fashion.

JP turned on the charm and told her that we were on a very tight schedule as we had to get to Epema in time to catch a boat to Boha before sunset. She looked spectacularly uninterested.

We went and got a coffee and kicked our heels for an hour and a half. Then, unable to wait any longer, we went back. To our delight there was now a man in a passably smart shirt and trousers sitting next to the woman. JP asked him if he was the moneyman. He nodded gravely and confirmed that he was indeed.

JP produced the form that he'd filled in earlier and gave it to Moneyman. Moneyman looked long and hard at the form – far longer and harder than the woman had done before. Again there was total silence. Finally, after what seemed like about five minutes, Moneyman looked up at us.

'We have no money,' said Moneyman matter-of-factly.

JP looked shattered. 'No money? But . . . You are a bank . . . How can you have no money?'

Moneyman shrugged his shoulders. 'Yes, we are a bank with no money. We had to pay the Americans yesterday. They have very big salary so we have no money.'

We asked him what Americans he was talking about. He told us that there was a UNHCR (UN Refugee Agency) camp just outside of town. We hadn't seen any foreigners and were completely unaware of their existence. JP reiterated to Moneyman just how important it was that we got some money. We had only limited time to get to the lake because . . . Moneyman shrugged and JP stopped his explanation. It was no use. As we started to leave there was a hint of guilt from Moneyman. He told JP that he could ask around the market and see if he could borrow the money. I looked out of the door at the motley collection of stalls selling little plastic bottles of petrol and assorted bicycle parts and thought this was most unlikely.

Nevertheless, Moneyman said he would ring us if he was successful or if any money came in. We returned to the guest-house to wait but already it looked like we wouldn't make Epema that night, let alone Boha. There had been no sign of Hermes and his friend from the WCS. They had been supposed to pick us up at nine but there was no answer from their mobile. Time was clearly a very relative concept in the Congo . . .

As we sat waiting outside our rooms at Le Rosier, I realized that I was secretly quite pleased with the delay. It meant one day less in the swamps, one day less of hardship. This is quite a common sensation for me. Whenever I was driving around looking to do a hidden camera stunt I was always relieved when something went wrong with the set-up and we had to delay things. Once I was actually in the thick of it I loved it, but the pre-tension was unbearable.

Finally JP's phone rang at around one p.m. It was Moneyman and he had managed to scrape together 350,000 francs. Someone had come in and paid some money over to someone in Brazzaville. It was not enough but JP hoped he could pay WCS by wire transfer and use the cash for porters and negotiations with the village chief. However, the problem was that we still couldn't get hold of the WCS driver to take us to Epema. It was incredible enough that there was mobile phone reception in Impfondo, but this was all part of the process of 'municipaliza-tion' that the government had implemented in the last six years in an attempt to ensure that all towns in Congo have at least one tarmac road and better public buildings. At the time of my visit the road from here to Epema had been built only four years previously, with Brazilian money, and was the only tarmacked road in the entire province.

JP went off to get the money from Moneyman before

Moneyman lost his money. I started reading *King Leopold's Ghost* by Adam Hochschild. Finally, at around five p.m., the WCS people arrived at our guesthouse. They seemed entirely unconcerned with being almost a day late. Hermes had brought his boss, a Rwandan and a man called Sylvestre who had been to Lake Tele four times. He told us it would be a two-night camp from Boha, with us arriving at the lake on the third morning. Today was Friday and we had to be back in Impfondo by Thursday morning to get the plane to Brazzaville. This left us with very little time to play with.

We went through the finances of the trip. Sylvestre wanted 5,000 Congolese francs per porter per day. He was going to come with us and his fee was 10,000 Congolese francs a day. He estimated we needed to pay around 100,000 Congolese francs each to the chief and that we would need 80,000 for food and supplies.

We went to the market for the supplies. We needed two bottles of water per person per day, tinned tuna, hamburger buns, pasta, rice, tomato sauce and some Babybel cheese. On our way back from the market we spotted that a large boat had docked in town and we went down to have a look. On deck was a white man: a rotund Frenchman who seemed rather surprised to see us.

The boat turned out to be a bi-national cooperation between the Central African Republic and the Congo. He had been working on it for seven years and knew the rivers very well. They would trawl up and down the river from Bangui to Brazzaville putting in buoys and arrows to show boats where to navigate. The Frenchman told us that it was a never-ending task, as the power of the river shifted the sand constantly.

I asked him if he had ever seen the Mokèlé-mbèmbé. He looked puzzled. He didn't know what it was. A Congolese crew member sitting on an oil drum and having his head shaved with a rusty-looking razor looked up.

'Mokèlé-mbèmbé? *Le dinosaur?*'

I nodded and ask him if he'd seen it.

'I haven't, but I know plenty of people who have.'

He got very animated and I feared for his scalp. He told us about a place on the river charts where everyone said there was a Mokèlé-mbèmbé. He said that all Congolese avoided this bend because of the beast. Another deckhand spoke up. He claimed that planes didn't fly over the Lake Tele area because the beast had a magnetic power that dragged them into some sort of aerial whirlpool before crashing them. While I was happy that they knew about my quarry, I hate stories like theirs. These were so ludicrous they made the reality of a Mokèlé-mbèmbé seem unlikely.

The Frenchman laughed and promised us that he'd keep an eye out. It was another four days downstream to Brazzaville from Impfondo.

Bangui to Brazzaville on a boat down the Congo – now *that* was an adventure. But sadly it would have to be for another time. We said goodbye to the Frenchman and scrambled back up the bank past a mother washing four little naked kids on top of an upturned dugout canoe.

Once back at the guesthouse we were finally ready to go. The Rwandan was driving a big white Toyota Land Cruiser, the vehicle of choice for charities and relief agencies worldwide. We squeezed into the back and set off out of Impfondo along the road that the Brazilians built. Now, I know little of the Brazilians' road-building capability, but let's just say that I hoped this wasn't the jewel in their crown. The road was essentially a series of joined-up potholes with the forest attempting to reclaim the route from all sides. We had to go at a snail's pace to avoid breaking the Land Cruiser's suspension.

Sylvestre was sitting opposite me in the back and I asked him if he believed in the Mokèlé-mbèmbé. He said that he hadn't seen one but he knew of many people who had. This seemed to be a stock answer round here and I hoped that I might get some first-hand experiences from someone in Boha.

It took about two hours to get to Epema and most of that time was spent listening to the government *conservateur* of the park having a screaming argument with the others about the Bible.

His French was very heavily accented and I couldn't follow everything but the main thrust seemed to be about vegetarianism and how Daniel, because he was a vegetarian, was not eaten in the den of lions as he didn't smell of meat. At one juncture they asked me what I thought and I admitted that I had no idea but I had heard that the Mokèlé-mbèmbé was vegetarian. They all nodded and said that, yes, it was a herbivore.

'I hope so,' I said, mock-nervously, and everyone roared with laughter. Outside the vehicle was total darkness. Occasionally I could spot the glimmer of a fire outside a hut through the thick trees. Every so often the headlights would catch the surprised face of someone walking in the pitch-black along the road. Where were they going? Come to think of it, where were *we* going?

We rolled into the WCS compound in Epema, where JP and I were given a very basic room with two beds. The sounds of the forest were all round us.

'I'm afraid that I snore,' I warned JP.

'No worry – I make gas,' he replied.

Sylvestre promised that he would wake us at five in the morning and that we'd immediately set off in a boat for Boha. We woke up at seven. Nobody had woken us up and we stumbled out and tried to get things going. Predictably everyone was still asleep and it took another good couple of hours before we were ready to get on the boat. I glanced at my iPhone and was astonished to find that I had reception.

I once did a show for Radio 4 about how extraordinary the mobile-phone boom has been for Africa. It's allowed fishermen and traders to check where they can get the best price for their goods as well as keeping migrant families in touch with each other. In the days before mobiles this was a major problem and would have made our already tricky trip almost impossible to coordinate. Now, though, men in day-glo orange vests patrolled the streets of every town we'd been in trying to sell people 'credit'. All the government had needed to do was erect some mobile-phone masts and the money started to roll in. Every African 'rich' kid wanted to get in on this boom business.

I sent Stacey a final text:

I'm getting on the boat and heading off into the unknown – laters xxx

Finally, Sylvestre, JP, the boat driver and I (plus all our supplies) set off down the misty river of Likouala aux Herbes in search of dinosaurs.

The river was bordered on both sides by a swampy savannah and you could see the high-water marks from the rainy season. Kingfishers swooped and dived all around us. On the banks perched large herons and the occasional vulture. Beneath us were crocodiles, hippos and possibly a Mokèlé-mbèmbé or two. I felt very vulnerable in our tiny boat.

Every so often we would pass fishermen standing tall on their long, thin dugout canoes, the rim just inches above the water level. As seems to be the international boat convention, everyone waved at each other frantically. Admittedly this was a friendly thing to do but why does this just happen in boats? Why don't we all wave at each other every time we see someone in another car? I made a mental note to start doing this when I got back home.

The sun rose higher in the sky as we ploughed on down the river at a steady but unexciting pace. The river was still and trees were reflected in the water as though in fantastical mirrors. After a time my eyes started playing tricks on me and tree stumps became men and logs metamorphosed into giant croco-diles. The herons all sat ramrod-straight on dead branches, seemingly contemplating life as they knew it. They appeared Zen-like in comparison to the hyperactive kingfishers, swoop-ing up and down looking for the slightest hint of a fish. I felt incredibly peaceful: to travel is better than to arrive – and I was slightly dreading the arrival. It was the calm before the storm.

Our boatman waved at a man sitting on a log by the river-side. The man beckoned us over and we turned sharply towards the shore and beached the boat. The man lived in a tiny hut with his wife and two little kids. He would catch fish and then smoke them on a wooden trestle table that hung over a slow-burning fire. Every month he would make the trip to Epema in his pirogue to sell the smoked blackened fish. We bought 2,000 Congolese francs' worth, which JP chucked into the front of the boat where their blackened, dead eyes stared balefully at me as we proceeded on down the river.

An hour or so later we rounded another corner and came across two men in their pirogues. One, who bore an extraordin-ary resemblance to Snoop Dogg, was holding an antique rifle and had a large dead python wrapped round it. The other, whom I shall call Bulldog, was a more physically intimidating-looking man and held a long, nasty-looking spear.

'We are in luck,' said Sylvestre quietly. 'These are the very men we need to talk to . . .'

It turned out that Snoop Dogg, who looked very young for the role, was the village chief, whereas Bulldog was a tribal elder (although not that elderly).

Snoop Dogg seemed to be in a good mood on account of his python kill, whereas Bulldog was friendly enough but a little distant. Aware of the constraints of time, we offered to tow them back to the village. They agreed and each sat in their dugouts holding on to the sides of our boat as we became a kind of DIY catamaran.

After ten minutes we turned right off the main river and down a side tributary. To our left we began to see the village half-hidden in the trees. Our arrival sparked much interest and most of the village rushed down to the river to watch us disembark. We climbed a steep mudbank and entered the village right by the chief's hut. He went inside and produced a couple of low, home-made chairs that he beckoned us to sit in. The chief, it quickly became apparent, was also the government's man in the village. He told us that he was responsible for any white man in his area and he wanted to be sure we had no ulterior motive for visiting the lake. He seemed quite smart, rather charismatic and young – maybe thirty? We told him why we were there and that we were on a very tight timeframe and needed to leave as soon as possible on that day to have a chance of reaching the lake and returning on time. He nodded and said it was possible to organize porters and do the trip, but that he needed his 'chief's fee' for this to happen. We discussed the fee and it was within our budget so we handed the money over and we shook hands. This had really been too easy. It looked like the travel gods were on our side. The chief stood up and said that he'd start thinking about who would go with us. While he did this, he said, we should go and greet the village elders and get their blessing for the trip. This was all going swimmingly and we set off through some quite thick forest to where the elders were assembling.

On the way I asked Sylvestre about Boha and how it was that the people here looked after Lake Tele since they were so far away from it. He said that the tribe used to live around the lake but they, like everyone else, were forced to move to the riverside so that the colonial authorities could keep an eye on them. So the tribe had moved to Boha but they were still custodians of Lake Tele and anybody going to the lake had to go through them.

Sylvestre pushed his way through a thick bush and we

found ourselves in another little village. It was all part of Boha but this area had definitely been built with a view to keeping a distance from the rest. This was where the elders lived and we could see a couple of their wives pounding manioc, their staple food, in the doorways of their huts. We rounded a corner and walked into a central area that was clearly used for meetings as there were two long low benches on each side. It was indicated to us that we should sit on one of these benches, and this we did. I looked around us. Directly opposite us were the elders. There were about five of them, including Bulldog, and they were all holding the rather nasty-looking spears we'd seen earlier. A couple also had machetes hanging by their waists. In the middle of them was a man who seemed to be a lot older than the elders. He looked fairly ravaged by life. His eyes were bloodshot and slightly crazed-looking. He wore a tattered old combat jacket that was open to the waist. He stared at us with a look that didn't immediately scream 'Welcome to the jungle.'

To our left sat about fifty men from the village all settling down as though about to watch a good match . . . Which they probably were.

JP, though normally pretty cool about things, was visibly quite unsettled by the amount of weapons on show.

'Will this take long?' I whispered to him. We needed to get cracking as soon as possible if we wanted to get any distance towards the lake before we had to camp.

'I have no idea what is going on,' replied JP.

A young, very tall man stood up. He was holding a wicker brush and another long spear. Sylvestre explained that he was the porte-parole. He would stand in between the elders and us and relay any messages. We were not to speak to the elders directly. Everything had to be directed through Porte-Parole. I couldn't believe this system at first but actually it wasn't that dissimilar to MPs directing their remarks to the Speaker in the

House of Commons. Supposedly it helped to avoid full-on arguments.

Proceedings started with Sylvestre, speaking through Porte-Parole, greeting the elders and telling them that we had come a long way to go and see the lake and wanted their blessing for the trip.

Porte-Parole relayed this to the elders, who all nodded and grunted in what looked like a fairly amenable manner.

Then the crazed-looking man in the combat jacket, whom I shall call Crazy (because, frankly, he was), started to speak. I say speak; it was more a series of shouts and gesticulations. Porte-Parole listened and, after a little pause, informed us that Crazy was happy that we'd come to see them and that they would give us their blessing if we paid them the sum of 250,000 Congolese francs. This was totally out of the question. Firstly, we had just paid Snoop Dogg for the privilege of making the trip to the lake and we were not about to pay twice. More importantly, we just didn't have anything near that sort of money.

Sylvestre stood up and thanked the elders for their kind offer but hinted that this was a little more than we had been expecting to pay. Both JP and I hissed at him that it was a *lot* more than we had expected to pay, since we had already paid. Porte-Parole took this all on board and passed it on to the elders.

The elders went . . . apeshit. Crazy started waving a machete at us in a distinctly unfriendly manner and Bulldog was shouting at the other elders and pointing at us.

I asked Sylvestre what was going on. Why were we negotiating to pay more money that we didn't have when we'd already paid the chief? Sylvestre explained that Snoop Dogg was chief but he was the government's man, whereas traditional tribal authority rested with Crazy and the Elders (good band name). They had no interest in what we'd negotiated with Snoop. As far as they were concerned he was an irrelevance. They were the top dogs and we needed to pay them for access. I asked Sylvestre why he had not mentioned this before and he shrugged in that infuriating African way. I could see JP subtly looking at how much money we had left and making a quick calculation of what we could afford. I already knew that it was not much and the clock was still ticking.

JP took the floor and did his flowery-French thing. He dropped the fact that he was a prince back home and said he knew how these things worked and didn't want to offend. He then went on to explain that we'd had a lot of unexpected problems on the trip and this had left us short of both time and money. He started off on quite a long allegory about a hunter going out into the forest and chopping down trees that were too big and took too long to chop down, and he didn't have enough provisions so he went home without the trees because it was dangerous in the forest at night. I was just about following this and hoped that Porte-Parole could convey it in full. Porte-Parole did his best but, when the gist became clear that we were not going to pay anything near the amount they wanted, Bulldog exploded. He ignored Porte-Parole and started screaming at JP and me while waving his spear about.

'If you don't like the price then go back to where you came from. We have no need for you here. Anyway, the *gros bébé* will never make it to the lake – he will die on the journey . . .'

It took me a moment to work out that the *gros bébé* in question was me. It took me a little longer to confirm that he was not threatening to kill me but was sure that the forest would . . .

I looked at JP and he looked at me with a sense of foreboding. We agreed to leave the clearing and discuss what we should do next. Curiously Snoop Dogg had now turned up and insisted on joining our discussions. I was already annoyed with him for taking a payment that gave us nothing, but joining our secret negotiations was a bit much. JP and I talked, and worked out that 50,000 Congolese francs was the best we could do and they would have to take it or leave it. Snoop Dogg nodded at this offer and said they would listen to it. I asked him whether he had at least organized the porters so that, should this sort itself out, we could leave immediately. He looked at me vacantly and I guessed the answer.

We returned to the clearing and I told Porte-Parole what we could offer. Bulldog would now not even look at us and Crazy had gone nuts again. He shouted and screamed for about five minutes until even the other elders looked a little disturbed by whatever it was he was shouting. Porte-Parole looked a little embarrassed and gave us what was clearly an edited version, saying, in effect, that we should get back on our boat and leave, pronto.

JP stood up again and laid on some more flowery prose. This was becoming like a weird poetry slam. He laid on the flattery very thick and basically said that we were now in a situation where they either got something or nothing. A couple of the elders seemed to accept this logic but Crazy and Bulldog were now competing with each other to shout at us. Finally JP played his last card. He offered 80,000 Congolese francs and said that this was the final offer: they should either take it or leave it – but, whatever, if we didn't leave immediately there would be no point in any of this. Porte-Parole spoke and I sort of felt that he pleaded our case a little as Crazy and Bulldog calmed down a little. Porte-Parole told me they were going elsewhere to discuss things. All the elders got up and disappeared into a nearby hut. Porte-Parole stood outside a little awkwardly as a guard.

They spent fifteen minutes in there and then emerged to return to their seats. Crazy stood up and spoke quite pompously for about eight minutes. Porte-Parole listened intently and then turned to us and said, 'They accept.' He smiled at me.

It had taken about two hours but we finally had a decision and we were good to go. We looked over at Snoop Dogg and asked him how long it would be before we could get going.

Snoop looked at his watch, except he didn't have one, and then said, 'Soon, but first we celebrate.'

Porte-Parole had slipped into a hut and was now coming out with about five bottles of something very dirty and visibly home-made.

'Oh no . . . Jungle gin,' said JP. 'We are all supposed to drink to the agreement.' He grimaced.

Now, having done a whole TV series for which I went round the world drinking revolting local alcohol, I do have some form in this area and I doubted anything would be more lethal than the 90-per-cent-proof Samagon that I drank outside St Petersburg. I was wrong.

Snoop poured me some jungle gin and I sipped it. It was quite horrific and I felt dizzy. JP pretended to drink but didn't swallow anything. The rest of the elders weren't so reticent and started knocking it back like it was Happy Hour at Hooters. More worryingly, so did the whole village. We tried to leave the circle but this was considered bad form so we had to stay and watch as everyone got blind drunk and started stumbling over spears and fighting and generally behaving like they were at a lock-in at the village pub. After a desperate hour of this, during which we pretended to drink along, we managed to slip away back to the main village to get ready.

We were done in ten minutes and we then stood around outside Snoop's hut looking hopeful. Our boat driver wanted to know if he could leave, as he wanted to get back to Epema before nightfall. I realized that once he'd gone we would have no way of contacting him until he came back to pick us up in five days' time. There had been no mobile reception since Epema and I was very wary of letting him go until we knew what was happening. I asked him to wait. He wasn't happy about this but I had a feeling that things were going to go weird.

I sat down with JP and Sylvestre and tried to make a plan. The big problem seemed to be that nobody was prepared to be specific about how long it took to get to the lake. Some people were saying two days while others were saying three. If it was three days each way, then we wouldn't have enough time to get back to catch the plane. I needed someone to give us a definite answer so we could make a decision.

Snoop Dogg turned up with three men whom he informed us were our porters. They were all totally drunk and stumbling about. It was becoming very clear that whatever happened nobody was going anywhere today. I needed to know if it was possible to do the trip if we left the following morning but Snoop wouldn't give me an answer. Finally I'd had enough and sat Sylvestre down in front of me. He'd been to the lake three times and was our best bet.

'Sylvestre, can we make the lake in two days' walk? Yes or no?'

Up until now he had been hinting strongly that it was possible in two days but we had never really pinned him down about it. He looked shifty and started to talk about how we'd need some manioc for the porters . . .

I ignored him and asked him again: 'Sylvestre, can we make the lake in two days' walk? Yes or no?'

Sylvestre's eyes flickered around in panic looking for a distraction but there was none. He looked at me, and his face dropped.

'No, it is impossible in two days; it is at least two days and a half.'

We were fucked. JP and I both knew that this news, plus the fact that we couldn't leave today because the whole village was blind drunk, meant we were not going to be able to get to Lake Tele.

JP and I went for a walk around the village to discuss our next move. I told him that I was there to get information about the Mokèlé-mbèmbé. We had to accept that we couldn't go to the lake but, since there was nobody living around the lake, I could still get some answers from the villagers . . . If they sobered up.

JP looked at me with worried eyes. He knew I was right – that we couldn't make the lake – but he'd promised to get me there and I could see he felt bad. I told him not to worry: shit happens. The important thing was to see what I could get out of the villagers about the Mokèlé-mbèmbé. JP agreed and we decided that, whatever happened, we would spend the night in the village and take it from there.

We returned to Snoop Dogg's hut, where a quite drunken crowd had now gathered and were hanging about. JP announced to them that the trip we had spent three hours negotiating was now off. There was an immediate air of great tension and too many machetes and spears suddenly appeared for my liking. Snoop went mental and asked us if we were mad – which was a fair question. JP tried to calm people down by explaining how our series of delays – first with King, then Moneyman, then the WCS, and now the drunken initiation – had left us with no time left to do the journey. He then attempted to explain the concept of Western time to the villagers, who looked absolutely bemused by the whole idea.

'You wanted to go today and you can go today?' said the chief suspiciously.

'We wanted to go today, early this morning, not today, this evening. We have no time left to go to the lake and back,' said JP.

'Why not? You can be there in three days?' said another villager.

'Because we have only five days in total for the journey now . . .' said JP desperately.

Everyone nodded wisely and then asked what time we now wanted to leave.

JP calmly explained again that we would not be going to the lake but that we wanted to talk to them about the Mokèlé-mbèmbé. Snoop Dogg now realized that we were serious and seemed to sober up quite quickly. JP and I sat down and opened a couple of beers while the Snoop discussed this peculiar new state of affairs with the drunk porters. We watched them all try to make sense out of this group who had suddenly arrived out of the blue one morning, organized porters, spent a spirited three hours negotiating forest access with the tribal elders, paid the money, and then cancelled the whole trip. It was clearly something that they would talk about for years to come but, for now, most of them were still a little ripped to the tits on jungle gin to really think about it.

An hour passed during which we had a bit of lunch from our plentiful supplies. Then a stressed-looking Porte-Parole appeared to inform us that the elders wanted to see us again. We groaned inwardly but trooped over through the forest to their part of the village. As before, the elders were sat around waiting for us. Bulldog, however, was not there – but Crazy was and he was waving an empty bottle of jungle gin. Crazy launched straight into Porte-Parole for about four minutes. Porte-Parole then told us that Crazy was confused by this extraordinary situation and that he was worried that they had taken money and not done the job. This was technically illegal and they feared that the police would come.

This was a lot more rational than I'd anticipated and, through Porte-Parole, we assured Crazy that this would not be the case. We told him we would not complain and that circumstances had just conspired against us to make us run out of time. He could, of course, simply return the money should he so wish . . .

JP launched into some flowery French again. He told Crazy that sometimes travel plans go wrong. Maybe God himself did not want us to make it to the lake and we would have been struck down by giant pythons?

Crazy nodded and confirmed that January and February were the very worst time for pythons.

JP was now on a roll: 'Maybe one day the elders have gone

into the forest to cut down a tree. They cut a little one down and carry on. Then they find a medium-sized tree, cut it down and carry on. Finally they come across a huge tree and start to try to cut it down but it takes ages and they there all night and their food and water run out and they are are in trouble . . .'

Crazy nodded at this story, which appeared to be the same one that JP had told earlier. Crazy said that he understood the point – although he personally did not cut down trees, as he was a tribal elder.

The elders then asked for a final promise that there was no problem between us and we assured them that all was fine. They could even keep the money: all we asked was that we could talk to them about the Mokèlé-mbèmbé.

Crazy agreed immediately and told us that the village was at our disposition. He went further: he said that he would person-ally get a group of elders together at five p.m. and they would tell us everything they knew about the Mokèlé-mbèmbé. He warned me that I would run out of pages in my notebook as he personally had so much to say on the subject. Porte-Parole told him that I had a magic notebook that used electronics and had no limits. Everyone nodded. Porte-Parole slammed his spear into the earth: the meeting was over.

We returned towards the main part of the village where tents were to be set up near Snoop's hut for us to sleep in that night.

On the walk back JP apologized for talking too much.

'I have to talk in pictures here – like with the tree story – it is the way an African speaks and it can be very long-winded.'

We laughed and followed Porte-Parole along the open scrub area that linked the parts of the village. We walked past a cool, shady spot under a tree where they were making palm roofs. Five kids ran out of a house and started shouting 'Hello' at us.

'My kids,' smiled Porte Parole. '*Petits* Porte-Paroles.' We all laughed.

Once back at Snoop's hut we sat down at a table that Snoop

had put under the cool shade of the tamarind trees. Snoop was looking concerned again and asked if he could speak to us. We nodded wearily.

He consulted a little child's maths exercise book in which he had written down our names.

'Mr Dominic Joly *et* Mr Jean-Pierre Samon . . . I will not talk for long . . .' he said, before talking for a very long time. The gist of it was that the village of Boha did not receive many tourists (sixteen in the last thirty years) and he wanted us to help him start a tourist industry there. JP and I nodded enthusiastically while looking at each other and thinking that this was probably not the best time to have this discussion. After a good twenty minutes of non-stop fast French patois it was as though we had been hit with a verbal machine gun.

'I am not the sort of person to talk for an hour . . .' he said, looking like he was winding himself up for another round. I told him that I had to talk to villagers about the Mokèlé-mbèmbé and slipped away, leaving poor JP to round two.

I talked to a man in a bright-yellow shirt emblazoned with photographs of the president. I had not seen this man before and he appeared to be the most sober man in the village. His name was Mandzamoyi Marcelin and he said he was the secretary of the village, whatever that might be.

He told me that Lake Tele was originally a little pool that their tribe, the Bakolou, would all hunt and fish around. Then the lake started to grow in size because the Mokèlé-mbèmbé would dig channels to allow themselves in and out. These channels obviously allowed more water into the lake and it got bigger and bigger. The Bakolou were unhappy with the Mokèlé-mbèmbé coming into the lake because they ate all the fish. So, in the time of Marcelin's great-grandfather, the tribe built nine wooden dams in an attempt to stop the Mokèlé-mbèmbé.

They soon spotted a Mokèlé-mbèmbé trying to come in and it managed to break through eight dams before the tribe managed to spear it to death at the ninth. People dived in and cut bits of the flesh off the huge body. The whole village celebrated the kill by cooking a great feast with the Mokèlé-mbèmbé meat. Unfortunately, everyone who ate the meat died. Marcelin said that it killed more than a hundred people. He said the channels were still visible around the lake.

JP came over as the story was finishing and I filled him in on the rest. I asked him why they wouldn't have dragged the creature out of the water on to land. He said that this was a very Western attitude. If an elephant was killed in the forest people would come with knives and cut off the flesh to take back home to cook.

Sylvestre suddenly piped up. He had been very quiet since the whole cancellation debacle. He said that on his first trip to Lake Tele he had brought a man from Congolese TV. They had got to the lake and had just made camp when they spotted a huge shape in the middle of the lake. He said the Congolese man had filmed it and the footage was often shown on local TV. I thought this sudden admission to be a little odd, since I'd already asked him if he had seen the Mokèlé-mbèmbé and he'd said no. I wondered whether he was now trying to get back into our good books. (I have since searched for this footage online but have found nothing.)

At around five p.m. Snoop Dogg asked us to sit down at his table. Our boat guy had zoomed off to get some beer. Forty minutes later, he returned with a carton of Congolese red wine made in Pointe-Noire called, rather confusingly, Baron of Madrid. It was the single most revolting thing I have ever drunk – and I've had Irn-Bru.

Crazy limped his way over and sat down. He looked angry, but then he always looked angry. He spotted the wine and announced that it was a woman's drink. He then poured himself a large glass and downed it. Snoop launched into a long introduction as to why Crazy was *the* man to tell us about the

Mokèlé-mbèmbé. Crazy had another large glass of wine and looked out towards the river disinterestedly.

When Snoop finished, Crazy started speaking. He spoke fast with loads of gesticulations and I got quite excited, feeling sure he was telling of some epic encounter with the Mokèlé-mbèmbé. When he eventually drew breath I looked expectantly at Sylvestre for a translation.

It turned out that Crazy was very annoyed that he had invited us to the elder's area and was then told that he must come to Snoop's hut.

'*Lui, c'est l'état!*' he screamed in French in case I hadn't understood his beef.

Crazy announced that he would not say a single word unless we came over to his area. Snoop laughed, obviously quite enjoying Crazy's discomfort. He said that it would soon be dark and that he did not go over to the elders' area in the dark because it was via a forest path and he worried about his security at night. Crazy shouted back at Snoop that us being at Snoop's table was an insult to the elders. Snoop told him to leave if he didn't like it, but we were his guests. Crazy crossed his arms in an overly dramatic gesture and sat sulking.

Nobody was going to give in. Then a man in another vivid-yellow Nguesso shirt stepped in and, in perfect French, explained that this had become a fight between the state and 'tradition'.

He looked at me and said: 'Get in your boat and leave. Your mission has failed and you are causing a fight between the chief and the elder.'

Crazy stood up and hurled abuse at Snoop before storming off with Porte-Parole. We all got up and followed him, including a very reluctant Snoop. Rather than walk the five minutes it took to get to Crazy's area, we all trooped down to the riverbank – where our boat guy was ordered to take everyone about 300 yards upriver, where we disembarked and walked into

Crazy's clearing. The whole thing was getting ridiculous but we were now at least in the correct place and were going to get some great Mokèlé-mbèmbé stories.

Crazy sat down in his favourite place under a tree and grabbed a spear for effect. He started by admitting that he had never actually made it to Tele himself because of his bad foot (and attitude). He said that we had gone about the search for the Mokèlé-mbèmbé in the wrong way. We had come in a hurry and wanted to leave immediately. The correct way was to come and spend three four nights (the very thought!) in the village and then set off on our trip with their blessing.

At this juncture Snoop interrupted and shouted at Crazy, saying that he was not setting the story up properly. Crazy ignored Snoop and carried on talking.

'In the old days the Badzama, who lived by the lake, would put their manioc in the water but every day it disappeared and they couldn't work out why. They accused another tribe . . .'

At this point an elder sitting next to Crazy tapped him on the shoulder and pointed to the sky. It was nearly dark and he reminded Crazy that tradition dictated that they should stop telling stories at this time. This was a full ten minutes after we had finally begun. I started to wonder whether I was the victim of Congolese *Candid Camera*. You couldn't make this farce up. The elders disappeared into a hut for some more jungle gin and we were left to troop back through the forest with a nervous Snoop.

I now just wanted to go to bed. I'd had enough of Boha politics. We were told that we could return for more stories the following day but both JP and I were reaching the end of our tether. The boat guy had set up our tents while we had been away. One was badly broken but the other one was OK save for a large hole in the roof. We ate a sullen meal with Snoop. His wife provided some smoked river fish with rice with peanuts. There was also a bowl of the local staple food, cassava. It's very easy to grow but has little nutritional value. The leaves are edible and known as *saka-saka* but it's the tubers on the roots that feed the Congo. First they're soaked, then cut up and dried until they're white and brittle and then they're pounded into flour by the women and made into *foo-foo*, the bland dumplings on the table in front of us. It is extraordinary how little the Congolese grow for themselves. As we came down the Likouala aux Herbes JP had been marvelling at how perfect the swampy flatlands are for growing rice.

'If the Chinese came they would be in rice heaven,' he'd said.

Snoop started ranting again about Crazy but we'd had enough and called it a night. We got into our tents. It had got seriously cold and I had no warm clothes and no cover. I lay on a mat and stared at the stars through the hole in the roof. I could hear something slithering around just on the other side of the canvas. I became convinced that it was a python and stayed rigid in the middle of my mat for about an hour as whatever it was slithered all around the tent. Unable to sleep, I used my head torch to read the part in Redmond O'Hanlon's book about when he visited Boha. This was a big mistake. There's a particular passage where O'Hanlon asks his friend where they should pitch their tents. His friend replies that only a crazy man would camp in Boha. He insists that they sleep in a hut with someone guarding the door.

'I'm not going to be axed through the canvas in the night . . .' says the friend.

I started to imagine a spear suddenly slamming through the thin canvas into my sides. I wondered what it would feel like. Would it kill me immediately or would I go slowly, groaning, my lifeblood draining away into the sand?

As it so happened, I was neither speared to death nor bitten by snakes in the night but I was woken by the sound of terrible, terrible singing very close to me. It was worse than my mother-in-law on a road trip. (She is a wonderful woman who loves to sing but nature has blessed her with the voice of a tone-deaf hobo. It's a cruel fate – like adoring animals but finding out that you're allergic to them.) And, like my mother-in-law, the singer here was not going to stop.

I got up and clambered out of the tent. It was about five in the morning and the sun had just risen. I strolled down to the river-bank where villagers were already setting off for dawn fishing trips on their pirogues. A thin mist hung low over the water. Birds sang lustily and, for a moment, Boha was almost a pleasant place. I climbed up from the riverbank and walked down the dusty main drag. On a whim I turned left near Porte-Parole's hut and followed a little track. To my astonishment and delight, the first hut I came to had the words 'Boha – Pilote – Dinosaur' daubed on the wall in fading white paint. I bumped into Porte-Parole on the way back and asked him about it. He said that the owner of the hut had done it about thirty years ago, when the first interest in the Mokèlé-mbèmbé had surfaced. He'd hoped that there would be a flood of visitors he could guide to the lake.

'And what happened?' I asked.

'Nobody came,' replied Porte-Parole ruefully.

I returned to the tents to find Crazy and Snoop standing outside Snoop's hut and having a furious shouting match. It was seemingly never-ending, like being stuck in a nightmare loony council meeting. JP was up and we went for a little walk and decided that things were getting a little out of hand and we should probably beat a retreat back to Epema. Bulldog had turned up again and was looking like thunder at us.

We returned and interrupted Crazy and Snoop to let them know that we were leaving. They immediately stopped fighting and Snoop produced a bottle of jungle gin and announced that, before we left, we must drink to celebrate. If I was honest, it was perhaps not the ideal breakfast drink and it burned my throat quite badly.

As we sat, Bulldog started accusing us of all sorts of things and got quite nasty. JP whispered that we needed to get on the boat and fast. Suddenly there was a commotion beyond Snoop's hut. A man appeared brandishing a machete. He was bare-chested and had cut himself all over his chest and arms and was approaching us fast and didn't look friendly. Blood was pouring from his wounds and it looked like a scene from hell. I recognized the man as one of the porters assigned to us the previous day. Had we left yesterday we would be in the middle of the forest with this man going crazy. It didn't bear thinking about.

He had an insane look in his eyes and they were focused right on me. Fortunately for me, two villagers grabbed him and there was quite a tussle with the man flailing away with his machete. He was eventually subdued and tied to a tree with rope.

We didn't wait any longer. JP and I headed for the boat with the entire village following us, shouting and screaming at each other and at us. We didn't hang about. Our boat guy was already in the boat with Sylvestre and JP shouted to him to turn on the engine, which he did. We hopped on and shouted 'Go!' to him. He needed no further urging: he'd been looking very uncom-fortable throughout our stay. We pushed off and were soon free of the reeds and in deeper water. Back on the shore the crowd had got into a huge argument and were screaming at each other again. The whole thing was more Asterix than Tintin. As we left the reedy channel and joined the main river we all breathed a huge sigh of relief.

On the way upriver towards Epema we stopped at the village of Mohounda to get some more petrol for the boat. Despite the fact that a young thirty-five-year-old man had died of a heart attack in the night, they were very welcoming and petrol was provided and we were soon on our way. As we made our way upriver there were a lot of pirogues on their way down. Many were full and precarious with seven, eight, nine people in them.

139

'They are all going for the funeral in Mohounda,' said Sylvestre. I asked him how long the ceremony took.

Three days and three nights of dancing and then they bury the body and everyone goes home.'

I was astonished at how quickly the 'grapevine' had informed everyone, all the way up to Epema, about the death.

We finally got back to the WCS camp and went to see the Rwandan boss. He said that he'd known that there was a problem when the boat hadn't come back. He didn't seem at all surprised. Carefully ignoring his part in our delay, he started slagging off the villagers – saying that if they behaved like this they would lose their rights to control access to the lake and that he would find another way in. He then told us that, six years previously, four Americans went to the village but refused to pay the huge sum they were asking and came back. It was nice of him to tell us all this now.

JP and I didn't want to be stuck in Epema. It was a total ghost town. Fortunately the director was embarrassed enough to offer to drive us to Impfondo himself. We were very grateful. After a minimal wait (in Congolese terms) of about two hours, while nothing seemed to happen, we were off.

The first part of the road out of Epema was in quite good nick and the director drove like a mentalist.

'This is the only road in the whole province of Likouala –' he said, half looking at the road and half at me – 'twenty-three thousand square miles and only a hundred miles of road . . .'

Up here, of course, the rivers were the real roads and this was what first excited the French and the Belgians: a ready-made artery of infrastructure for them to transport first ivory and then rubber to the coast for transport to the West.

We eventually arrived in Impfondo after a long talk about Pygmy discrimination. They were seen by locals as 'sous-humain' and appallingly discriminated against.

We got dropped off at Tropicana and discovered that they

had rooms as well as a restaurant. After Boha, it seemed like a five-star resort, and we had a fabulous meal of lamb, potatoes, rice and a lot of *ndongo*. We passed on the sautéed antelope.

Everyone was much more relaxed and Sylvestre was like a new man. The director asked us our plans. We were uncertain but worried that we might bump into King, who would surely make us pay more money as we did not have a *permis* to *not* go to Lake Tele. Everyone laughed. If you can't laugh, then Congo travel is very much not for you.

Sylvestre told me about a Swiss man who had come to Epema and wanted to see gorillas. They'd stayed in the forest for six days and didn't see a single one. The Swiss man went totally mental and was blaming Sylvestre and threatening him.

'I must make remote-controlled gorilla so I can control them,' laughed Sylvestre.

Sylvestre and the director left to head back to Epema. We headed for our new rooms to chill out. They were much better than those at Le Rosier, which had felt like they were modelled on a prison exercise yard. Our new rooms had a TV, air con and a shower. I was excited. I turned on the air con as it was boiling hot – but there was no electricity. JP went and made enquiries and found out that it would come on between six and nine in the evening. It was four-thirty, so I lay on my bed in a pool of sweat and read a book. At six-forty-eight p.m., the electricity came on. I know this because there was a sudden violent flash and some smoke from two bare wires hanging out of the wall above the bed. I tried the lights and a light bulb turned on but I received a moderate electric shock as penance. I turned on the air con. There were no life signs: it didn't work. I plugged in the TV very gingerly but that didn't work either. I went into the bathroom and turned on the shower: a tiny trickle appeared and I stood under it, desperately trying to get wet. After two minutes I had enough water on me to start lathering up and I attempted to get the forest off me. Just as I'd covered myself in soap, the water stopped completely and the electricity went off. I was left stumbling around with foam all over me – this was not good. I managed to find a towel and wipe as much off as possible. I then felt my way to the bed and lay down on it, still soapy and wet. The electricity came back on and another small firework display burst from the wall wires. I was wet and that doesn't mix well with electricity. I carefully returned to the shower but there was no more water. I gave up and lay back down on the bed. I was foamy and naked but I didn't care any more.

I continued reading my book. For the next hour or so I could hear quite a commotion on the terrace that ran past my room. There was much laughing and shouts and it felt like there was quite a crowd out there. I ignored it and carried on reading. The man I called Crazy turned out to have been the chief of Boha when Redmond O'Hanlon visited in 1995. There was even a photo of him, bare-chested, clutching his favourite spear and looking quite the young warrior. He looked about forty and fit as a fiddle. There was simply no seeing him as the haggard, rotting old man we had been dealing with. Among its many other properties, it was clear that jungle gin was not good for eternal youth.

At eight-twenty there was a knock on the glass door of my room. Both the door and window of our rooms were mirrored, which was quite disconcerting. I caught a glimpse of myself in the door. I looked like I'd just been to a San Franciscan foam party. I opened the door an inch to find JP looking a bit embarrassed.

'I think it's best you close your curtains – you are becoming something of a town exhibit . . .'

I didn't have the foggiest what he was talking about so I put on some shorts and stepped out on to the balcony. I looked at the window to my room which, in the daytime, had been mirrored and impossible to see in through. Now, however, with the lights on inside, the mirror had turned into a sheet of clear glass – as had my door. Unbeknown to me, for the last hour and a half I had become the equivalent of the women exposing themselves in windows in the Reeperbahn. The show, although catering to quite specialist tastes, had apparently been very popular. I was mortified and when I got dressed and entered the restaurant the whole place was awash with smirks, glances and laughter. I felt violated in a most curious manner. I ate an omelette and some *ndongo* as quickly as I could before heading off to bed. This time I closed the curtains – not that this mattered now, as the electricity had cut out again for good.

About an hour later I started to feel unwell – very unwell – and I spent the rest of the night sitting on the loo with a head torch while I shed half my bodyweight into the Impfondo sewage system (which I'm guessing meant the river just below the hotel).

The following morning at breakfast I was still feeling delicate and very, very drained. Fortunately I had thought to bring some Dioralytes and these helped a lot. JP said that if we didn't make a journey it was because God didn't want us to. I'm not a religious man but I thanked the Lord for not allowing me into the swamp forest with a man so crazy he had to be tied up while I was shitting my insides out over holy ground.

JP was trying to work out how we would get back to Brazzaville. We'd checked the two boats in town the night before, including the one owned by the Frenchman we had met previously. However, both boats were going upstream to Bangui, so this option was a no-no. JP needed to try to get some money from Moneyman as there were rumours of a rogue plane headed for Brazzaville the following day.

We said hello to Moneyman who explained that, sadly, he once again had no money – but that he was fairly confident he'd have some at one p.m. The most common phrase you hear in the Congo is this: '*Vous savez, avec ça le grand probléme c'est . . .*' and then a reeling out of all the possible problems ahead of you in whatever you're wishing to do. Actually, scratch the word 'possible' – the problems will definitely happen . . .

Back in Tropicana I lay on my bed in the infernal midday heat. I would not have liked to be here in the wet season. Then, according to the Rwandan boss, the whole town – a grid of dirt tracks and shacks – becomes a mud bath and almost impenetrable.

At about two-thirty we got good news. JP had got money from Moneyman and thought he'd managed to swap our previous airline tickets for two on a flight to Brazzaville the following day. The man in question said that he would bring the air tickets to us at six that evening. If I was a betting man, I wouldn't have put a single Congolese franc on this happening.

Come six p.m. we were seated in the Tropicana garden having a beer. Nobody showed up. There was, however, a bit of drama unfolding to keep us entertained. A little man in a shiny suit came in, surrounded by three bodyguards. The man was a caricature of a self-important African oligarch. He was on his mobile and very upset. He was talking so loudly that he made my *Trigger Happy TV* character look like an amateur. He was complaining to the local police inspector that he had just been beaten up by a crowd in the street. I knew nothing of the affair but my sympathies were almost immediately with the crowd. I tried to get some footage of this buffoon but one of the bodyguards spotted me and charged over to demand why I was filming. I professed total ignorance and claimed I was cleaning my camera. There was a brief stand-off but the guy backed off. Next, a large group of excitable youths entered the garden and surrounded the buffoon. I rather hoped that they were the crowd in question, here to finish him off, but he stood up and gave them a rousing speech at which they all roared their approval. His speech finished, he proceeded to lead the youths out of the garden as though to battle.

Suddenly a new character – a huge, fearsome-looking woman – entered the garden in a voluminous, multi-coloured, all-encompassing dress with a repeat pattern made of the colours of the Congolese flag and the face of the president. The woman squared up to the buffoon, right in his face, and started scream-ing that, if he wanted to cause problems, he should do so in parliament in Brazzaville – not here, where she had to live.

The waitress whispered to us that the buffoon was a senior member of the ruling party and this woman was his sister. He backed away as she continued her verbal assault. The buffoon was having a bad day. A policeman turned up but appeared to be nervous of both parties. He tried to separate them and they both turned on him. Eventually the whole circus poured out into the street and marched off shouting at each other.

As if on cue a tall, thin Congolese man wearing a Pete Doherty cast-off hat pressed 'play' on a PA system that he had been setting up in the garden. A gritty rap song blared out. The hook phrase, endlessly repeated, was, 'I know you niggazzzz wanna fuckkkkkk meeee . . .' On the grass three five-year-old kids danced innocently a yard away from the speakers, apparently transfixed by the hypnotic groove of this appalling tune.

JP and I downed another Ngok and prayed that the plane would take us away from all this tomorrow.

The rap stopped and now Phil Collins's 'Against All Odds' polluted the African night. The girls looked disappointed and stopped dancing: some things have no frontiers. We called it a night at ten. There was still no sign of the airline-ticket man, whom I was now convinced was a close relative of Moneyman. Whatever, this was the Congo and tomorrow would be what it would be . . .

My stomach was feeling a little better, possibly because it could find little else other than my vital organs to get rid of. I had weird dreams about being on the shores of Lake Tele watching Motörhead playing 'Ace of Spades' on a floating platform before they were attacked by a Mokèlé-mbèmbé and drowned. The subconscious is a curious creature.

I awoke at eight a.m. and watched the fishermen out on the river. Lonely silhouettes on calm waters. JP was in the restaurant and he had still not heard from Ticketman but he was confident that we could get on the flight. The only thing I could be sure of was that you can't be sure of anything in the Congo. We had a final *ndongo*-peppered omelette. The only other person in the restaurant was a rather shattered-looking man from Benin. He'd been on our flight up from Brazzaville and was supposed to stay for a week but, like us, was going back today (although, also like us, he had no ticket).

'It is impossible to do business here – it is like the Stone Age. I have not managed one meeting, one discussion; nobody turns up for anything. It is beyond belief. This country is dead.' He wandered off looking distraught and quite frazzled.

We said goodbye to the nice waitress at Tropicana, who had never understood why we were there or what we were doing but had delivered the closest to decent service that we'd encountered in this country.

At midday we hopped on to the back of a pickup and roared off to the airport. There it was predictable chaos. JP found Ticketman, who wanted more money for the tickets but gave in when JP went apeshit. We then fought our way through the laughable screening process but were pulled out of the line by the same officials who'd hassled us on our arrival. They were now demanding money for an 'exit tax'. JP was close to nuclear explosion. The officials said that we could not get an exit stamp without paying. JP pointed out that, as were not leaving the country, we didn't want an exit stamp.

Everything kicked off big style. JP and I eventually marched out of their room and joined the line again. The officials followed us and were by now really hassling us, but there appeared to be a VIP in front of us and he became interested in what was happening. The officials backed off and we got through the screening.

A soldier checked my passport and thought my Iranian visa was my ID page. He spent ages checking it was in order. In the end he nodded and we were on the tarmac waiting for the plane to land so that we could get the fuck out of Dodge.

The mystery plane eventually landed six hours late and only after it missed the actual airport twice and overshot the runway once. There was another rugby scrum to get on to the plane.

Onboard every other passenger seemed to have a plastic bag full of smoked fish and the smell was absolutely astonishing – like an abattoir in a fish tank. A woman sat down next to us with an open bag and I very nearly passed out and thought I was going to vomit. Fortunately we were by the emergency exit and the stewardess told her to move: women are apparently not considered responsible enough to operate emergency exits. Normally this kind of sexism would appal me but, on this one occasion, I let it slide. It would be no exaggeration to admit that, for the duration of this flight, I became a little more religious. It lasted only an hour but both JP and I were absolutely convinced something else was going to go wrong.

In between thoughts of imminent death I reflected on the problems inherent so far in monster-hunting. I certainly wasn't dispirited. There was no rulebook for this. I was flying by the seat of my pants and trying, in a series of short trips, to do what some people spent years doing. The main problem seemed to be trying to distinguish between native beliefs and cold, hard facts. The stories of the monsters in the Okanagan and the Congo had come from the indigenous peoples and had been subject to osmosis by settlers or travellers who seemed to have some problem in interpreting what was real and what was spiritual. At least the Hibagon was a relatively new (though short-lived) creature: very rare in Japan, the land of a million ancient monsters. Whatever, I had at least had a sighting – something that many firm believers in these creatures would never have. It was all turning out to be as varied and weird and downright exciting as I'd hoped it would be. It was good to be alive and I couldn't wait to set off on my next expedition, one of the daddies of the monster world: Bigfoot.

That evening, safely back in Brazzaville, JP and I headed out to the best restaurant in town – a posh riverside place called Terminalia. We both ordered pizza and sat gazing over the mighty Congo at the lights of Kinshasa dancing on the moonlit waters. We were happy and in a slightly euphoric post-adventure mood. We went over some of the 'highlights' of the trip and the alcohol flowed freely. The pizza took a while but we were busy chatting and it was only when a terrible tiredness came over us both after an hour or so that we realized that nothing had arrived. The waitress wandered past and I asked her if there was any sign of our pizza.

'*Oui, oui – ça arrive tout de suite*,' she said, walking on.

Another twenty minutes elapsed and finally Jean-Pierre went inside to remonstrate. He came back out half-laughing, half-stressed.

'The oven is not working,' he said.

I asked him why they hadn't just told us that from the start.

'It's the Congo, my friend: nothing is normal here . . .'

We got up and wandered out through the gates and into the streets of Brazzaville.

'Do you feel like visiting Kinshasa tomorrow?' asked JP playfully. I looked at him and he was laughing.

'Maybe next time, Jean-Pierre, maybe next time . . .'

Bigfoot

'Darwinian man, though well behaved,
At best is only a monkey shaved.'

W.S. Gilbert

I settled into my seat on the flight to San Francisco. As I did so
the one in front of me was tilted back violently by a very fidg-
ety Indian gentleman. We were still on the tarmac and I knew
my rights: no tilting until after take-off. I gave his seat a shove
back and battle commenced.

'I have the right to put my chair back – this is why it is
designed in this manner!' shouted Fidget.

'Not until we take off. Seats must be upright until we take off;
that is airline law,' I countered.

'You are British? This is why you lost the Empire: for this sort
of arrogant behaviour. It is why you lose the cricket as well.' This
was a very left-field argument but it stumped me momentarily. I

considered mentioning that it was a shame we had not taught our former colonial subjects the basics of travel law, but realized that I'd be hoiked off the flight by the steward.

'As a matter of fact, England are currently the best cricket team in the world.' It was checkmate.

'Go fuck yourself.' He had run out of steam and he knew it.

His chair stayed up until we'd taken off, when he immediately titled it back to the full extent. Sometimes I hate travelling.

Arriving in San Francisco I braced myself for the usual torment of entering the United States. In my experience, if you happened to have been born in an 'enemy' country, as I was (Lebanon), then you could expect a five-hour wait, a dumb interrogation and, if you're lucky, an internal examination. To my utter joy, however, it turned out that the whole NSEER system has finally been abolished, having caught precisely zero terrorists and turned everyone who went through it into an anti-American since its hasty introduction by panicky Neo-Cons post-9/11. I sailed through and was soon riding the futuristic monorail to the car-rental agencies. I wondered how long it would be before monorails stopped looking futuristic.

There can be few things more liberating than driving over the Golden Gate Bridge with good music blaring, off on a road trip into the badlands of Northern California. When the purpose of said trip is to find Bigfoot, it's off the scale.

I'd done most of this journey before. The very first travel piece that I ever wrote was for the *Independent*. In it, I set off to find the Giant Redwoods I'd heard so much about. Like most tourists, I stopped at Muir Woods, about twenty minutes north of the bridge, and walked around craning my neck upwards and marvelling at these natural monsters, unaware that they were mere minnows compared with what awaited me further north.

California is an extraordinary state. To me it's a microcosm of the United States, with the deserts and lush hills of the south, the seaboard cities and then the wild of the north that even includes a 'Lost Coast'. My destination this time was Willow Creek: Bigfoot Central and home to a museum dedicated to the Sasquatch, as the Native Americans call him. Willow Creek is inland from Eureka, a large(ish) town on the coast about 250 miles north of San Francisco. As you drive north from San Francisco you go through several areas. First you pass the outskirts of Sonoma and Napa, wine country. Then it's into beer country, dotted with hundreds of microbreweries. Finally, you enter marijuana country and all bets are off. Willow Creek is in Humboldt County, famously the home of hundreds of reclusive weed farmers who hide their crops in the woods and are renowned for not liking strangers wandering about. Maybe unsurprisingly, Bigfoot territory lies slap in the middle.

I'd left San Francisco at about three-thirty in the afternoon so I wasn't going to make Eureka that evening. I drove up Highway 1 for a while. This is one of my favourite drives in the world: it's like rolling through an enormous Hitchcock set. I got to Bodega Bay, where he filmed *The Birds*, before turning inland and stopping in Ukiah, a little beer town, for the night.

I'd stayed here before on my Redwoods trip and had been billeted in a bed and breakfast with a woman who lived with a giant turtle. I hate bed and breakfasts. This time I checked into the Economy Inn Motel. The reception smelt of curry and a tiny woman gave me the key in exchange for forty bucks. The room was like every motel room you've ever seen in American movies: slightly grotty, but sort of strangely exotic at the same time.

The last time I was in town I found an oasis called the Ukiah Brewing Company & Restaurant – a haven in a town full of beauty parlours and combat gear. It was only three blocks from my motel so I popped in to get a drink and some supper. There were several groups of draft dodgers in various corners and I installed myself at a high table in the window. I ordered a beer and steak and watched the Patterson/Gimlin film of Bigfoot on my laptop. This is probably the most famous piece of monster footage ever. The film was shot on a sixteen-millimetre camera on 20 October 1967 by Roger Patterson and Robert Gimlin on the Klamath River, near Orleans in Northern California. The film shows a large female (she has big bosoms) Bigfoot walking away fast along the bottom of a creek. The creature has come to be known as 'Patty' by cryptozoologists. It's either a hoax or the most important piece of wildlife footage in history. The Wikipedia entry about the encounter goes like this:

In the early afternoon of October 20, Patterson and Gimlin were at Bluff Creek. Both were on horseback when they 'came to an overturned tree with a large root system at a turn in the creek, almost as high as a room.' When they rounded it they spotted the figure behind it nearly simultaneously, while it was 'crouching beside the creek to their left.' Gimlin later described himself as in a mild state of shock after first seeing the figure. Patterson estimated he was about 25 feet (8 m) away from the creature at his closest. Patterson said that his horse reared upon seeing (or perhaps smelling) the figure, and he spent about twenty seconds extricating himself from the saddle and getting his camera from a saddlebag before he could run toward the figure while operating his camera.

He yelled 'Cover me' to Gimlin, who thereupon crossed the creek on horseback, rode forward a while, and, rifle in hand, dismounted (presumably because his horse might have panicked if the creature charged, spoiling his shot). The figure had walked away from them to a distance of about 120 feet (37 m) before Patterson began to run after it. The resulting film (about 53 seconds long) is initially quite shaky until Patterson gets about 80 feet (24 m) from the figure. At that point the figure glanced over its right shoulder at the men and Patterson fell to his knees; Patterson would later characterize the creature's expression as one of 'contempt and disgust.'

At this point the steady middle portion of the film begins. Patterson said 'it turned a total of I think three times,' the first time therefore being before the filming began. Shortly after glancing over its shoulder, the creature walks behind a grove of trees, reappears for a while after Patterson moved ten feet to a better vantage point, then fades into the trees again and is lost to view as the reel of film ran out. Gimlin remounted and followed it on horseback, keeping his distance, until it disappeared around a bend in the road three hundred yards away. Patterson called him back at that point, feeling vulnerable on foot without a rifle, because he feared the creature's mate might approach.

Next, Gimlin rounded up Patterson's horses, which had run off before the filming began, and 'the men then tracked it for three miles, but lost it in the heavy undergrowth.' They returned to the initial site, measured the creature's stride, made two plaster casts (of the best-quality right and left prints), and covered the other prints to protect them. The entire encounter had lasted less than two minutes.

Those two minutes had a profound effect on me as a kid. I first saw only still images taken from the film and reproduced in the Arthur C. Clarke book. This was obviously in the days before the Internet and there was no way for a schoolboy in Oxford to access the footage. I finally saw the shaky, mysterious film on a repeat of the Arthur C. Clarke show on television. I watched it once and was transfixed. Now you can go on the Internet and see it endlessly looped, slowed down, analysed . . . Back then, however, it was an elusive experience and I longed to know more about it. Was it a hoax, as many had claimed? One of the problems was that Patterson had rented a very expensive sixteen-millimetre camera and couldn't remember what film speed he'd filmed it on. This made reconstructions quite difficult. I wanted to know more about the film, to try to get near to where it was shot, speak to people who knew the pair. A couple from New Jersey seated next to me – presumably because I was the least dangerous-looking person in the room – were eager to chat. I told them that I was hunting Bigfoot and they told me that there was one in New Jersey. I tried to look sceptical, as though I was something of an expert in the field. They appeared impressed – but then again, they also appeared impressed by metal cutlery.

I told them about my wine/beer/marijuana Northern California division and informed them that they were right on the beer/marijuana frontier. They looked very excited and asked me whether I could sell them any dope. I patiently explained that I was 'not from round here' and they nodded, unconvincingly. They ended up asking the waitress, who told them about medical marijuana. It was readily available: all you needed was a note from a doctor. They asked her if she was a doctor. She replied that, no, she was a waitress. I started to weep quietly.

Just before I left, I went to the loo and found the old New Jersey guy talking to the chef, who appeared to be a doctor because some deal was clearly going down.

My motel room would have made a fabulous murder scene in a TV show. I turned on the telly but Piers Morgan popped up so I turned it off feeling dirty and violated.

Surprisingly I got a great night's sleep, despite the man next door to me snoring so loudly through the paper-thin wall that I thought this might be my first earthquake. I awoke to the sound of the snoring man weeping loudly. I'd had enough exotica and headed out for breakfast before hitting the road north again.

The scenery just got more spectacular the further north I went. Mist clung to the hills and the moss-covered coastal oaks had a haunting air about them. I was now most definitely in weed country. I drove into Garberville, a town that boasts a 'Cannabis College'. The town looked like a movie set from 1972, with long-haired hippies shuffling about and sitting on the sidewalk strumming guitars tunelessly. Everywhere I looked were smoke shops and shady-looking men in pickup trucks buying disproportionate amounts of lighting equipment. It was all a bit *Twin Peaks*.

Just to the north of Garberville is the magnificent Avenue of Giants – a truly majestic stretch of road about twenty miles long that is bordered and overlooked by some monster redwood trees. Unless you have actually seen a redwood or a giant sequoia, it is difficult to describe just how mind-blowing they are. It is no coincidence that a group of them is known as a cathedral. There is something immensely spiritual about them.

Would you like some redwood facts? Here you go then.

They are the world's largest trees in terms of total volume. They grow to an average height of about 280 feet and 26 feet in diameter. Record trees have been measured to reach 330 feet in height and more than 55 feet in diameter. The oldest known giant sequoia based on ring count is 3,500 years old. I thank you.

Back in my enormo-vehicle, I was really enjoying my leisurely cruise down the Avenue of Giants. At times the trees were so tall and so thick that it was almost dark. Then a lone shard of sunlight would find a way through the foliage and light up a section of the road like a movie spotlight. I kept taking photo-graphs; I just couldn't stop as the trees were so impressive. The problem was that it was almost impossible to take a successful photograph because I could never get the whole tree in my viewfinder unless I lay on the road and looked straight up – and even then it was a bit weird.

Suddenly, to my left, I spotted a fallen giant. The trunk was about thirty feet in circumference, and its decaying root system looked like a small city's infrastructure. The Avenue was totally devoid of traffic so I stopped right in the middle of the road and took some more photographs out of the window.

Then, from out of nowhere, a beaten-up old truck came speeding down the Avenue honking violently at me. There was no problem in getting past me and the driver would have spotted me from a good 200 yards away, so they were just trying to be jerks. I ignored them and carried on taking photos. I think that my fearless attitude might possibly have been slightly emboldened by my new status as a monster-hunter. Canoeing down the Congo changes you somehow: honking pickup trucks do not phase you . . .

The truck drove up alongside mine. I looked into it. To my surprise all three occupants were women. They were in their mid-twenties and looked like they spent their weekends beating up lumberjacks.

'Asshole!' they all shouted in unison before giving me the rigid digit and zooming off.

Assuming that these 'ladies' were not simply people who didn't appreciate my TV work, I considered this to be totally uncalled for. In fact, I'm ashamed to admit, a red mist descended upon me in this, the calmest and most reflective of nature's places. I gunned my engine and set off in hot pursuit of the rogue females. After two or three minutes I'd caught them up and observed with pleasure the driver's startled look in the mirror. I started honking and flashing my lights. I was behaving like an idiot, but I was really angry. I had no idea what I'd do if they stopped; I just wanted to register my displeasure. I imagined Stacey in the seat next to me screaming, 'For fuck's sake, Dom, stop . . . What are you doing, you bonehead?'

But Stacey was not here and I was a monster-hunter and my pride had been dented. We careered on down the Avenue of Giants, nose to tail. Suddenly they screeched to a stop, forcing me to steer madly to the left before halting just behind them. I pulled myself together and thought about remonstrating with them but feared that they would laugh at my English accent.

I can do quite a good 'Southern' accent – a hybrid Mississippi/Louisiana thing I use when I'm online playing *Call of Duty*. I like to assume the role of a moronic redneck and tease Brit gamers by feeding them every American stereotype in the book.

The girl in the passenger seat got out of the car and I wound down my window and, in my finest hick, shouted, 'What the heyyl do yooo asshooles think you're all doing getting all uppity and sheeeet . . . ?'

The girl ignored me and went straight to the boot of the car. She leant in and pulled out a crowbar. I didn't hang about. This cowboy got out of Dodge as fast as his steed would take him. I hit the gas and shot off past them. In the mirror I saw her jump back in and they started chasing me.

I really panicked now. I was being chased by a truckload of homicidal killer ladies. We roared down the Avenue of Giants aping a scene from *Need for Speed*. I thanked the Lord that California has tougher gun laws than say, Nevada, where the woman would have probably pulled a bazooka out of the back. I looked in the mirror again. They were now right behind me and I could see their faces, twisted in anger. I was genuinely scared. This was like a cross between *Deliverance* and *Duel* (with women). It would actually have been quite a strong movie synopsis had I not actually been living it out for real. We burst out of the redwoods and into a town called Myers Flat. I saw a sign advertising a tree that you could drive through and, right in front of the sign, a huge wooden statue of Bigfoot waving at me. It was my very first sighting and he was taking the piss. I shot through town with the murder gang still on my tail. I sped up and rounded a corner, almost on two wheels.

I was slightly ahead now and, for a moment, they couldn't see me. I spotted a little track to my right and I acted instinctively. I pulled hard right on the wheel and skidded off the tarmac. I prayed that they hadn't seen me turn. I kept driving for about five minutes but there was nobody in the rear-view mirror. I turned off the track into a little grove and parked the car behind a big tree so that it couldn't be seen. I sat in silence for five minutes. I was sweating and my heart was beating fast. Nothing happened and I started to relax a little. I opened the car door and listened for the sound of murderous banshees. There was nothing, just an eerie silence. I got out and closed the door gently. I locked it with my key fob. It beeped to let me know that it, unlike me, was now safe. The beep reverberated like an explosion in the silence of the redwoods. I tensed up and waited but everything stayed silent. I didn't want to go back on the road for a while so I decided to go for a bit of a walk into the forest. Maybe I'd get lucky and find Bigfoot first go? I wandered off, away from my car, along what seemed to be a vague path. The trees surrounding me were even bigger than the ones on the Avenue. I felt tiny and very alone. I was utterly dwarfed by nature.

I kept walking, the only sound being the muffled *clump*, *clump* of my Reeboks on the spongy forest floor. As before, occasionally the sun burst through and lit up a little clearing, but predominantly it was dark and primeval.

My mind started to play tricks on me and I could easily see how people might believe that monsters lived here.

I started to hum to myself as the silence had become quite oppressive. I hummed 'A Forest' by the Cure: 'Suddenly I stop/ But I know it's too late/ I'm lost in a forest/ All alone . . .'

I kept on walking deeper and deeper into the magical forest. It was like being on the set of *The Hobbit*. Every tree seemed to be bigger, thicker, taller than the last . . .

Suddenly I stopped . . . I spotted the unmistakable outline of a bear about fifty yards ahead. Fortunately for me it was looking the other way, down into a leafy crevice. I froze to the spot and then started to lower myself to the floor in tiny little movements. This was totally crazy: I'd been chased by killer lady rednecks and now I was about to be eaten in a forest by a bear. The bear did not move and nor did I. I lay perfectly still on the soggy, mushy ground for what seemed like an hour but was probably no more than a couple of minutes. The bear was totally immobile; it seemed to be focused on some unseen prey. My broken foot started to ache and I crawled forwards a little until I was behind a bush. I waited there for another couple of minutes or so thinking about my options. I could get up and run away. Then I remembered the sign in the Okanagan: 'Under no circumstance should you run away from a bear unless you have somewhere to go . . .'

I had nowhere to go. Other signs I'd read in bear country suggested having a bell with you and ringing it if you saw a bear. I'm not sure if this is to scare the bear or to alert the search party to where your remains could be found. Whatever, I didn't have a bell on me now so I was stumped. The bear was still not moving. I crawled a little bit nearer . . . It was a weirdly shaped log. Actually, it was a scary bear-shaped log. Your mind plays extraordinary tricks on you out there.

The balance between human and nature is completely inverted among these natural giants. The place gives you a constant slightly freaked-out feeling, an age-old instinct telling you to be on the *qui vive*. It had been the same in the misty mountains of Japan, the steamy forests of the Congo and the dark, impenetrable waters of the Okanagan. When nature decides to turn on the creepy mood music it's incredibly effective.

I was by now exhausted from this adrenaline roller coaster. I retraced my footsteps and found the car. I got in and locked the door. I needed some normality. My phone had no network so I plugged it into the car and played a Kermode/Mayo podcast. Never had the Good Doctor's ranting (this one about some arsey new film by Gus Van Sant) been so reassuring. I drove back up the track and on to the Avenue of Giants. I turned left and headed back the way I'd come. Very soon I was back in Myra Flats and spotted the statue of Bigfoot. I wanted to park and get a good photo of it but as I was about to pull up outside a bar I spotted the three women. They were sitting outside drinking beer with three men who looked like they enjoyed a spot of butchery at the weekends. Somehow, in a country in a county full of hippies, it looked like I'd angered the Manson family. I drove by trying to look as inconspicuous as possible. Fortunately my Chevy blended in and couldn't have been that memorable as they didn't seem to recognize me. One of the women looked up and stared at me as I drove past but I just looked straight ahead and headed out of town. The moment I was through I hit the gas and didn't stop until I got to Garberville, where I ducked into a bar and had several glasses of chilled Sauvignon Blanc to soothe my frayed nerves.

In the space of about two hours I had gone through every American-backwoods cliché that I'd ever seen in a movie except bumping into the Ku Klux Klan and some incredibly racist fat police chief. I looked out of the window to check for burning crosses or a roaming cop car but there was nothing but a dread-locked hippy strumming a guitar under a tree. I needed some medicinal marijuana to calm me down – the only problem being that it always makes me paranoid and I didn't need that right now. I got up and left. Outside I had to step over two parody hippies complete with headbands, guitars and John Lennon glasses. They were seated on the pavement just staring vacantly at the traffic. I had a huge desire to tell them that Vietnam was over and that whatever they were running away from could all be sorted out with a haircut and a good bath. I realized that I'd become 'the Man': I was a 'suit' and a 'total square'. I walked on without saying anything but slightly depressed. I passed two hemp shops, got into my car and drove a couple of miles to where I was staying, the Benbow Inn, a mock-Tudor building that felt rather incongruous slap-bang in the middle of Hippy Country. In its heyday this place had served as a bolt-hole for Hollywood luminaries looking for some privacy and a spot of fishing. Guests had included Spencer Tracy, Clark Gable and, more recently, the King of Jordan and Cher (though sadly not at the same time).

My room was a joy, with a four-poster bed and a stone balcony overlooking an old bridge over the Eel River. Sometimes even monster-hunters need a bit of downtime.

I posted some video footage of me lost in the woods on Facebook. People asked whether this was for a TV programme. I told them that it was for a book called *Scary Monsters and Super Creeps*. Inevitably, a cyber-twat started accusing me of 'ripping off' David Bowie. He seemed to think that he was the only person who had spotted that the title of this book was lifted from a Bowie album. I told him that this was not exactly a secret and, as a huge Bowie fan myself, it was a nod to one of my heroes.

He wasn't having it: 'You're a relentless asshole riding on his coat-tails.'

I was genuinely unsure as to what his beef was. If it was with me personally, then why on earth was he following me on Facebook? If it was with the appropriation of the name, did he think I was trying to con people into buying my book by making them think it was actually a David Bowie album?

I hit the bar and ordered a Grey Goose up with a twist. All was good with the world. After a couple more beige birds I was ushered into a rather fussy dining room where I was constantly asked what I thought of the food by a waitress called Bambi.

The food was very good but, like in the UK in 1972, Bambi

started putting chairs on tables at nine p.m. Out of spite I hung around playing with my overly elaborate pudding until nine-thirty. (I'm a bit rock 'n' roll like that: no sleep till bedtime.) I eventually left the dining room as the lights were about to be turned off. As I walked through the hotel I started to look at it properly through drunken eyes. There were teddy bears everywhere. Back at the bar, a solitary gentleman propping up the corner and nursing a short turned out, on closer inspection, to be a seven-foot teddy bear. It's a universal truth that a building with more than two teddy bears on display is telling you that its owner was probably sexually abused and is now a predatory serial killer. I hurried to my room and locked it securely.

I left early the next morning. It didn't take me too long to make it to Eureka. This is a weird city, quite industrial in parts and with an area containing some quite extraordinary Victorian Gothic mansions. The main one, the Carson Mansion, is an unbelievable piece of fantasy architecture reputed to have provided the blueprint for some of Walt Disney's ideas for Disneyland. I was staying at the Carter House Inns, a hotel owned by Mark Carter, a local bon viveur and wine aficionado. One of the hotel buildings is another example of crazed Victoriana. Painted bright yellow and orange, it's an exact reproduction of a building that stood in San Francisco until it was destroyed in the Great Quake of 1906. I checked in and was shown to a rather magnificent cottage that turned out to be entirely at my disposal. I had an enormous living room and kitchen, a master bedroom, two bathrooms (because one is never enough) and a terrace. This was going to be hard to leave.

On the table was an envelope with my name on it. I opened it.

Mr Joly

Welcome to Carter House Inns. We hope you enjoy your stay here. Your companions, Corey and Kirsten, left a message saying that they would be arriving at midday.

Reception

I reread it wondering what on earth they were going on about. I had no 'companions' and wasn't expecting any. I wondered if this was hotel code for letting me know that a couple of complimentary hookers were being provided. Corey, however, sounded like a man. This was California so maybe they were just hedging their bets? I checked my watch; it was ten-forty a.m. Whoever my companions were, they were arriving in twenty minutes.

I opened my laptop and got online. I searched for the names Corey and Kirsten on my Facebook pages. The name Corey came up and I clicked. Now I remembered. Back in the early days of Facebook, when *Trigger Happy TV* was out in America, this fifteen-year-old kid called Corey had contacted me and we'd chatted occasionally about stuff like music and comedy. He'd been going through a tough time (his parents were divorcing) and I'd felt bad for him. He'd also given me a lot of cool music recommendations. I now also remembered that his pages had always been littered with photos of a girl called Kirsten. When I'd been in San Francisco a couple of years before Corey had contacted me and tried to meet up; I'd been filming, so we'd been unable to. He'd said he was at Humboldt State University, in a town called Arcata, just ten minutes from Eureka.

Before I left for California this time I'd put out a 'can anybody help me' message on Twitter and Facebook and it looked like Corey had answered the call. I checked his Facebook page. He was now married to Kirsten and living in Sacramento, the state capital – about seven hours' drive from Eureka. I hoped to God that they hadn't driven up from there. If they had, then they would be expecting to accompany me on some serious monster-hunting – and I normally prefer to do this kind of thing on my own. I'm an inherently selfish traveller and like to do things when and where I want to, without worrying about others.

Fifteen minutes later there was knock on my door and I opened it to find Corey and Kirsten staring at me. He was a tall, thin and slightly Goth-looking guy of about twenty-three and Kirsten was slightly shorter and pretty.

'Hey,' I said.

'Hey,' they said.

'You came,' I said.

'We came,' they said.

'Not from Sacramento?' I asked.

'Yeah, it took us seven hours,' they answered.

'Shit,' I said to myself quietly.

I let them in and we all sat down slightly awkwardly. Actually, *I* was awkward – they seemed to think that this was the most normal thing in the world. They *ooh*ed and *aah*ed about my hotel 'complex' and I nodded as though this was my life all the time. I longed to show them the photo I'd taken of the Economy Inn Motel in Ukiah but I thought I'd keep up the pretence of being 'Dom Joly' for a while. They told me that they were in town for two days. I nodded and they asked me what the plan was. Obviously the plan was to find Bigfoot, but I'd heard that nearby Arcata was the US's hippest town and who knew what this could turn up? So I asked them to show me around.

Corey had spent three years at the university and was the ideal guide. The campus was dotted all over the little town. The main square comprised weird little shops around a grassy park in which very stoned students were all playing Frisbee. I counted nine sets of dreadlocks and five didgeridoos in plain sight. Corey told me that he'd shared a room for a year with a guy who did nothing but smoke dope and play the didgeridoo. Personally, I would have thought these were grounds for justifiable homicide.

We popped into a 'head' shop that sold innumerable variations of bongs and . . . Frisbees. According to Corey, everyone just got stoned and then wandered off to play Frisbee golf in the woods. I didn't believe him so we headed off into the woods where, sure enough, we found a Frisbee-golf course and a large amount of stoned students aimlessly holding Frisbees.

This seemed a bit weird to me. Surely Frisbee golf isn't the obvious first thing that comes to mind when you're stoned? I remember my own light dabblings involving watching a lot of really rubbish TV and eating crap. Apparently whatever they smoked up here gave you Frisbee cravings. Corey told me that, apart from Frisbee golf, sport's not really that big a thing at Humboldt State. The university football team is called the Lumberjacks and Corey told me about a headline in the local paper that had simply read, 'THEY WON!'.

Our tour of Arcata complete, Corey and Kirsten looked at me expectantly. The plan was for me to drive (alone) to Willow Creek the following day and start my hunt there. If you look at a map of Bigfoot sightings in the Northern California area then Willow Creek is the geographical epicentre and also the home of the Bigfoot Museum. This was the idea for the following day but right now I needed something to do with Kirsten and Corey.

Then I remembered reading about a place called Tall Trees Grove about an hour north of Eureka. It's supposed to have some of the largest trees in the world and there have been two Bigfoot sightings nearby. I figured we could start there. I asked them if they knew where it was; Corey rang a friend who told us how to get there. The decision was taken and the hunt was on. We were off to Tall Trees Grove for my first Bigfoot hunt.

We drove through Orick, a 'town' that seemed to consist solely of four roadside stores selling extremely weird wooden statues. A couple of miles later we turned off the scenic coast road and started to drive up into the mountains. We drove for about twenty minutes and then the tarmac road became a dusty track. We kept climbing higher and higher.

'I hope you're not axe murderers?' I said semi-jokingly.

This was exactly what you were not supposed to do on an Internet first date: drive miles and miles from anywhere into deep woods. To divert myself I read a warning leaflet that we'd got from a park ranger we'd met at the bottom of the mountain. It was called 'What to do if you meet a mountain lion'.

1. Do not run!
2. Do not crouch or bend over
3. Remain calm
4. Yell loudly, wave arms and throw objects
5. If the animal attacks – fight aggressively

You had to wonder who wrote these things. There was nothing about what to do should we meet a Bigfoot.

We found the trailhead and parked the car. The trail descended very steeply into what looked like the Lost Valley. We walked down and down and down. It took us about half an hour to reach the bottom. When we did, it was like stepping back in time. Towering ferns bordered gargantuan trunks of monster trees that soared high into the sky like vast wooden spires. All the trees had massive burls, growths that resembled gargoyles, their twisted shapes metamorphosing into hideous creations. It was further proof, if needed, of how spooky surroundings could really feed a hungry imagination. We all instinctively started to talk in hushed voices as though in church. At the very centre of the ring of tallest trees, we stood in complete silence for a moment and listened to the earth's heartbeat . . .

I know this all sounds like I'd either had a huge spliff or become a hippy overnight, but I have never, ever been so profoundly affected by the sheer presence of nature. These are the tallest trees you can visit anywhere in the world. There are individual taller ones, but most are on weed farms and protected by armed and paranoid hippies. One interesting fact (despite my not really liking *Star Wars*) is that the moon scenes of Endor, when we meet the Ewoks in *Return of the Jedi*, were filmed here. George Lucas lived in Northern California and it's very obvious that the idea for Chewbacca was influenced by tales and descriptions of Bigfoot.

We spent about an hour just chilling in this magical place before realizing that it was getting dark. We didn't want to be stuck down here at night: it would definitely get very spooky. There was no sign of Bigfoot on the long, hard walk back to the car. Fortunately, we didn't meet a mountain lion either.

Back in Eureka, Corey and Kirsten headed off to find their hotel while I chilled in my cottage at Carter House Inns. I had an hour before I had to meet a guy called Richard, whom I'd contacted on the Internet, at the Lost Coast Brewery. Richard was the media manager for the Humboldt County Visitors Bureau and had promised that he could help me with accommodation and introductions to some Bigfoot enthusiasts who were known as 'squatchers'. It was through his influence that I'd got the beautiful cottage to stay in so I liked him already.

The Lost Coast Brewery was a big shed-like building about four blocks away from my hotel. I walked in and a good-looking, urbane guy of about my age stood up and greeted me. This was Richard and he'd clearly done some research on me, as he knew what I looked like from the Net. He looked a bit like a news reporter: square jaw and round glasses with a soft Southern lilt that betrayed his roots in Georgia. He was a very easy-going guy and we chowed down and got talking about Bigfoot. Richard said that a lot of Bigfoot 'scat' was found in the woods. A local Indian had confirmed that this was no human scat as it would have 'split a human apart'. Some stools had supposedly been found that measured up to two feet long. Local wags claimed that this accounted for a lot of the screams heard at night in the forests.

He also told me about Bigfoot 'nests'. These are very similar to those gorillas build in Africa: thick branches bent over and made into a type of bed. This really got my interest and Richard showed me some photographs. They did indeed show quite intricate constructions with thick branches having been weaved together into a rather cosy retreat. Were Bigfoots really sitting and constructing such things? It was another thing to look out for.

We poured over a very detailed map of the Bluff Creek area where the Patterson film had been shot. The place looked very remote – two hours' drive from Willow Creek on tarmac road, an hour of off-road driving and then a two-hour hike. Richard seemed keen to come with me and, as he knew the area and could get me permissions, I was all for that.

Corey and Kirsten turned up and I introduced them to Richard, who couldn't get his head round the fact that they'd come all the way from Sacramento despite never having met me before. I think it somewhat increased my kudos as a world-famous monster-hunter. We had a couple of drinks before I called it a night and headed back to the hotel.

The next morning, Richard insisted that Corey, Kirsten and I went to the Samoa Cookhouse for breakfast. This was a place that used to feed the hungry loggers three times a day and then, as now, they didn't really go in for calorie counting. The food was homicidally filling, all doughy biscuits and beans and bacon and thick black coffee. We met the owner, Jeff Brustman, who told me that the local Indian tribes used to call the Sasquatch 'Omah'. They were convinced that the creatures were a lost

Indian tribe. They were also convinced, laughed Jeff, that hippies were living proof that Bigfoot had mated with humans. I told him that hippies were too skinny to be descended from any missing link – though they did share a pungent odour with the Sasquatch.

He told me about the very first Bigfoot sighting, before he was even known as Bigfoot. It was reported in a letter to a columnist on the local paper. I found it later online.

Humboldt Times, 21 September 1958

I am writing regarding a queer situation my husband has encountered while at work. I have read your column for a long time and have noticed that you often dig into things of various natures. This happened when my husband recently took a land-clearing job up on Bluff Creek, near Weitchpec.

The rumor started among the men at once of the existence of a 'wild man'. We regarded it as a joke and even added fuel to the story by passing on bits of information. It was only yesterday that my husband became convinced that the existence of such a person (?) is a fact.

On their way to the job, the men found tracks going down to the road. The tracks measured 14 to 16 inches in length. The toes were very, very short, but there were five to each foot. The ground was soft and the prints were very clear. In soft places the prints were deep, suggesting a great weight. The tracks were quite wide as well as long and things such as fruit have been missed by the men camping on the job. There are at least 15 men that will swear this is true, among them, my husband. Have you ever heard of this wild man?

The newspaper columnist replied:

> Well, honestly, no! I wonder if anyone else knows about this. Please help. Maybe we have a relative of the abominable snowman of the Himalayas, our own Wandering Willie of Weitchpec.

Weitchpec was on our way to Bluff Creek and it was cool to hear about such an early sighting. I wasn't quite sure why they'd called it 'Willie' but assumed that it was just good alliteration. Whatever, the report was a classic Bigfoot encounter. I couldn't wait to get over the hills and into Bigfoot territory proper.

But first I went for a wander round the 'old town' with Corey and Kirsten. They had made such an effort to join my curious adventure and I wanted to spend a little more time with them.

As we walked around the four blocks of nice old buildings and reasonable shops that constitute 'Old' Eureka, I hoped that they weren't too disappointed; but they were a quiet couple and didn't say too much.

We popped into a great bookstore and started browsing. I checked out some books from the seventies on Bigfoot. They were all pretty much the same. Like the ones on Ogopogo, they tended to be self-published, rather dry accounts of sightings. It was all part of this desperate need to be taken seriously, but it took all the fun out of it. In the far corner I spotted Corey and Kirsten looking at a book excitedly. I went over. They were the most animated I'd seen them yet.

'What's the book?' I asked.

'Only the greatest book ever written,' replied Corey.

I looked at the cover and a sudden, nauseous feeling swept across me. The book was called *The Fountainhead*.

Wasn't this that book so beloved by extreme right-wing Aryan Brotherhood types? I seemed to remember Louis Theroux doing something about it. I looked at Corey and Kirsten again.

She was of Scandinavian origins while Corey had piercing blue eyes and slightly Preacher-esque sideburns. Oh ... My ... God ... Were these two Nazis? Had I unwittingly been hanging out with a pair of white supremacists? On the way to Tall Trees Grove I'd found a Christian religious book in the back of their car but I hadn't mentioned it. Thinking about it, they didn't swear and seemed to eat only fish – but surely if they were white supremacists they would eat only raw meat? Corey had been to university in Humboldt State, hardly the epicentre of Nazi power. Maybe the hippy with the didgeridoo had sent him crazy? I didn't want to ask them straight out but how could I broach this kind of thing?

'Yo, what about them Negroes?'

We left the bookstore and continued our walk but I found myself actually distancing myself from them. A Chinese man walked past us and I subtly watched to see if they showed any sign of disapproval. They didn't and we walked on.

'There's a great bagel place here?' said Corey.

'The best in the USA,' said Kirsten enthusiastically.

I spotted my chance.

'That's weird – why here? After all, bagels are a *Jewish* thing ...'

I really over-emphasized the '*Jewish* thing' but they didn't seem to flicker. We went into the bagel place. It was called Los Bagels. In the window there was a sign in Spanish saying that the staff spoke English. The staff were all Latinos. I tried again.

'Jesus Christ, this place is totally run by Mexicans. Don't any Americans work?'

I looked across at them for a reaction but they were looking at me a bit weirdly. Maybe they thought I was one of them now? We walked out, munching on our Jewish-Mexican bagels, and headed back to my hotel. I was totally freaked out now. I wanted to dump the Nazis. I told them that I had to pack and head off for Willow Creek. This was something I needed to do alone, I said. They took a couple of photos of us all together and then said goodbye. They were going to drive all the way back to Sacramento . . . Probably for a Klan meeting.

I waved from my porch as they drove off. I very nearly gave a Hitler salute to see if they responded but decided against it. The moment their car disappeared round the corner, I rushed inside and googled the book.

The Fountainhead is a totally legitimate 'classic' about an architect who fights against the system. There's nothing right wing or dodgy about it at all. The book I was thinking about was *The Turner Diaries*. I've absolutely no idea why I confused the two. Corey and Kirsten were not Nazis and I was a complete idiot who appeared to be in the early stages of mental illness.

I packed up and checked out of the hotel. I got into my car and drove the hour inland to my final goal: Willow Creek, considered to be Ground Zero for squatchers. There was the Bigfoot Museum to go to and Richard had kindly set up a meeting with Al Hodgson, a local Bigfoot expert who had made plaster casts of Bigfoot feet. He was the guy who told Patterson that Bigfoot had been spotted in the area and prompted him to set off on his expedition.

The town's pretty much a one-street affair, so as I drove in I quickly spotted the museum: there's an enormous wooden statue of Bigfoot outside that must be thirty feet tall. I parked up and was let in by a woman called Peggy McWilliams, who let me look round. She told me that the museum was normally closed from October to May but that she opened up for visitors if they contacted her. She was very chatty and told me that there had just been a Bigfoot sighting over the border in Oregon. A woman saw a Bigfoot cross the road right in front of her car. I was thrilled and pumped her for more information – had anyone taken a photo? She didn't know much more about it.

I asked her whether there had been a dip in sightings.

She made the point that the only dip had been in footprints, because more and more roads were now tarmac and early sightings were all on fresh-cut dirt roads that had been built into new areas for logging.

She also told me that Al Hodgson was a bit doddery and had just lost his wife so he might be a bit late. I told her not to worry and started looking around the museum. The exhibits were mostly casts of big feet, which was probably to be expected. There was a tape on loop playing an old black-and-white TV show about Bigfoot. It was quite interesting and showed some new footage that I hadn't seen of a hairy figure running fast over a prairie-type landscape.

Having finished watching the tape I read some of the newspaper clippings that were pasted on the walls, one of which was the article that coined the term 'Bigfoot'.

Al Hodgson eventually turned up after Peggy phoned him. He was a nice guy but a bit deaf and, yes, a touch doddery. I asked some pretty stupid questions and he seemed to be on autopilot. He told me that at the time of the Patterson film there had just been a huge flood in which Bluff Creek had been stripped bare. He said that, should I try to go there now, I'd find it was very different and totally overgrown. It would be very difficult to find the actual spot where the Patterson film was taken. He understood why I wanted to go to the actual site but, if I wanted to see a Bigfoot, I had as much chance anywhere in the surrounding area. He told me about a recent sighting only four miles from where we stood. A local lady driving a produce vehicle had spotted a Bigfoot on the road at four in the morning. He knew this woman and said she had no reason to lie about it. I asked him if this was the same incident that Peggy had just told me about. He replied that no, this was a different one and happened very near to where we stood. I was really excited. I was definitely in with a chance of at least spotting Bigfoot. This was the stuff that little boys' dreams are made of.

Al started asking me about where I was from. I got the distinct feeling that he was a bit bored of talking Bigfoot. He told me that his family was originally from Leeds. I nodded as though Leeds was my favourite place in the world. In the end the conversation went a bit dry and I thanked Al for meeting me and he pottered off to talk to Peggy.

I had another look round the exhibits before wandering over to where Peggy and Al were shooting the shit. Al showed me a plaster cast of a Bigfoot print that he had taken himself at Notice Creek in 1955. I fell in love with it instantly. This had to be the best travel souvenir I'd ever seen and had to have one. I asked him if it was for sale and he said that he had one I could buy. For twenty dollars, this was the best thing I'd ever bought on my travels. Al's lift turned up and we said goodbye but I stayed on chatting to Peggy, who was turning out to be a lot more interesting than Al. She said that Hoopa, the nearby Indian reservation, had the most Bigfoot sightings and that I should go and talk to people there – although, she warned, they were not that keen on 'snooping strangers'. A local man came in and said hello to Peggy. On a whim I asked him if he had ever seen a Bigfoot.

He looked at me and said, 'Nope – but then again, I've never seen a mountain lion and they exist. There's something out there; I know too many people who've seen stuff.'

I was getting hungry and left the museum and had a look round town for somewhere to eat. I walked past the Bigfoot Motel, which looked suitably awful. It had a large cage in the car park supposedly there to capture a Bigfoot should one wander into town. After lunch in a little Mexican place I went into a coffee shop to get an espresso. On the television hung on the wall behind the counter was a show about the 'Skunk Ape', another creature that's supposed to roam Florida. I presumed the show was on a loop and that this was part of the local monster industry. It wasn't, though: it just happened to be on the telly, which was a weird coincidence. I'd read all about the Skunk Ape when I was thinking about where to go on my trips.

Florida certainly has a lot of 'wildlands'. I wondered whether an ageing Bigfoot, bored of living among the weed farmers of California, had decided to retire to Florida?

I had very little left to do for the rest of the day. Willow Creek is a town that can be 'done' in well under an hour. Richard had organized for me to stay in one of a series of rather posh cabins that were normally for people coming up to fish in the nearby river. He was joining me the following day so that we could head off on our trip to Bluff Creek.

I checked in and sat outside my cabin reading until it got dark and then went to bed to watch yet another Republican Presidential Hopeful debate. When it had finished I despaired for America.

The next morning, Richard turned up in a decidedly dodgy-looking car. It was quickly agreed that we should take my rental on our expedition as his had seen better days.

We first went to my Skunk Ape café, where we had some muffins and coffee. We looked at maps again and Richard started talking quite loudly about Bigfoot, causing several local heads to swivel round to look at us suspiciously. Richard certainly seemed to know his stuff. It turned out that his father-in-law had a cabin near the mouth of Bluff Creek. I had lucked out and seemed to be with something of an expert. Before we set off, I popped into the local mini-mart and bought some beef jerky and water. There was a huge sign outside saying that they sold buffalo meat. I took a picture of the sign. When I got to the checkout the woman working there was looking at me distrustfully.

'They say you took a photo of the store . . . Why?' I think she suspected me of some Federal Government snooping.

I over-Brit-accented and told her about how weird it was to see buffalo for sale. She immediately warmed up and started to chat.

'Do you guys not eat buffalo, then?'

I told her that, no, we didn't and that this was clearly our loss. I asked her my default question: 'Have you ever seen Bigfoot?'

'No, sir, I've never seen him, but I know a lot of good folk who have round here.'

This appeared to be the default answer to the default question.

I joined Richard in the car and we set off out of town on the so-called 'Bigfoot Highway'. We hadn't been driving for long when Richard asked me to pull over at a forestry station. He wanted to find out which roads were open and which were closed, as there was still snow in the mountains. Forest Ranger Jim was behind the desk and was busy issuing permits to a group of Mong (a displaced Burmese border tribe, not a bad Ricky Gervais joke) who were off mushroom picking. The Mong were taking ages and quibbling about the fee.

Forest Ranger Jim eventually finished with the Mong and we had a chat. He told us that we were better off asking at the forestry station in Orleans as it was much closer to our destination.

I asked him about Bigfoot and he went very weird with us.

He announced that he didn't speak to the media since the National Geographic Channel had come to talk to him.

'They reduced my hour-long interview to just twenty seconds, then they got my name wrong, and then the bastards ignored all my referrals to serious people who have really seen Bigfoot. Instead they talked to some woman who claimed she fathered a Bigfoot in Arizona. So I'm sorry, but I don't talk to media no more . . .'

He then proceeded to talk non-stop for about half an hour about various sightings. He told me that when the original logging tracks were first built into the wilderness, a logger friend of his complained that something was messing about with his machines. They were being vandalized, with something hurling big heavy rocks at them. He also found several sets of footprints.

Forest Ranger Jim was on a roll.

He told us about how many creatures previously unknown to science there were discovered every year under the sea. He mentioned the recent discovery of a type of deer that scientists had thought extinct.

It was safe to say that Forest Ranger Jim was a believer but we couldn't stop him talking. It felt like the whole world was being sucked into some time-space vortex from which we would eventually have to extract ourselves if we were to go anywhere that day. Despite this I was quite stoked to find a forest ranger who believed in Bigfoot. These guys were officials who had spent all their lives in this environment. It seemed to me that he was a pretty credible witness.

We drove on through Hoopa, the Indian reservation. Richard's father-in-law had been the dentist here in 1969, after he'd left the Marine Corps, and so he knew quite a lot of the people. Richard had rung the tribal museum to ask whether we could come and talk about Bigfoot, but they'd hung up on him. They didn't like people cheapening the Omah story and without their cooperation it was very difficult to gain access to any valid information on the reservation. We drove on through. There was trash everywhere and shanty-type trailers with old cars and junk lying about. To be honest, it was a bit of a shit-hole.

Once out of the reservation we soon came to the town of Weitchpec. This was the site of the very first reported sighting of Wandering Willie of Weitchpec. We stopped at the local store, which had more than a touch of *Deliverance* about it. We bought turkey jerky, which was a first for me. Richard chatted to the old guy behind the counter, who looked like Uncle Jesse from *The Dukes of Hazzard*. He was the descendant of a Norwegian who'd married a squaw and he very much gave out the impression that he was in charge. I asked him whether he knew anything about Wandering Willie. He nodded slowly as though he knew everything about it. I waited for him to expand but nothing came and it was fairly clear that nothing would.

We drove on again, the road running above the raging river and through some staggeringly beautiful scenery. As I looked up into the thick woods bordering the roads it was easy to see how something could stay undiscovered there if it so wished. We got to a bridge that spanned Bluff Creek where the creek ran into the main river. We parked the car and clambered up the sides of the hill to get a better view. As we climbed, I noticed a weird, unpleasant smell. Was it Bigfoot or was I being paranoid? We climbed higher and I had to push my way through some thick bushes. The smell was really bad now and the hairs on the back of my neck were standing up. I bustled through another thick bush and the ground flattened out into a little plateau on which stood a loo. It was weird – we were about fifteen minutes from the road, in the middle of nowhere, and suddenly we'd stumbled on a loo. It stank to high heaven and I opened the door while holding my shirt over my nose. It was a mess. It looked like somebody had exploded in there. What on earth was this thing doing here in the middle of nowhere? Did bears shit in the woods? I was definitely on the lookout for Bigfoot scat but hadn't expected this. Richard was totally confused. He had no idea what this was doing where it was. It was oddly freaky and we climbed back down to the car quite speedily. I looked up the creek for a while and imagined spotting a creature down on the shoreline fishing for salmon. It would look up startled and then move off in that curious gait, back into the thick undergrowth. This was just what a fisherman had seen on this river very near Willow Creek. Bigfoot was not showing himself for me, however. I was rather pleased. Nobody would believe me if I spotted one anyway, but in Bluff Creek of all places it would be ludicrous.

We got to Orleans, once a serious conurbation with a

population of 6,000 inhabitants but now a bit of a ghost town with a population of less than 600.

We found the forestry office and popped in. An elderly woman was sitting in the back and seemed very surprised to see someone. We asked her a question but she couldn't hear too well, so she got up and started walking towards us so slowly that I estimated it took her about seven minutes to traverse the twelve feet or so between us. She was also wearing glasses so thick that you couldn't see the eyes behind them. When she eventually reached us we asked her about roads and whether they were open. We wanted to try the Go Road. Originally built to join Orleans with the next valley, this was the closest proper road to where we needed to go. Local Indians had complained that it crossed over sacred ground and building work had stopped. Now the Go Road just went to a dead end miles up in the hills. It was therefore known by local wags as the No-Go Road. The Forest Ranger Lady knew nothing about the road but offered us some posters and Smokey Bear goody bags. Out of politeness we said yes and to our horror she announced that she would have to go find them. She started to move off on what looked like the beginning of an extraordinarily long trip. Richard and I glanced at each other in despair.

As we waited, an unkempt man called Bud turned up and seemed to know all about which roads were closed and which were not. He said that the Go Road had snow and was not really passable. I asked him the default question.

'Have you ever seen a Bigfoot?'

'I have not personally, but I know a lot of people who have . . .' This was getting to be very repetitive.

He told us about having to rescue 'some idiots' from very near the Patterson Gimlin site. They had hiked down there having heard a story of a Bigfoot massacre. Forest rangers had supposedly killed ten of the creatures and were covering the whole incident up. The hikers had got completely lost and had no food with them. Bud told us that they were lucky to have been found.

'It's a big place out there . . .'

I asked him, just for clarity, to assure me that forest rangers had *not* carried out a hushed-up massacre of Bigfoots and he confirmed that, no, this had not happened. I asked him what had started the story.

'Who knows? Some wacko writes something on the Web and then it's fact. Those sorts of things get in the way of real sightings.'

I later looked up this theory and could find only a confused story claiming that Patterson and Gimlin, on an earlier trip, had stumbled on a clan of Bigfoots and had shot dead several of them. They then panicked at their similarity to humans and buried the bodies. Supposedly, when they returned and shot their famous film, 'Patty', the Bigfoot featured, had been in the process of digging up the bodies.

The world of cryptozoologists is indeed a weird one.

We thanked Bud and got back into our car. I was a bit depressed about not being able to go up the Go Road. This meant that we could not get near enough to the Patterson Gimlin site to hike in. Richard looked at me like I was crazy.

'Sure we can go up there. He said what he had to say, I said what I had to say, but the body language was all about understanding that we were going up there anyhow.'

I hadn't picked up on any of this at all; I just heard that the roads were closed and that was that. But Richard clearly knew the area and I trusted him. We filled up with gas at a petrol station run by Indians. There was a sign on the door with a drawing of a nasty-looking gun:

If you are found here tonight, you will be found here dead tomorrow

The Indians seemed pleasant enough but you certainly wouldn't mess with them. With a full tank we headed uphill on the Go Road. It was a rather magnificent thing and we cruised up it in bright sunshine in high spirits. We spotted mile markers, which were useful because we needed to turn off at the seventeenth mile; there we would start heading down to the end of Cedar Creek Road and walk from there. I couldn't help feeling that we were a little underprepared but Richard didn't seem worried and he knew the area so I rolled with it.

I adore driving, especially in snow or sand – the fun stuff. We saw nobody on our way up, although there were supposed to be the paranoid weed farmers hidden away all over the place and they don't like strangers. On we drove until, at the ten-mile marker, we started hitting some patches of snow. It was mainly lying on the side of the road and not too bad so we cracked on. Any part of the road on the south side was exposed to the sun and had no snow but we slowly came across more and more stretches of road that were on the north side and in shade with a lot more snow on them.

There were a couple of tracks through the snow, and my rental was an all-wheel drive, so we carried on. I motored through a particularly deep bit, just keeping the car under control and on the road and preventing us from falling off the drop on the right. I got a massive adrenaline rush and Richard seemed impressed with my driving. The short snowless stretches gave us confidence to face the next lot. I started to drive and film at the same time and this made Richard a little more nervous. He hinted that, should I need a cameraman, he could be of assistance. On we ploughed as the road got steeper and darker and snowier. As we passed the fifteen-mile mark we came round a corner and the road got very steep and the snow extremely deep. I gunned the motor and flipped into low gear. We made steady progress but it was tough going. About half a mile further up the slope I veered out of the tracks and into deeper snow. The SUV stalled and we were stuck.

We were not overly concerned. We both got out to film the situation and made jokes about what idiots we were. It was noticeably colder than down in Orleans, even though it was only around one in the afternoon. Richard was all for calling Bud and getting him to come up and help us out but I was rather embarrassed that we had not heeded his advice. My manly pride kicked in and I thought that we should try to do this ourselves. I had a look at the car. We were not that stuck and I thought that, if we dug the snow out from under the car, we should be able to move back into the tracks and reverse back down to a better spot. Richard didn't seem so convinced. I was slowly coming to realize that he was about as practical as I was: i.e., not at all. We were two idiot city boys stuck in the middle of nowhere.

We set about digging the car out and soon had all four wheels fairly clear of snow so I got back in and started the engine. Richard was at the front pushing and, after a while, a wheel gripped the snow and we moved back on to the tracks. I was elated and whooped with excitement. Richard shouted at me not to stop and to keep reversing downhill until I got to an easier spot. Over-adrenalized, I shot off way too fast. For a while I managed to keep the SUV on the road but suddenly I skidded very badly and the car screeched into a ditch on the side of the road and smashed against the bank. We were now well and truly stuck. Richard came down looking concerned and I announced ruefully that we were not getting out of this one. It was clear from his face that he already knew this. I said that maybe it was time we called Bud. He picked up his mobile and peered at it for a while before putting it back down.

'You not going to call him?' I asked.

'We haven't got any reception,' he answered. The first shiver of uncertainty shot through my body. I'd seen this before in Ray

184

Mears's TV shows – the gentle progression from adventure to big trouble. Nobody knew that we were up here, unless Richard's 'body language' theory was right (which I was starting to doubt). We had no way of contacting anybody and we had only four hours of daylight left. We had to get the car out. I looked around and spotted a fallen tree. I told Richard that we had to get some of the thick bark on the trunk and then put it under the tyres to create traction. He looked rather impressed by this. I waded into the deep snow and ripped some bark off in long strips. We put them under the car and I tried to rock back and forth using the engine but the car was stuck fast.

We struggled for a while but it was useless.

We needed to make a decision as to what to do. We were stuck in the middle of nowhere, very high up a mountain, and it would get extremely cold at night. Richard thought that we should start walking down the road and he would soon get cell reception. I couldn't help remembering Ray Mears's golden rule of survival: always stay by the vehicle . . .

That, however, was surely when you were lost in the middle of nowhere? At least we knew that there was a town seventeen miles away down the road we'd come up. Sure, there were bears, mountain lions, paranoid and armed weed farmers and possibly a Bigfoot, but there was a town at the end. We got our coats out of the SUV. We put our three bottles of water and a pack of turkey jerky in a bag and headed off. Confidence at this stage was fairly high. We would simply walk downhill into the sun where we would get cell-phone coverage.

For the first mile or so we kept stopping to hunt for the elusive single bar, but there was nothing. I told Richard that we needed to be near Orleans before we got any signal. He admitted he hadn't had any there either. I started to realize that we were not going to get cell coverage. We needed to find someone to help us or it was going to be a very long trek.

I thought humans averaged about four miles an hour

walking speed so I estimated that it would take us about four hours until we hit Orleans. It would be dark in three. It was doable but we had to be careful. Richard said that weed farmers tended to 'SSS': shoot, shovel and shut up.

Many of the local Indians were also a law unto themselves and not really who you wanted to bump into. I'd heard a story about Jeeps Colgrove, a physically imposing Indian woman who used to wander about with a razor stuck in her hair. She'd committed several murders and used to pick people up off the side of the road and then ask them, 'Do you know who I am?' She was from the Hoopa reservation, which was not a huge distance away.

We really didn't fancy any of this. I'd stupidly left my passport in the car and was worrying about that as well. It was also getting darker quicker than we anticipated. I had a little panic. Had we really fucked up here? Were we going to become the poster boys for idiots from the city? I was wearing a T-shirt and a Prada anorak – what a twat. Then I remembered another Ray Mears tip: survival was all about keeping a positive frame of mind.

We started telling stories. Richard and I were actually quite similar: he used to work in Congress and for CNN whereas I used to work in Parliament and for ITN. We were both passionately interested in American politics and we discussed the upcoming presidential campaign. We both thought that Obama would scrape back in, but only because of the lack of serious opposition.

I was quite pleased with my pace, especially considering the old foot injury I have.

We reached the twelve-mile mark only to find a long uphill slope that we didn't remember driving over. The slope sapped our strength and we both realized how far we still had to go.

Had this been a script, this would have been the perfect time for Bigfoot to find us after we'd fallen unconscious by the roadside. I would awake in a Bigfoot nest to find the beast gently breastfeeding me.

We got to the ten-mile marker at four-thirty. We had one more hour of light, if we were lucky. It was getting very cold and I longed to see a car: even if we got *Deliverance*-d maybe they'd let us go afterwards?

Richard kept saying, 'You've been in worse scrapes, right?'

And I kept thinking, *Yes, but with people who knew what to do.*

I tried to imagine the headlines: 'Idiot comedian dies in Californian hills looking for Bigfoot. But is it a hoax?'

We reached the eight-mile marker and my feet were really starting to hurt. It was almost dark and getting rather creepy. We spotted some tracks going straight up a steep bank of red clay. We couldn't work out what had made them and, for a moment, we forgot our plight and got quite excited. Richard tried to clamber up the hill beside them and they were a big size. There seemed to be smaller tracks of something like a deer followed by far bigger tracks, bigger than a human foot would make. What puzzled us, however, was the steepness of the slope. It was almost vertical. Richard was having difficulty getting any traction but whatever had made these prints had gone straight up and over. Richard re-joined me on the road and we started trying to figure out what might have made them. It was not a bear, as there were no claw marks; these tracks had toes and did look pretty human-like. As we stared I heard a voice – and then, a miracle. I spotted someone coming out of the woods further down the road. He was wearing a blue T-shirt and was carrying a basket. Was he a crazed weed grower? He didn't appear to be and I couldn't see a gun. To my shame we forgot all about the tracks and approached our potential saviour like desperate castaways to a friendly boat. He gave us a big smile as though he'd been expecting us. His name was Peter and he was picking mushrooms to eat. He had a car hidden out of the way down a side track because, 'There are dangerous folk around here.'

I asked him what he meant and he listed a series of people whom we really would not have been thrilled to encounter: local rednecks, homicidal Indians, bears, mountain lions, armed weed farmers . . . It appeared that we had been picked up by the only safe man in Humboldt County.

He seemed more than happy to give us a lift and we walked towards the car. I had never been so pleased to see anyone ever in my life. Peter seemed like a really cool guy. His parents ran a 'dude ranch', a place that harked back to the tradition of 'soft' East Coasters coming west for a vacation where they could redis-cover their manliness by taking part in cattle drives, shooting guns, riding horses, etc. He was polite enough to leave the matter unsaid, but it seemed clear that he felt that Richard and I were prime candidates for this experience. Surprisingly, Peter had not seen Bigfoot himself but he knew lots of people who had . . . I told him about the tracks we'd seen and he said that they were probably deer or bears. By this stage I was too tired to care.

Peter clearly realized that we probably shouldn't be left alone again and he insisted on driving us the twenty miles to Richard's father-in-law's cabin. I'd expected this to be some small two-room hut. How wrong I was. Seemingly in the middle of nowhere, a set of gates swung open and led us up a drive and past two fish ponds to a giant log cabin complete with swim-ming pool. It was idyllic.

Richard's father-in-law was a very charismatic Irish ex-Marine. He was most definitely a man's man and I felt that, on the inside, he had to be howling with laughter at his effete son in law and his Brit girlfriend.

He was polite enough to keep his thoughts to himself and ushered us inside where a roaring fire was burning and several bottles of rather good red wine awaited us. Never had I been so cosy or so happy. We started to tell him about our experience and make light of it but I realized that we had made a really stupid mistake; it could have all gone very wrong.

We headed out for dinner with his neighbours. I sat in the back of his pickup truck on a veritable arsenal of guns and loose bullets and hoped that nothing would go off.

The neighbours were extraordinary people – uber-smart Berkeley types who had got away from it all. We were fed ginormous steaks and given more wine. Out of adversity come the best things.

At about ten I looked over the table and saw that Richard was nearly asleep. Our adrenaline rush was fading and we were cream-crackered. My foot was hurting really badly. We headed back to the cabin and, after a final tumbler of single malt, I hit the sack and slept the undeserved sleep of kings.

The next morning we woke early and headed back up the Go Road to retrieve our car. We had two big pickup trucks equipped with powerful winches and strong, tough men. As we reached the halfway mark a pickup truck roared down past us going towards Orleans at a rate of knots. Everyone joked that the Indians had found the car and pillaged it.

We passed the point where St Peter picked us up and I asked the guys to stop so we could look at the tracks – but it had rained hard overnight and the slope was washed clean. We kept on climbing. It was a very long way up to the car and even Richard's father-in-law was quite impressed by the distance we'd covered. Eventually we got to the car. It was safe; nobody had broken into it. Everyone had a good laugh at my bark-track attempts and Richard and I were gently moved aside as the real men winched the vehicle up and pulled it out. I then drove it gingerly backwards for a mile down the hill until I found a turning spot. We were free.

It felt really good to be under our own steam again and not reliant on others. Also, I had learnt a valuable lesson: I am a moron.

We headed back to the cabin for some beers in the sunshine.

Then we went on a tour of the property. Richard's father-in-law was a very devout Catholic and he'd built a beautiful chapel on the edge of a cliff. Richard had met his wife at a retreat here. I realized how different Americans are to us. Back in the UK, if someone's Christian it kind of defines him, whereas here in the USA it's a sort of given.

'Have you seen Bigfoot?' I asked Richard's father-in-law, anticipating the stock answer.

'No. I don't believe in that stuff. The Indians will tell you any old story you want to hear.'

At last, a different perspective.

We said our goodbyes and headed back to Willow Creek. I had been going to drive to Garberville to talk to the head of the Cannabis College but she hadn't emailed me back so I figured that I'd stay on in Willow Creek for another night. When we got there, however, my room was empty. All my stuff had gone and I panicked, thinking it had been stolen. It turned out that the owners had rented the room to some fishermen and moved my stuff out. They'd booked me into the Bigfoot Motel. Suspecting that even Bigfoot wouldn't stay there, I passed and decided to drive through the night to San Francisco.

Richard and I went to the Mexican place for a last meal. I asked Gonzales, the owner, if he had seen Bigfoot.

'No, I have not personally, senor, but I know many, many people who have . . .'

On the way out of town Richard suggested that I pop into Bigfoot Books, a small bookstore that was the centre of the new generation of Bigfoot hunters. I spoke to the owner, Steve Streufert, who was initially a little suspicious of me but eventually warmed up. He showed me some photographs of a trip he'd made to the Patterson Gimlin site in Bluff Creek. It was unrecognizable, but he was convinced that they'd managed to pin it down. There were various arrows pointing to trees and other identifiable things from the original film. I tried to take a photograph of the photograph on his computer but he got a bit shirty about it all. It reminded me of people hiding their JFK assassination 'evidence' from others. Surely we all just want an answer?

I asked him the question.

'No, but I know a lot of folk who have . . .'

I picked up a copy of the *Bigfoot Times* and said goodbye.

Outside in the car park I bade farewell to Richard. We'd shared quite the adventure and there's nothing that bonds people together quicker.

On the drive down to San Francisco I had time to think about matters Bigfoot. Before I'd actually gone to the area, my main problem had been that it was simply impossible for a largish tribe of Bigfoot to be roaming an area of the United States without them having been scientifically discovered. Now, having been right into the heart of this vast region of almost impenetrable and empty forest, I was more convinced. The sheer volume of sightings by people who lived in the area and were not likely to mistake a tree stump for a bear, along with the disinterest in publicity a lot of them shared, made me think that there was something out there. As for the Patterson/Gimlin film, I remained uncertain. I really wanted to believe it, and that was maybe the problem: it's almost too good. A man goes off in search of Bigfoot with a sixteen-mil camera and hits the jackpot? It would be like a comedian sitting in his hotel room and spotting a monster in the lake through the window . . .

Everything is possible.

Six hours later I spotted the flickering lights of the Golden Gate Bridge through my windscreen. I had a little bit of time to kill before heading off to the airport so I went for some breakfast at the farmers' market in the ferry-terminal building. A lot of tourists had confused it with the nearby Occupy San Francisco shantytown. I watched as one woman peered into some grebo's tent and was spat at as she tried to take photos. Meanwhile a weathered-looking Indian woman was screaming at a police-man who had taken a piece of paper off her. She had been brandishing it in his face while refusing to vacate a seat reserved for 'Seniors for Peace'.

'This is my land! I was here thousands of years before the blue eyes came . . . !'

Everyone gathered round to watch the fight. Meanwhile some Maoists were having a huge argument with some anar-chists. It turned out they were both supposed to have a stall in the same place and nobody was giving an inch. It was a truly depressing place. The only unifying thing about the whole encampment was the noxious odour of the great unwashed that floated off them all.

In a way they kind of reminded me of monster-hunters. Everyone obsessed with their particular theory or exclusive photo and not wanting to share it or listen to anyone else. It was Crazyville.

I headed off for a pulled-pork sandwich. Rather aptly, it was called the 'Pigfoot'.

Yeti

'There is precious little in civilization to appeal to the Yeti'

Edmund Hillary

The call for my flight came over the Virgin Lounge Tannoy. 'Would all passengers bound for New Delhi please proceed to Gate 22.'

I was off: first to New Delhi and then on to Kathmandu, where I'd catch another little plane high up into the Himalayas and then trek up into thin air looking for the Yeti, the Abominable Snowman. The Himalayas are so vast that I'd been slightly at a loss as to where to go for this particular quest. There's a monastery in Khumjung, within sight of Everest, that claims to have the actual skull of a Yeti. It would be a hard slog to get there and I eventually figured that this should be my destination; I would learn what else I could along the way.

My favourite Tintin book has always been *Tintin in Tibet*. Quite why it's called *Tintin in Tibet* has never been clear, though, as Tintin clearly landed in Kathmandu. I presume *Tintin in Nepal* just didn't sound as good. Maybe Hergé couldn't resist the alliteration? Whatever, Tintin had headed off to Nepal to try to find his Chinese friend Chang, who had been in a plane crash. The Yeti made a guest appearance in the book. I was rather hoping that he might make a similar appearance in mine.

Along with the Loch Ness Monster and Bigfoot, the Yeti is probably the most famous monster in the world. Pre-Buddhism a lot of Himalayan peoples reportedly worshipped a 'wild man', an apelike figure said to carry a stone for hunting. From the moment Westerners began to attempt to climb the peaks of the Himalayas, starting in the early twentieth century, reports came both of sightings of a bipedal, apelike figure and discoveries of footprints. Probably the most famous of these were the photographs Eric Shipton took of huge footprints. Shipton was a respected mountaineer who was attempting to climb Everest. He took them at an altitude of about 19,500 feet and the footprints looked human except for the size and the fact that they were made by someone or something wearing no shoes. I came across these photos as a kid and was blown away by them. I think it was the fact that so many reports and sightings came from well-known mountaineers like Edmund Hillary (he saw footprints in 1953) who were not in the business of self-promotion. A lot of them were serious, scientific types and this gave the sightings great credibility. Of all the monsters I'd been after so far, to me, the Yeti was the most credible given the extraordinary remoteness and inaccessibility of the Himalayas and the constant drip-drip of sightings from visitors to the region.

The flight to India was uneventful except that Virgin seemed to have kindly upped my minor-celebrity status as at least three people came up to my seat, shook my hand, and hoped everything was fine on board. Then, when we landed in New

Delhi, a lady was assigned to meet me at the plane and take me through immigration to get my luggage. There was no queue jumping and no special doors; just the normal procedure but with someone in uniform standing next to me all the time. It just made me feel like a rather simple child being shown how an airport worked.

Flights to and from Kathmandu are notoriously late so I hadn't booked any connecting flights on the same day. I'd therefore decided to spend the night in the Indian capital, which was no real hardship.

I awoke the following morning at four and packed before heading downstairs to the lobby. As I got out of the lift a man standing in the middle of the lobby wearing a trendy leather jacket said, 'Mr Joly?'

I nodded at him and settled my bill before following him outside. I got into a tiny old Ambassador, the signature car of 'old' India. I slumped down in the back seat as another man drove us out of my hotel, amusingly named the Claridges. An armed guard at the gates bowed as we exited on to the relatively empty streets of pre-dawn Delhi. The airport was only twenty minutes away and we drove in silence for about ten minutes before the man in the leather jacket turned to talk to me from the passenger seat.

'We will stop somewhere for breakfast on the way,' he said.

I thought this very kind but a touch unnecessary.

'Thank you,' I said. 'I'm OK, I'm not hungry.'

'OK, we shall see later but it is up to you.' Leather-Jacket Man wobbled his head about in that peculiar Indian fashion.

The car drove on and I started to think about Nepal. It was late February and, technically, still too early to trek: things normally don't get going until March as the weather is too cold before then. I was going to climb to about 13,000 feet (that's two and a half bloody miles straight up into the sky, if you're reading this on a beach). I worried about whether I was fit enough to do this.

'First time in India?' Leather-Jacket Man was talking to me again.

'Uumm, no . . . I've been twice before: Delhi, Mumbai, Goa, Hampi and Agra.'

The man looked at me in surprise.

'You have been to Agra before?'

I nodded, not sure why this was odd.

'The Taj is truly magnificent but normally people do not revisit; there is so much to see in India.'

I half-nodded, not really taking in what he was saying.

'Is there any specific part you would like to visit that maybe you were unable to do so on your last visit?'

His sing-song voice suddenly caused me concern.

'Sorry, what do you mean?'

'I am saying that if you would like, we can organize a different itinerary than possibly the one you did on your last visit to the Taj . . .'

'I'm going to the airport . . . To get a flight to Kathmandu . . . You know that, right?'

'You are Mr Crawley?'

'Joly . . . I'm Mr Joly.'

'Oh blimey . . .' said Leather-Jacket Man. 'You are the incorrect fellow.'

By this time we'd been in the car about thirty minutes and were well on our way out of Delhi towards Agra to start Mr Crawley's tour of the Taj Mahal. Leather-Jacket Man was very kind. He ordered the driver to take me to the airport while he telephoned the Claridges to tell a no-doubt concerned Mr Crawley that he was on his way.

I was flying on an airline called JET to Kathmandu, which was a short hour-and-forty-minute flight. The flight was two and a half hours late, though – which, according to the guy sitting next to me, wasn't too bad. Apparently you need 8,000-feet visibility to land in Kathmandu, as there's no facility for an instrument landing. Visibility was currently 160 feet. This was a predictable problem when you wanted to land in one of the world's highest capitals. I was disappointed to learn, however, that Kathmandu, at an altitude of some 4,400 feet above sea level, only just slips into the top-ten list. What's the world's highest capital city, then? The answer is quite complicated. It should be Lhasa, the capital of Tibet, at 11,975 feet, but since the country has been annexed by China Lhasa is now technically not a capital. The honour, therefore, should really go to La Paz, in Bolivia, at 11,811 feet. Unfortunately, although La Paz is the default capital of Bolivia, with most of the government institutions there, the official capital is actually Sucre. So the world's current highest capital is Quito, in Ecuador, at 9,350 feet. There's one for the pub quiz.

The first thing to hit me as I got off the plane in Kathmandu was the sweet smell of incense and a sense of restrained chaos. While filling out my form for a visa I managed to leave my iPhone on the desk. I discovered this only in the luggage hall. In most countries that would be it: there would be no way you'd be allowed back into the immigration department. Nepal, however, is a relaxed place and I wandered back through the airport without anybody even questioning me. I gratefully retrieved my phone and exited the terminal building. To my delight the weather was glorious: very sunny with clear blue skies. There was no sign of the mysterious thick cloud that had delayed our arrival.

I hopped into a car that had been sent to meet me and headed towards my hotel, the appropriately named Yak and Yeti.

The hotel was very plush and filled with Buddhist monks all bustling around a sumptuous buffet in the ground-floor restaurant. I chucked my bags into my room and went out to have a look round the city. I needed to get some hiking equipment for my trip and I'd been told I could rent it. I wanted a warm down jacket, a walking stick, a decent hat and a couple of maps. I turned on to the Old Kings Way and walked down to the Royal Palace before turning left and heading into Thamel, a bustling area of little streets containing hundreds of shops groaning with trekking stuff, hippy gear and Nepalese/Tibetan art shops. The streets were packed with tuk-tuks, motorbikes and little cars all hooting and barging their way past pedestrians. I loved it. Every hundred yards or so, however, men walked past very close and whispered, 'Grass?' or, 'Wanna smoke something?' or, 'Marijuana sir?' This was definitely not my bag so I walked straight on, trying to look as though I knew my way around. This is always the secret in these types of places. If you look hesitant for even a second then you'll be swooped upon. Fortunately there were far greener horns than myself wandering about and I was mainly left alone. There was one ratty-looking little guy who spotted me and made a beeline towards me. I tried to swerve and move but he was fast and right next to me in seconds.

'You want tiger balm?' enquired my new friend in hushed tones.

I looked surprised. 'Tiger Balm?' I asked him.

'Shhh, police! You want tiger balm? I have best tiger balm in Kathmandu.'

I was confused: wasn't tiger balm some muscle relaxant easily available at any major pharmacy? Why was this guy 'dealing' tiger balm when it wasn't even illegal?

'No, thank you. I'm OK for tiger balm right now.' I tried to dismiss my new friend with a lofty wave.

'My friend, this is best tiger balm in Kathmandu – premium gold standard, sir . . .'

I really didn't know what to say and just kept walking until he finally gave up and picked on someone else. I walked on wondering whether I'd possibly misheard him. Maybe he'd been selling tiger bum? Maybe this was a new dastardly area of

Chinese medicine now that they'd finished with tiger penis and dolphin nose? Were they experimenting elsewhere? Sadly, I shall never know.

I rented a thick down jacket, a water flask and a walking pole for my Himalayan monster-hunt then walked back to the Yak and Yeti. There I had to meet Robin – an Englishman who had been in the Gurkhas and had then driven out to Nepal in 1978, literally moments before Afghanistan and Iran made that particular trip inaccessible. Robin had lived in Nepal ever since, and was helping me with my expedition. He'd arranged a Sherpa guide for me. His name was Mingmar and he'd come along with Robin to meet me. The plan was to fly into Lukla, one of the world's most spectacular airstrips, perched on the edge of a cliff. From there we were going to trek up the Khumbu Valley towards Everest and the town of Namche Bazaar (two days' walk). From Namche it was half a day's walk to the monastery at Khumjung where I hoped the monks would show me the scalp of a yeti. Mingmar had been born in Khunde, a village right next to Khumjung, and knew everybody up there. He had a very wide smile and seemed to be happy that we were trekking at this time as there would be very few people about.

Robin warned me about altitude sickness. It is a problem above 6,500 feet and could affect anybody, especially those who don't acclimatize and climb too quickly. You could be an incredibly fit marathon runner and it still could affect you whereas 'someone like you' – Robin looked at me slightly disparagingly – 'might totally get away with it; you just don't know.' He recommended that I take a pill called Diamox twice a day. Although not actually designed to help with altitude sickness (it's for glaucoma and epilepsy) this thins your blood and climbers have been using it for ages. Robin said it would help but warned me once again that you never knew how altitude was going to affect you. If he was trying to freak me out then it was working.

I said my goodbyes to Robin and, as he walked away, wondered whether I should have mentioned my intense loathing of walking uphill. It was too late, however: he'd disappeared into the Kathmandu night.

I certainly wasn't going to find a Yeti sitting around the hotel. They did have a rather pathetic footprint in a rock in the garden, which a sign claimed 'had been found when the hotel was being built . . .' Yeah, whatever . . .

I sat down in the lobby to read a bit of the only book I could find on the Himalayas: the one written by Michael Palin to accompany his TV series. The book was, like Palin, very charming and enthusiastic. I'd met Palin once at a show we were both doing in memory of Peter Cook. He was utterly charming, like a rather lovely uncle whom you could be fairly certain wouldn't abuse you.

I was pleased to see that he'd also stayed in the Yak and Yeti. I started to read about his director being kidnapped by Maoist rebels while they were trekking but couldn't really concentrate as there was a pianist playing 'Baa-Baa Black Sheep' in the centre of the lobby. He then moved on to murdering a ropey version of 'Let It Be'. Why are there always pianists in bloody bars? Nobody wants them there. It's like music in lifts. Who decided that lift muzak could be either pleasant or necessary? Were 'they' scared that, left alone with our thoughts between the first and third floors, we might find it all too much and blow our heads off with concealed handguns?

Maybe lift muzak accounted for the biggest news story to hit Nepal since Everest was conquered? (George Mallory, the English climber who disappeared on Everest in the 1920s, hated the term 'conquered'.) In 2001 the crown prince shot dead the king and queen and seven other members of the Nepalese royal family before killing himself. Perhaps he had been in a lift with no muzak? More likely he'd had to sit in the lobby bar of the Yak and Yeti listening to this God-awful pianist. Whoever was to blame for that tumultuous event, it had led to the deposing of the monarchy and the establishment of a democratic system that was currently still finding its feet. The poor Maoists who kidnapped Michael Palin's director had lost their mass appeal as they found themselves to be just another potentially corrupt political party. Being a guerrilla was so much more fun.

I got to a section in Palin's book in which he describes asking his Sherpa about the Yeti. The man told him that Yetis liked to drink so locals attempted to catch them by leaving out dead dogs full of alcohol. Unbelievable: Bigfoot loves menstruating women and the Yeti is an alcoholic.

The pianist was now playing 'Delilah'. It was definitely time for supper and bed. My adventure started the following day and I wanted to be in good spirits. I had an early start and reading about Palin's altitude sickness was making me nervous again.

I joined the seemingly endless hordes of Buddhist monks pigging out at the hotel buffet. It appeared that, like their Benedictine counterparts, Buddhist monks don't do the ascetic thing. They like the good life. I opted for à la carte as I can't trust myself with buffets. Humans, in my experience, when faced with unlimited food, will just keep eating until they can't walk. It's the inner hunter-gatherer instinct within us all. This is a basic truth as relevant to Buddhist monks as much as to porky comedians from the Cotswolds.

I slept well and left the hotel at five in the morning, having left my main suitcase with the concierge for the duration of my trek. I had managed to get what I needed into a smallish rucksack. A very tiny man, flirting with the frontiers of dwarfdom, picked me up and drove me through the deserted streets of Kathmandu. Occasionally the headlights would pick out groups of Nepalese police deployed in strategic corners and covered in protective riot gear. My tiny driver was perched on two big cushions that just about enabled him to peer over the dash at the pockmarked road ahead.

The domestic terminal was a place full of exotic-sounding airlines like Buddha Air and Yeti Airlines. Yeti Airlines were sadly in the process of changing their name to the less interesting Tara Air, which was a shame. I was pretty sure that this had something to do with the terrible crash they'd had at Lukla's Tenzing-Hillary Airport, the very airstrip we were now headed for. It happened on 8 October 2008: there was very heavy fog but, for some reason, the pilot still tried to land on the tiny (1,500 feet long and 65 feet wide) runway. He missed and smashed into the cliffs below, killing all eighteen passengers. The pilot was the only survivor. I was flying on Tara Air and hoped that they'd done more than just change their name. As my Sherpa guide, Mingmar, joined the scrum for tickets I realized that I was feeling rather out of control. I worried about how I would fare with the altitude – Robin had said that 99 per cent of people suffered from it and around 20 per cent were totally incapacitated. I opened my bag and necked my first Diamox. I felt a bit wimpy. Even at our maximum height, at Khumjung Monastery, we would be at roughly 13,800 feet – only half the height of Everest. I have a neighbour in my village back home with the unlikely name of Kenton Cool. He has apparently climbed Everest loads of times. I should have popped in to see him before I went, except I would have probably felt even more of a wimp.

The plane was a Twin Otter – a name that I presumed represented the total power of the two tiny engines. There were twenty of us crammed into the thing: five trekkers (obviously one of them being a Kiwi: international law forbids any interesting journey taking place without a Kiwi) and the rest red-cheeked locals. The plane took off very steeply and, as we flew higher, we bounced around as though we were in a fairground ride. The cockpit door was wide open and I could see no sky through the windscreen, just monstrous snowy peaks that seemed to loom above us even though we were miles up in the air. I thought of Chang, Tintin's friend whose plane crashed high in these mountains. Despite Hergé having never travelled, his depiction of Kathmandu was remarkably accurate. I hoped that this would not extend to this plane trip.

We landed on the sloping runway at Tenzing-Hillary. It was eight in the morning and cold. We were at 9,350 feet and I almost immediately felt a little dizzy and disorientated. I wasn't sure if it was altitude, hypochondria or nerves. It was not unlike the feeling I'd had when I wandered into the *I'm a Celebrity . . .* camp. Then, as now, I'd found myself in a desperate private battle to retain control. There was another bunfight for the luggage as the departing passengers were bundled on to our plane and it rocketed off down the runway to be flung into the abyss by the ramp at the end. They didn't muck around up here. The total turnaround time from landing to take-off was about seven minutes. I presumed they didn't want to risk a build-up of ice on the wings.

We walked out of the one-room airport and climbed a path that ran above the runway and then down into the village of Lukla itself. Mingmar signalled that I should follow him into a guesthouse, where he was warmly welcomed. I had some cheesy scrambled eggs and hot coffee and read a rather alarming leaflet on 'Acute Mountain Sickness'. I was still definitely feeling a little light-headed but I hoped that it wouldn't get worse as the symptoms listed were 'extreme nausea, vomiting, unconsciousness and death'.

Cheery stuff. We had a four-hour walk ahead of us to where we would be spending our first night in a village called Monjo.

The secret to trekking at this altitude, said Mingmar, was to go very slowly. This was absolutely fine by me and I assured him that he would get no speed out of me whatsoever. The beginning was rather nice as it was downhill to the valley floor below us. The only problem was that I was acutely aware that everything I descended I had to climb back up again.

The first half-hour was pretty easy-going and I just took in the scenery. Locals had to carve steps out of the steep landscape to enable them to grow anything. These descended like a curious set of giant stairs to the raging river far below.

The sun came out and it got rather hot so I immediately started shedding the layers and layers of protective clothing I had donned that morning in Kathmandu. I asked Mingmar if Yetis were ever seen this low. He replied that there were occasional sightings but that most occurred above 13,000 feet. He told me about a girl from Khumjung who had been attacked by a Yeti and survived. She had said that it smelt really bad. It had ripped out a huge clump of her long hair and thrown her into a nearby river. She had played dead and the Yeti left her alone and killed three of her yaks as she watched out of her half-closed eyes. Mingmar said that she would probably talk to me but that she would want money. I supposed that it was a way to earn a living telling tales of being attacked by the missing link. One of the unifying themes in the creatures that I'd gone after was that they smelt bad. Was being hygienically challenged a must for any self-respecting monster? It crossed my mind that the smell might not actually come from the monster but actually emanate from the witness, their body switching into automatic fear-response pong mode.

Mingmar told me that there were two different types of Yeti: a yak attacker and a man attacker. I asked him which type this one had been as it seemed to have done both. He said that it was a yak attacker – otherwise she would not have survived.

We walked on and on down the path, slowly descending towards the azure-blue river roaring beneath us. Every so often we'd come to a stupa that tradition dictated we had to pass on the left. Most had prayer wheels that you spun as you passed: 'for clean soul', said one sign. There were also enormous rocks decorated with multifarious symbols; most were money rocks and were supposed to bring good luck.

Keeping a steady pace behind us was another trekking couple – a crusty-looking Australian and his German companion, who seemed to be constantly weeping. We stopped for a breather and they did the same, with the German girl ripping off her Converse shoes and attempting to puncture several nasty-looking blisters. They were headed for Everest base camp, a full seven days' trek away. I was highly doubtful that they were going to make it.

In one village we passed a group of four British-Asian trekkers. They did a double take as I went past and then, when I was a hundred yards away, one of them bellowed at the top of his voice, 'Hello! No, I'm in Kathmandu and it's *rubbish* . . . !'

Technically this was stupid as we were nowhere near Kathmandu, but that's British geography skills for you. I ignored them and walked on as they all creased up in peals of laughter. Mingmar was very confused and I tried to explain that it was from a TV show I'd done but I don't think it got us anywhere.

Going downhill was OK except you really had to watch your footing. It was the occasional uphill parts that really took it out of me, and this was the easy day. I'd been getting fairly fit in the previous months, having bought a running machine, but the foot I broke in Argentina was still giving me big problems. The thin air left me breathless and my foot was starting to ache; this was not a good sign but I cracked on and we reached Phadking in two hours, which was fairly good going. We stopped for lunch and I decided not to have a beer but went for a Coke (sugar energy) and the rather wonderful option of yak and chips. It was pretty good – a little stringy if I was being picky, but tasty.

We sat around for an hour chatting. I asked Mingmar what he thought my chances were of seeing a Yeti. He smiled and said that everything was possible. I was already starting to smell like one and hoped that this might attract one to me. We set off again and soon crossed a long and rather wobbly suspension bridge to the other side of the 'Seven Rivers Join' river (it possibly lost a bit in translation). I noticed that every Sherpa who passed by had a long red line on the top of their cheeks as though wearing rouge. I worked out that, because they had such angular faces, the strong Himalayan sun hit their cheekbones hard. This wasn't going to be a problem for me.

We started walking along the left bank of the river and I really began to understand the sadistic logic of the topography. If the path went down for a bit, it inevitably started going up soon after. After four hours of walking my legs were starting to feel like dead weights and my broken left foot was screaming in agony. I had to stop and indicated so to Mingmar, who pointed to some flat stones overlooking the river. We sat and I quizzed Mingmar more about the Yeti.

I asked him whether he had ever seen one. He laughed and said no. I asked him why he was laughing. Did he not believe in the Yeti?

'No, no, Eti he exist – just I no see him.' He said he'd heard the Yeti howling and made an echo-ey, throaty sound that reverberated across the valley to demonstrate. 'When we hear this we burn juniper branches – Eti no like.'

I'd seen villagers burning pine all along our path through the valley but this juniper Yeti-preventer tip was good.

'Also Yeti kill my father's yak.'

This was excellent stuff. I enquired further. They'd had three yaks in the family and one went missing. He and his father went into the mountains to look for it and they found it dead.

'It was rip apart, in two pieces. Eti kill yak.'

I nodded and asked him if he by chance had any photos of this.

'No, it was before mobile phone with camera. Now everyone have camera. My cousin he take photo with mobile phone of

Yeti footprint in snow at 13,000 feet.' He drew a huge footprint in the sand.

I asked him if it could have been a bear or a yak footprint.

He said, 'No: this very big.' This was promising. He said I could talk to his cousin in Khumjung. I was stupidly excited.

We moved on and every step was torture now. I kept having to take more and more frequent breaks. Mingmar was really sweet and pretended that he was exhausted, but he was a rubbish actor. Finally, after five and a half hours' walking, he pointed to a village high up on the hill above us.

'Is Monjo – we sleep there.'

I could hardly breathe, both with the excitement of the news and because I was near death. We came round a bend and the path snaked steeply down back to the river where a little bridge crossed it. On the other side I could see the path wind suicidally up an enormous hill towards Monjo. It was the final push but I had hit the wall and it took me a good twenty minutes and several breaks before we got up the hill and finally walked into town. Mingmar pushed open a little gate to a sweet guesthouse. We'd made it.

I felt unbelievably relieved. The crusty Aussie and his weeping girlfriend (who was no longer weeping) were already there as they hadn't stopped for lunch and had pushed on through in a supreme effort that made me reassess their abilities to reach Everest base camp in Converse trainers.

We greeted each other like warriors back from a battle and agreed to meet for a beer a little later. I found my room, a sweet little prison cell with MDF walls and a rickety bed. I flopped down and immediately started to worry about the next day. The path up to Namche Bazaar was straight up the mountain for a good three hours. I reckoned I'd make it in about eight if I didn't start getting ill from altitude sickness. My left foot had swollen up and I could barely get my boot off. This was not looking good. I had to get up to a serious altitude to find this

Yeti scalp. I wasn't going to have another disappointment like the one in the Congo. I limped over to the main building and ordered a beer. It was a real *Ice Cold in Alex* moment as I downed the cool, lovely liquid in one go. The Aussie came in and, despite sounding like a New South Wales sheep farmer, turned out to be British and had only been working in Australia for two years. This was a man clearly desperate to change countries, as there was zero sign of his English upbringing. They were travelling on a shoestring and I felt very spoilt. His German girlfriend, Carina, soon joined us. She seemed in much better spirits and appeared to have forgotten her earlier unhappiness. I had some Eccles cake (my secret drug of choice for the trek – I'd got it from an outdoors shop in Cirencester. It's basically pure sugar and gives you a real kick) and I gave them one for the trip. I also gave them a couple of Diamox as I had way more than I needed. They clearly had very little money and they reminded me of what Stacey would have been like when she trekked here in the early nineties. They'd already been for a wander round the village and said that I shouldn't bother. There was nothing to do or see.

'Just a place renting a horse to anyone who doesn't want to walk. Can you bloody imagine?' The Aussie/Brit looked disgusted.

He asked me something else but I wasn't listening any more. A horse? That was the answer. I'd rent a horse. I wasn't here to bloody trek; I was a monster-hunter and I needed to get to where I was going as fast as possible. Also I knew that the less exertion you went through the less chance you had of getting altitude sickness. Also my foot was really hurting and . . . I knew I was just making excuses but all I wanted to do was to go and rent the bloody horse. I was too embarrassed to broach the subject with the Aussie/Brit and German so we had supper together in the communal room. A wood stove was giving out great heat and a couple of cute little cats wandered about stealing our food.

I had a second culinary first in the same day: water-buffalo curry. It was good, but the yak and chips just edged it. After supper I slipped out of the room and wandered down to where they'd said the horse lived. I found the lady owner and we did a bit of bartering. I managed to get a horse to take me up to Namche Bazaar for forty pounds. It was the best money I would ever spend. I returned to my (by now freezing) room and got into the first of my two sleeping bags and fell asleep almost immediately.

Mingmar woke me up early the next morning and we had a breakfast of eggs and black coffee. I broached the subject of the horse slowly with him. I told him that, as he knew, I was a leading scientist here to do some serious investigative work and I couldn't have my injured foot prevent me from reaching my goal. I told him that I'd come across the lady with the horse and had rented it for the day. He seemed totally astounded by this but nodded politely and said this was fine, although I could almost see the words 'You total wuss' appear on his forehead. Once breakfast and my embarrassing admission was over, we packed up and I prepared to meet my horse.

The horse was walked through the village to the guesthouse, as though for an execution, by the lady owner. Her name was Tiza (the horse, not the lady) and she had one look at this large foreigner and took an instant dislike to me. Undaunted, I hopped on and grabbed the reins. I'm a pretty good horse rider. I did quite a bit as a kid in Beirut and I've ridden all over the Atlas Mountains so I was certainly going to show Tiza who was boss. I urged her on but she refused to move. I gave her a couple of prods with the stirrups but she ignored me and wouldn't budge. I did the weird 'click click' sound that horse riders around the world have variations of. Nothing, Tiza was going nowhere.

The horse's owner meanwhile, a thin scary lady, was sizing me up and already regretting her decision to rent me the horse.

There are temples in China on top of steep hills where lazy pilgrims can be carried up the innumerable stairs in hammocks suspended on a bamboo pole between two porters. The only catch is that the porters charge per weight of the pilgrim. While very sensible on the porters' behalf, this is rather humiliating for the larger pilgrim when being put on the scale and having their fee shouted out for all to hear.

Scary Lady had had enough of my equestrian demonstration. She grabbed the reins off me and set off ahead leading a still, reluctant Tiza.

Great, I was going to be led all the way up the Himalayas like a fat child at pony club. I'd envisioned more of a macho riding role for myself. This really made me look seriously Kenton Uncool.

Off we trod through the street of Monjo. Trekkers were preparing for the day ahead, sorting out their poles, stuffing their backpacks. All to a man just stopped what they were doing and stared at me as we trudged past. I could hear snickering from some and words in many languages that didn't sound complimentary. I looked straight ahead as though thinking about some great mission ahead of me but it was no use. It was a little like being paraded through the streets with the word 'paedophile' slung around your neck. The sense of general disdain was palpable. Thankfully we were soon out of the village and going along the path.

We came to a gate where there was an army checkpoint that wanted to see our papers. As the soldier took my passport he said something to Mingmar, looked at me and laughed. Mingmar laughed as well. As the soldier started to carefully peruse my passport I got off the horse and wandered towards a sign I'd spotted on the gate. It was in English and welcomed visitors to this 'special area'. It then went on to urge visitors to:

1. Refrain from taking life
2. Refrain from anger
3. Refrain from jealousy
4. Refrain from offending others
5. Refrain from taking excessive intoxicants

Bugger: this place was going to be no fun if I couldn't take lives and offend people. I decided to rely on a sensible amount of intoxicants.

On we plodded until we came to another wobbly metal suspension bridge that crossed the raging torrent below. UK horses would have been literally shitting themselves looking down through the thin metal lattice. Tiza, however, was made of sterner stuff and crossed over without a hint of concern. Once over the bridge the path climbed steeply up the mountain through thick pine forests. Mingmar told me that this was a new path: just three weeks ago massive winds had knocked down hundreds of trees in the valley and left the old riverside path impassable. I was amazed at how quickly it had been built. Since this was the only way up the valley and eventually to Everest, the livelihood of the whole valley depended upon it – and this was a powerful incentive. We climbed and climbed and I could feel Tiza breathing very heavily so I made us all stop and take a breather. I offered Tiza some Eccles cake but she wasn't interested. I was convinced that she was plotting about how best to chuck me off the vertiginous slopes to our left.

We rounded a corner and came across the Aussie/Brit and the German. They had left far earlier than us and were therefore unaware of my equine conversion. We passed them as they struggled up the steep hill. I waved an embarrassed hello. They were sweet enough to wave back but you could see that they thought I was a total arse.

We came to another bridge. This one was built by Edmund Hillary, who had clearly done a lot for the people of this valley.

Mingmar had been educated at the Hillary School in Khumjung, which was how he learnt to speak such good English.

At the bridge I got off, as the exit from it was a ludicrously steep drop straight down which then immediately started to climb back up again. This was the beginning of the arduous three-hour climb up to Namche. The first bit had just been a warm-up.

When I say arduous, I know that I was on a horse and that any keen trekker reading this is poo-pooing it as a Sunday stroll. Well, my Sunday stroll is up the hill to the pub – a distance of about 300 yards with an altitude differential of about 13 feet. This was a three-hour steep climb going up more than 2,000 feet while already nearly two miles in the sky. We were already approaching the height of some of the highest peaks in Europe. Rant over.

I got back on to Tiza. I was totally out of puff from my five minutes on foot. This was pathetic but it also made it clear that if I wanted to see this Yeti scalp I was not going to do it without Tiza.

Up and up we (Tiza) climbed. The path took a sharp zigzag pattern with very little let-up. Tiza was clearly finding it quite tough as she had started farting profusely. Every time she did so Scary Lady looked back at me with an accusing glare. I smiled back, assuming she would recognize her own horse's farts. By the third such instance, however, it was obvious she was convinced it was me.

'Not me: horse . . .' I said, pointing at Tiza's arse. Scary Lady just shook her head in disgust and trudged on.

We passed a descending pair of German trekkers. They looked at Tiza and then they too looked at me in disgust. I tried to indicate that I had a broken foot but they continued on down, confident in their moral superiority. After an hour and a half's steady climb we reached a tiny plateau where a lone Sherpa woman sat with a bowl of tangerines for sale. I dismounted and bought one. Considering the effort she had made to get them there, it was the least I could do.

'You want to see Everest?' enquired Mingmar, as though he was showing me an interesting bird.

I walked past the tangerine lady and there, through a gap in the pine trees, was the tallest mountain on earth, the roof of the world. We were unbelievably lucky: it was another clear day and the peak was clearly visible, with a thick plume of cloud being blown off the summit towards Lhotze, the fourth-highest mountain in the world. I was dumbstruck. Everest is so much part of schoolboy folklore and here I was standing next to my flatulent horse looking right at it with my own eyes. I just stood and stared for about five minutes. Suddenly there was a new arrival on our little plateau. It was an Australian who had been on the same flight as me up from Kathmandu. He was crazily fit and had been full of talk about all this being quite easy compared to 'two weeks in the Bush'. He'd set off from Lukla at the same time as me with a Turkish guy he'd met. They'd gone at breakneck speed and told us they were aiming to get to Namche Bazaar in the same day. Mingmar looked very doubtful and warned them about altitude sickness and how long the trek was. They hadn't listened and set off confidently. The Aussie had even strapped a heart monitor on to his chest and he had a watch that constantly beeped at him to relay various medical information.

Now, halfway through the next day and here he was: alone and clearly not in Namche Bazaar. He looked extremely surprised to see me ahead of him. I didn't tell him about the horse for a while and asked him where the Turk was. He told me that he'd got terrible altitude sickness just out of Monjo, the village where we'd spent the night. He'd felt dizzy and was vomiting and they'd been forced to return to Monjo and overnight there. The Aussie had left the sick Turk and headed on alone that morning. I showed him Everest and he completely freaked out. He started filming himself and narrating at the same time. I left him to his video diary and clambered on to my horse. As I said goodbye, the Aussie looked up from his camera and noticed the horse. His face told me that our brief bonding period was over.

We climbed for another hour until finally we rounded a corner and I got my first glimpse of the curious village of Namche Bazaar. Set in a half-bowl on the mountainside, its multi-coloured buildings cling to the steep slopes in symmetrical rows. I rode into town praying that no Westerners would see me. A German couple did, but they looked the types to have several prisoners incarcerated in their basement back home. We locked each other in mutual stares of contempt. They changed tack and tried to give me a condescending look but I'd figured that the attitude to take now was that you only walked if you couldn't afford a horse. I was a king riding into town saluting his poor pedestrian subjects.

I was eager to try this new approach on others but it was Saturday and everybody was at the bazaar, of Namche Bazaar fame. People come here from as far as Tibet to barter and trade their goods. I got off Tiza gingerly and walked down the main street giving the distinct impression that I had a cucumber stuck up my arse. I found a place that would give me cash off my credit card and I paid Tiza's owner. It was money I would never regret spending.

We checked into the Yak Hotel and I had lunch, some *momos* (Tibetan dumplings) and a bottle of sugary Orange Fanta. As I sat alone in the wooden dining room, I spotted a photo on the wall of the Dalai Lama. He was being led through some snowy mountain pass while seated on a yak. Not only that, but he was carrying an umbrella to keep the sun off him. This all made me feel a little better about my horse problem. If it was good enough for the Dalai Lama then it was certainly good enough for me.

I still felt absolutely fine, although I was very aware of the thin air and how it makes you behave a little like an old man. I shuffled around Namche to have a look at the place. It was the biggest village in the Khumbu but there was still not much to do. As in everywhere on earth and no doubt, when we eventually get there, on Mars, there was an Irish bar. I have no idea how the concept of global Irish bars started. Was there somewhere in the world an enormously rich Irishman who kicked all this off? Who was behind this worldwide conspiracy?

The other staple of world travel is, of course, the Kiwi. I wouldn't be surprised if there was an Irish bar run by a Kiwi on the summit of Everest. I hadn't been in Namche for more than two hours when I spotted my first one. He was wearing his All Black rugby shirt (it is illegal, as a New Zealand citizen, to wear anything else abroad) and wandering vacantly down a little alley. He spotted me.

'Excuse me, mate – do you happen to know a spot selling toilet paper? I'm bloody desperate and the guesthouse doesn't provide any. I think – pardon my French – if I don't find some soon I'm going to drop the kids off right here in the street.'

I pointed to a little shop down some stairs that I had just climbed up. It seemed to sell everything. He thanked me and ran towards the place in a cautiously desperate manner. I continued on toward the far end of town, where very little was going on. The day of the bazaar, always a Saturday, is also a holiday in town so lots of places were shut. I started back towards the Yak Hotel. Every step was a bit of an effort and I felt a little like an asthmatic pensioner. I shuffled into the street of the Yak Hotel and bumped into the Aussie/Brit and the German. They were both looking remarkably chipper. It had taken them only four hours to do the trek. I had clearly completely underestimated their stamina. There was no mention made of my horse; it was the elephant in the room.

I suddenly felt very tired. Just the walk around town had wiped me out. This is one of the symptoms of altitude sickness and the reason that I needed to acclimatize there. I spent the afternoon in bed, sleeping and reading. At six Mingmar knocked on my door and came in. He asked me if I was OK. I said yes but he didn't believe me and told me that it was important to tell him if I wasn't. I insisted that I was fine, just sleepy, and we went down to the wooden dining room, very like a European-style ski chalet. Two climbers were watching *Touching the Void*. Although a brilliant film, it really isn't the one I'd watch before going climbing. In five days' time the Everest climbing season (March and April) would start and there would be several expeditions going through Namche.

I still felt fine but incredibly lethargic – everything was a bit of an effort and I went upstairs and got into my sleeping bags and read some more Michael Palin. He was now in Tibet and his soundman had been hospitalized with acute altitude sickness. I felt very lucky and drifted off to sleep but I had terrible dreams. A Yeti smashed my window and dragged me outside. He put me over his shoulder like a rag doll and bounded up the mountainside. I didn't seem overly concerned about the Yeti's intentions but I kept shouting at him: 'I must acclimatize! I simply *must* acclimatize.'

The Yeti didn't seem interested and we eventually ended up in a cave covered in blue ice, where he threw me down in a corner and started to watch *Downton Abbey* on a television. When *Downton* finished the Yeti was weeping loudly and he came over to my corner and started shaking me . . .

I awoke to find Mingmar shaking me and looking concerned.

'You OK?' he asked. I nodded, blinking in the bright morning sunshine. 'You were screaming.'

'Bad dream, but I'm good . . .'

I really was feeling OK and a lot less lethargic than the day before. I had another full day acclimatizing in Namche ahead of me before we set off for Khumjung. Mingmar wanted to take me to the top of the mountain behind Namche to visit the

Sherpa Museum. We walked up a set of steep steps that seemed to go on forever. Every step in this thin air was torture. Eventually we got to the top and I was rewarded with an epic view of Everest. Once again the sky was swimming-pool blue and a thick plume of wind roared off the peak like a mini-tornado. Mingmar told me that I was very lucky to get this sort of weather in February.

We visited the Sherpa Museum, a lovely place commemorating all things Sherpa and especially their climbing achievements. Mingmar introduced me to Lhakpa Sonam, his cousin. He ran the museum and was a veritable fount of knowledge. He was, however, very deaf – something very common among the Sherpa people and put down to iodine deficiency. He asked me to write down any questions I had about the Yeti.

I started asking him any questions I could think of. He told me that the name Yeti was a Sherpa word, *'ye te'*, meaning 'mountain monkey'. He was convinced of its existence as so many people had stories of encounters. The Yeti, he said, was supposed to have huge breasts – so if you came across one you should run downhill, as these breasts tended to knock it off balance. If you ran uphill the Yeti would sling the breasts over its shoulder and could climb very fast. It was supposed to have brown hair and be very similar to a large monkey. Sightings by locals all claimed it was bigger than a gorilla and he said that it existed on both meat and berries. He also repeated what Mingmar had told me about there being two types of Yeti: one that attacked yaks and another that attacked humans.

The vast majority of footprints and sightings were found between 16,500 and 19,500 feet. He said that when Hillary found footprints he became fascinated in the whole story. I asked him about the Khumjung scalp. He said Hillary had negotiated its loan from the monastery and it was taken to London to be examined. There it was ascertained that it was definitely not a bear. They said it had to be a very large creature but they did not know what it was.

I had to see this scalp.

I walked back down into Namche Bazaar and spent the rest of the day sitting in the sun outside my hotel, watching people go by. I saw the Aussie/Brit and the German again and we agreed to meet later for a drink.

Come five p.m. we headed for the Irish bar, but it was closed. Instead we went to a nearby bar from which ear-splitting house music was coming. Inside, the walls were festooned with T-shirts signed by visitors from around the world. Nearly all were friendly and funny – except the British ones that were invariably of the depressing 'Lads on tour'/ 'Smash it up!'/ 'Foreign bastards!' variety.

There were two locals playing snooker and a hectic international field-hockey match on the blurry TV. We sat at the bar and I must plead guilty to taking excessive intoxicants. The German told me that they'd climbed up the steps to try to take photos of Everest but when they'd got to the viewpoint they hadn't been too sure which peak it was. This was hardly surprising as it turned out they'd based their identification on a comparison with the mountain on the Toblerone packaging – they were convinced that was Everest.

I had to tell them that it was actually the Matterhorn.

We said our goodbyes and I wished them well. They were heading off towards Everest tomorrow and I was off to Khumjung. I'd spotted another horse for rent and hadn't been able to resist. I didn't tell my new friends.

I headed back to the Yak. That night was the coldest yet and I slept with my hat on with only my nose peeking out from beneath my two sleeping bags and three blankets.

I was awoken to the sound of very loud Buddhist chanting from one room next door and the heavy smell of dope from the other.

Some trekker was clearly having a rest day. I felt on top form, particularly knowing that I had a horse on hold. My new steed was a lot better-looking than Tiza and went by the unusual name of Hermann. Apparently Hermann used to be owned by a German baker who plied his trade in Namche to hungry trekkers. Whatever, I was very pleased to mount Hermann as the route out of Namche was a veritable Kamikaze climb. I had given up all embarrassment about riding a horse: anything that got me to where I wanted to go without killing me was fine by me. A helicopter back to Kathmandu was the ideal scenario the moment my investigations were over. Sadly, this was not an option unless I fell off a mountain. It looked like I was going to have retrace my steps all the way back to Lukla.

Hermann and I set off uphill and, after fifteen minutes, passed a group of three Germans who looked to be very near death. They were at a stage way beyond contempt and I could now see a vicious, desperate sort of jealousy in their vacant eyes. They looked capable of ripping me off Hermann and claiming him as theirs. I kept his adopted nationality quiet and remembered the Dalai Lama. I passed by them quickly with a regal wave.

We climbed and climbed and Hermann made amazing progress. After an hour and twenty minutes we reached a plateau where Hillary had built the highest airstrip in the Himalayas: Syangboche.

This is a dust track ending in an aircraft-carrier type ramp from which to fling the planes into the void. He'd had it built to help evacuate stricken climbers. What I hadn't known was that, just three months after its completion, his wife and daughter died in a plane crash.

Hermann, Mingmar and I plodded over the deserted runway and entered a forest of short, stubby juniper trees. The ground was now an endless lawn of coarse grass and it reminded me very much of plateaus in the High Metn in Lebanon where I used to picnic as a child. On we plodded until we came to a corner with yet another magnificent view of Everest. We continued through patches of rhododendron, pine and juniper; it was by far the most incredible scenery of the trip so far. Here I was, riding a majestic German/Nepalese steed through the unexplored Himalayas. They would surely write books about my bravery in years to come. Only the very boldest made it here . . .

Suddenly up ahead there appeared an elegant, low-slung modern building. I asked Mingmar what it was.

'Everest View Hotel . . . Many Japanese, they come for one night to see Everest . . .' He looked slightly appalled by the concept.

I was dumbstruck.

'But, how do they get here?' I asked plaintively.

'They fly little plane from Lukla to Syangboche and then taken to hotel for one night. Is for very lazy tourist.'

'More lazy than me?' I asked, sitting on Hermann.

'Much badder than you . . .' Mingmar grinned from ear to ear.

'But you can't just fly into this altitude and not get bad altitude sickness?' I asked.

'No, they have oxygen in rooms but many get very sick; is big problem.'

'Well, I suppose, since it's here, we might as well go in for a cup of tea,' I said.

'OK, but very expensive,' warned Mingmar.

I got off Hermann and looked around vainly for valet parking. I tied him to a rhododendron bush and we marched up the imposing steps into reception. It was all minimalist swank inside and we were soon ushered on to the Everest-View Terrace for the pièce de résistance. The view was un-bloody-believable, possibly the best I've ever seen from a hotel, and once again I found myself staring slack-jawed at Everest.

We sat down and had a cup of tea. We were not alone on the terrace. To our left was a group of about twenty Japanese residents. The waiter told us that they had arrived only an hour ago. Looking at them, most seemed to be quite near death – but they were still bravely trying to rustle up enough energy to strike some gangsta camera poses. It was clear, though, that their hearts weren't in it. As we watched, one man dropped his camera and ran to the edge of the balcony and vomited profusely over the railings. A couple of the group started taking photos of the vomiting man while several started to suffer from the inevitable gag reflex. It was time to move on.

We walked down from the hotel through a small rhododendron forest until we reached the bottom of the valley and entered the village of Khumjung. I was really chuffed. Hermann dawdled through the dusty streets. He'd clearly had enough and knew that the end was in sight. We came into the main square in which sat a guesthouse run by Mingmar's brother. On the other side of the square was a stupa and the Hillary School where Mingmar had been a student.

We had lunch, the ubiquitous vegetable curry and rice. While we ate Mingmar told me that the woman who was attacked by a Yeti and thrown into a river would talk to me . . . For 6,000 dollars.

I nearly spat out my curry. I politely declined and suggested that I could possibly go to thirty dollars. Mingmar apologized but said that some Japanese TV crew had paid her this sort of money for an interview and she now refused to talk to anyone who wouldn't stump up the same sum. Bloody Japanese, they were really ruining this area . . .

I told him that for 6,000 dollars I wanted an exclusive interview with the Yeti himself. Mingmar laughed but he was obviously a bit embarrassed about the whole affair. He said that she had gone a bit doolally since the attack anyway. The Japanese crew had brought a Yeti costume with them, as they wanted to film a reconstruction of the attack. It turned out that they hadn't bothered to mention this to the woman in question. When the fake Yeti appeared she went totally mental.

Realizing that this interview was never going to happen I asked Mingmar if we could go to the monastery. He nodded, pleased to get off the loony-Yeti-attack-woman subject.

We left the guesthouse and Hermann, who was tied up outside, visibly flinched. I patted him on the head and assured him that his work was over before walking through a maze of waist-high stone walls towards the monastery, which I could see at the top of the village. We passed by locals sitting in the warm sun doing their washing or chopping wood. There was a house whose roof was ripped off in the terrible winds two weeks ago. About ten people were hard at work repairing it and it looked like a sort of Sherpa barn-raising ceremony.

After five minutes or so we arrived at the monastery, the Khumjung Gomba. A large money stone was positioned right outside the entrance. This was rather appropriate as it turned out that nobody could see the Yeti skull without paying a 'dona-tion' to the monastery. This Yeti business was . . . A business. A warty Buddhist monk stood outside the main door and greeted us with a beatific smile as we entered a courtyard filled on three sides with wooden benches and surrounded by cloisters. Mingmar whispered that once a year the whole valley came here for a five-day festival.

Then an elderly looking man, not in monk clothes, made his way slowly down to greet us. He pointed to a hidden door covered by a golden drape. He lifted the drape and unlocked two stiff padlocks. He opened the door and it creaked open in a rather satisfyingly *Scooby Doo* manner. We stepped inside behind him. It was a shrine and a rather beautiful one at that. Large multi-coloured Buddhas lined the rear wall and formed the backdrop to the central shrine. Hundreds of sticks of incense burnt everywhere in the room, creating a pungent, mystical fog. On both sides of the room were hundreds of little cubicles in the wall with the edges of prayer cloths hanging down from them. Just to my right an enormous gong hung from the ceiling. Both

Mingmar and the old man set about bowing and lighting candles while my eyes darted around the room looking for the elusive Yeti skull. They eventually alighted on a locked lime-green metal cabinet that seemed at odds with everything else in the room. I waited until Mingmar had finished his ritual and then pointed at the cabinet.

'Is that it?'

'Yes.'

'What now?'

'Please make a donation.' He pointed to a slot in the side of the cabinet that I hadn't spotted before. I pushed a tightly folded 500-rupee note through the slot and the Keeper of the Skull (this appeared to be his title) unlocked the cabinet and dramatically swung open the doors. Inside was a glass box with the words 'Yeti Scull' daubed in white paint on the wooden frame. The box had a white silk shawl draped over it. I bent down and lifted the shawl off the box. Inside was a cone-shaped object, about twelve inches high. It looked like someone had lopped the top off the head of a cone-headed animal. The hair was a reddish-brown colour and, on first impression, it looked pretty convincing.

I asked Mingmar to ask the Keeper whether he could bring the box out of the cabinet. The Keeper said no, we couldn't touch it; it was forbidden. Mingmar spoke to him for a while and then told me that the Keeper had kindly agreed to get the box out of the cabinet and put it on the top for a mere 200 dollars. I was starting to get a bit hacked off with the financial nature of anything Yeti. It was an expensive business, this monster business. I told the Keeper of the Skull that for 200 dollars I wanted the case unlocked and for me to be able to put the skull on my head while levitating. Mingmar communicated this to the Keeper, who didn't seem very amused. We eventually agreed that if I gave 200 rupees to the Keeper personally, as opposed to making a donation, Mingmar would be allowed rotate the skull in the cabinet so that I could photograph and film all sides of it.

The Keeper told me that this was a special honour and that I was not to tell anyone, so . . . You didn't hear it from me.

It was a bit annoying because I was pretty sure that I remembered footage in the original Arthur C. Clarke TV show in which a much younger Keeper of the Skull danced around the courtyard with it on his head.

I handed over the money and Mingmar gently rotated the box a full 360 degrees as I snapped away. One side of the skull had a vertical split all the way down it. Mingmar showed me a piece of paper on which was written, in dodgy English, the history of the skull.

Before the Khumjung monastery was established the peoples of the valley celebrated the festival of Dumji in the village of Thane. A dispute arose over who should organize the festival and the people of Namche, Khunde and Khumjung went it alone with Khumjung chosen to be the new host. As the new hosts it was expected of the people of Thane to give a worthy present in tribute. They gave them the Yetis Scull. They were so offended by this gift that they kicked it all the way home (hence the split) the scull was kept in the monastery and it was only in the twentieth century that its significance was realized.

I asked the Keeper if he had seen a Yeti. The Keeper said he had never seen a Yeti but he had heard them many times. He said that they sounded like a crying baby and that he often heard them at night. He did the cry for my camera and I have to admit that it was a touch spooky.

He then told me a story about a local villager who was at 19,600 feet with his Yaks. It started snowing really hard and the man wanted to move down lower into the valley. On the way down he saw a figure ahead of him in the snow. He thought that it was someone from his village and he shouted and the figure stopped. As he approached it the Yaks went crazy with fear and he smelt the creature (you guessed it: it was the Yeti) and it was not a good smell. The creature disappeared into the blizzard. When the man got back to the village he was crazy with fear and got very ill.

The Keeper now looked at us expectantly, like someone telling a ghost story to a bonfire of Scouts. There was silence for a moment. I wanted to hold the skull in my hands and it wasn't going to happen. The Keeper locked up the cabinet and ushered us out into the courtyard. We thanked him and he began the long, slow shuffle back up to his cloistered quarters.

We exited the monastery and walked back down to the square. I had a look round the Hillary School. It was very impressive. Mingmar went up to Khunde to visit his parents and I sat in the sun writing up my notes and soaking up the silence.

That evening Mingmar returned with his brother, the owner of the guesthouse. It was another freezing night and we sat around the communal stove drinking beer and talking. They told me about their other brother, who had climbed Everest. He had taken photos of a Yeti footprint in the Makalu region – again at the seemingly preferred Yeti altitude of 19,600 feet.

Then, out of the blue, the brother in front of me started telling me about a trip he'd made up the Holy Mountain the previous October. The 'Holy Mountain' is the name for the mountain that stands right behind the village; Western climbers are not allowed on to it.

The brother told me that they had built a big drinking-water construction project on a ridge on the other side of the Holy Mountain. One night, they were camping up at the site when the temporary water supply that they'd set up stopped working.

The brother climbed uphill to where they had set up a big water tank, only to find that it had been knocked over. Nearby were a set of huge footprints in the snow, just like the ones his brother had photographed. He said that he took two photos of the tracks on his mobile and then scarpered, as he was very afraid.

I asked him where the photographs he'd taken were. He said that they were on his computer. I asked him whether I could see them. He nodded and beckoned me through into the family bedroom. In the corner he had an old computer set up on a table. He fired it up and, when the home screen appeared, clicked on a file in the bottom right of the screen. There, on his computer screen, were two photographs of a set of large foot-prints. They were not the best quality, and he hadn't put anything next to them for scale, but they were clearly large foot-prints and he said that they were not of any animal he knew of. I saw no reason for him to lie.

Back on my night out in Namche, I'd noticed a painted Yak skull in the bar and I had told Mingmar how much I liked it. His brother had one that he'd bought in Tibet and he and Mingmar presented it to me as a present. I was so chuffed: it was a really beautiful thing, painted in yellow with Tibetan script on it.

I thought about it all night and in the morning I had to tell them that I couldn't take the painted skull: I'm always bringing stuff back from my travels and I worried that this might well end up being the straw that broke Stacey's back. Also, I was unsure as to whether I could get a skull through UK customs. Hillary apparently got the Yeti skull back to England with the help of the actor Jimmy Stewart's private jet. (Stewart happened to be holidaying in India at the time and helped Hillary out.) I had no such high falutin' assistance (as Jimmy might have said).

That morning it was crazily cold and there was a heavy frost on the ground. The plan was to walk all the way down to Monjo without a horse. We waited until the sun snuck over the nearest peaks and then set off. I'd rather hoped that Hermann would be waiting outside for me but his owner had retrieved him like a horse thief in the night.

The first twenty minutes were awful with a steady slog up a set of very steep steps. I huffed and puffed like a big bad wolf but, once we reached the top and passed a little stupa, it was downhill all the way. And I mean *downhill*. We crossed back over the dirt airstrip and kept going down. We threaded our way through the dwarf-juniper forest dotted with the occasional bulbous rock. Soon – ridiculously soon, in fact – we got to a point overlooking Namche. The view was wonderful but the descent into town was perilously steep and my knees were really starting to hurt as they took all the downhill strain.

A short history of my left leg

I suppose I'd better take you through the history of my unlucky left leg as I keep grumbling about it. Back in 1987, when such things might have seemed a touch cooler and I was still sporting guyliner, I was the proud owner of a pink Honda Camino Scooter (49cc). I was on my way down the Gloucester Road to my girlfriend's house when I overtook a bus and was hit by a Sloaney woman in a Peugeot 205. Her bumper went straight into my left knee and I went flying off the bike and into the doorway of a pub. I ruptured all the ligaments in my knee and had to have quite an operation that left me on crutches for three months. It also left me with quite a cool scar shaped like a question mark that I tell my kids was the result of a great-white shark attack.

Then, in around 1996, I was on a Greek island called Evia, visiting my lovely sister who lives there. I went with my then girlfriend, who had a PhD, allowing her to call herself 'Dr' Burr. (Weirdly, I have dated two PhD 'doctors'. One, the aforementioned Dr Burr. And the other? Dr Gurr. I kid you not.)

Anyway I wanted to rent a scooter but the Greek guy at the rental place persuaded me to take a motorbike instead. I had absolutely no idea how to ride a motorbike. We were in the town of Styra and Dr Burr was on the back when we came to a stop at some traffic lights. Dr Burr, who was also unused to motorbikes, started wobbling and the whole bike fell over, crushing my left knee.

Dr Burr was uninjured but I my kneecap was smashed into four bits. I was forced to fly back to the UK where (proper) doctors wired it up and tried to fuse the thing back together. While recovering in hospital I became rather attached to a button that would give me a hit of morphine every time I squeezed it. This helped a lot when Dr Burr came to see me in said hospital and dumped me unceremoniously.

Then, in 2011, I agreed to do *Celebrity Total Wipeout* in Argentina. For those of you not 'up' with shit TV, this is an insane assault-course-type competition where you are thrown into water and bounce off huge red balls for the sadistic pleasure of the viewing public. I agreed to do it because they flew me out to Buenos Aires club class and, as I was going to Antarctica afterwards via Patagonia, it was all going to work out nicely. Sadly, in the qualifying round, I found myself in second place and took an ambitiously competitive leap into the void and landed very, very awkwardly on my left foot, snapping three metatarsals. It's a wonder, frankly, that I can still walk. And, yes, I am both left-handed and left-footed.

Anyway, back in Namche, the descent had killed my knee so we stopped in a store that was doing a roaring trade in knee supports and painkillers. I slipped two on and two in and I felt much better. We continued on down towards the river. Ten minutes out of Namche we walked past some panting trekkers.

'Don't worry, only twenty minutes to go,' I said to them and they smiled and I smiled back. We were all trekkers together in one big happy trekking world and nobody needed to know anything about my horse problem.

Then the painkillers kicked in and I felt a bit woozy and evil. We spotted another pair of trekkers struggling up the hill, about thirty minutes away from Namche.

'Keep going – three more hours and you're in Namche,' I smiled as they both physically crumbled before my eyes and sat down disheartened on the side of the trail. I walked on feeling no guilt and blaming my behaviour on the drugs and altitude.

As we carried on down Mingmar told me a story about when he'd gone to work in Japan for a year. He was doing construction work with ten other Sherpas and he now spoke fluent Japanese. When they'd first arrived, however, they didn't speak a word of the language. One of their gang went off to buy some food and came back with various tins of things and they cooked up a very good dinner. The following night they invited some other workers from a nearby camp to share a meal. When these Japanese workers arrived for dinner they saw the tins and were horrified.

'That is bruddy cat food!' they shouted.

Tears rolled down Mingmar's face as he told me the story and the sound of our laughter echoed off the steep valley walls.

After two and a half hours we reached the bottom and crossed the suspension bridge over the river. As we crossed we passed two trekkers walking along happily, seemingly without a care in the world. Little did they know of the fiendish ascent right ahead of them. It was like driving along on the empty side of the motorway having just passed a five-mile traffic jam on the other side and seeing people driving towards it unaware of what was to come. It made you feel good . . . Or maybe that's just me?

We walked along the riverbank until we stopped for lunch.

We had vegetable curry, rice and some powerful chillies. The chillies certainly woke me up, and afterwards we made good time and were soon in Monjo. This was where we'd stayed on the first night and I was under the impression that we were stopping there. Mingmar, sadly, had other plans and so we marched on. He wanted us to sleep in Phadking, the village where we had stopped for yak and chips on the first day. It was another two hours' walk and my knee groaned in agony. I slipped on my headphones and listened to music. I started doing a much better pace, no doubt also helped by us having descended more than 3,000 feet. I marched to Bon Iver, Lana Del Rey, the Stranglers, Marianne Faithfull and the Divine Comedy. My legs were like lead and my knees ached with every step but I was managing not to stop for too many breaks. Eventually we crossed the final bridge and it was but a short five-minute walk up to the Green Village Guesthouse. As if on cue, on came 'Glad It's All Over' by Captain Sensible.

Walking through the main drag of the village there were several hectic games of Phadking underway. This is a game not unlike billiards but played with checkers on a flat piece of wood. The player must slide his or her checker across the wooden top and try to knock his or her opponent's checker into a small round hole cut into the corner of the wood. The table is sprinkled with flour to make it slippery. As the game was named after the village, I presumed it originated there – but apparently different versions of it are played all over the world. Either way it was certainly popular.

We climbed the stairs into the Green Village and I threw my bags on the bed and collapsed. I was filthy. A thick film of dust and dirt covered me but I couldn't have cared less. I was lying down and only three hours from Lukla and the flight back to Kathmandu. I remembered the steep walk down on the first day and I already knew that I had taken my last steps in the Khumbu Valley: I needed more horse.

Later that evening, as we sat around the wood stove in the centre of the Green Valley dining room, I broached the subject with Mingmar. He seemed unsurprised by my request and rang someone on his mobile to organize it. The stove was gloriously hot and I could feel the heat seeping into my tired bones. Outside the skies had darkened and the clouds had rolled down the valley, lowering the temperature by ten degrees in a second.

I was sick of beer so I bought a bottle of XXX Rum for us to drink. It did the trick and Mingmar was soon three sheets to the wind and suggesting we move on to the local drink, *rakshi*. This is made from millet and I'd had enough local spirits to know that it was going to be rough. I was wrong. It was utterly delicious, subtle, and really hit the spot. We sat around the Sherpa Aga and talked bollocks for hours.

My horse arrived early the following morning and, to my surprise, it was Tiza, my second day horse. The look of horror in the poor animal's eyes as she spotted me was unmistakable. She backed away, trying to turn round and bolt for home, but Scary Lady now saw me as a total cash cow and grabbed the reins for dear life.

The climb up to Lukla wasn't nearly as bad as I remembered and on the frequent flat bits I felt very embarrassed when passing fresh-faced backpackers heading off on their treks and staring at the lazy bastard on a horse. The last half-hour, however, was reassuringly steep and I was very pleased to have Tiza. I think I can confidently say that she didn't feel the same way. It started to snow quite heavily. We looked back up towards the Holy Mountain above Khumjung and it was white. We'd got out just in time. Mingmar thought otherwise.

'Snow good for Eti tracks,' he said ruefully.

Damn it, he was right – but I wasn't going back. I'd had enough and wanted a warm bath and my legs back. We trudged on up the path until we came to the final slope, where a memorial to the victims of the Yeti Air crash reminds trekkers that these are dangerous mountains. We passed by and crossed under the arch demarking the end of the trail. As we entered the town I quickly hopped off Tiza and walked in before anyone could see me. I paid Scary Lady off and patted Tiza on the nose. Tiza turned her head very slowly to look at me.

Our eyes met and we shared a brief moment and then she said, clear as day, 'Don't ever come back here again, you fat bastard.'

I jumped back in surprise and looked around to see if anybody else had heard her. Nobody appeared to have done so. I have had many such occasions, when I have been convinced that animals have spoken to me. It's either a very special skill or the first signs of severe mental illness. My son, Jackson, claims that every cat he encounters winks at him. It appears to be a family trait.

We said goodbye to Tiza and Scary Lady and trudged through the snow into town to my last guesthouse. I had to get a plane to Kathmandu the following morning and it wasn't looking promising. Given the height and the variable weather conditions, flights had sometimes been cancelled for up to a week. With the snow still falling hard, I had a sneaking suspicion that I might be getting to know Lukla rather well.

I spent the rest of the day writing up my notes and drinking cup after cup of sweet black tea. It was bollock-numbingly cold and, for the first time, I got out my rented down jacket and put it on in the communal room of the guesthouse. As with all Nepalese guesthouses, there was a wood burning stove in the middle of the room – but it wasn't lit. Various members of the guesthouse family came in, turned on a telly and watched an Indian show called *Dance India Dance*.

This was a succession of terrible dance acts, one being a woman dancing round her ironing board while another was a man in drag dancing inside a closet . . . Subtle it was not.

The judges all spoke in Hindi/English saying anodyne things like, 'Very sweet act; I wish you the best of luck.' After the panel had spoken a rather creepy man in a leather chair (who reminded me of Cyril from *That's Life!*) appeared to make the final decision. He slammed anyone male but was incredibly complimentary about any woman performer: 'You have a most fabulous form and such a charming smile . . .'

The Nepalese family *ooh*ed and *aah*ed at every act as I desperately hinted that it might be time to light the stove. They ignored me and so I poured green chilli all over my Sherpa stew hoping it might warm me up. I went to bed at seven p.m. and had the coldest night I have ever spent in a bed (and I have slept in two ice hotels).

I woke at five-thirty absolutely certain that all planes would be cancelled. Miraculously, however, the day became clear and sunny and the runway had been magically cleared of snow. I had a coffee and walked over to the airstrip. Mingmar came to say goodbye and gave me a white silk scarf for 'safe travels'. He was going to walk all the way back to Khumjung to help his parents build a new house. We said our goodbyes and parted. He was a great guy but I felt totally emasculated by him.

At seven a.m. a siren sounded to indicate the imminent arrival of a plane. Not only was it clear in Lukla, but conditions in Kathmandu were good too. The plane landed and passengers got off while porters hurried to offload baggage and hurl ours on. Meanwhile someone constantly rotated the propellers manually so that they wouldn't freeze up.

The engines roared and we started hurtling down the slope towards the drop. At the last moment the plane went up the ramp and was catapulted into the void. Everyone screamed, as the plane appeared to almost come to a standstill in mid-air. Then, somehow, it got some invisible traction and we were off. People started breathing again and unclenching their fists. The fat woman next to me let go of my arm and I felt blood start to flow to my fingers again. I looked out of the little window at the snowy peaks to my right. As I did I could almost swear that I saw a large hairy creature, about eight feet tall and covered in a reddish-brown hair. As I stared the creature raised its right hand and extended two fingers in the international sign of dismissal. I rubbed my eyes and looked again, but the mountains had disappeared and we were enveloped in soft white clouds that would carry us back to Kathmandu and the drudgery of the known world.

Nessie

'Whoever fights monsters should see to it that in the
process he does not become a monster.'

Friedrich Nietzsche

I couldn't really be an English monster-hunter and not go after
the Loch Ness Monster, possibly the most famous monster in
the world.

'Nessie' has somehow grabbed the world's imagination: you
can mention her anywhere and people know the story. The term
'monster' was first coined to describe Nessie in 1933 by Alex
Campbell, a water bailiff and part-time journalist, in an article
he wrote for the *Inverness Courier*. This was the year in which
the legend really kicked off, with a plethora of sightings of a
large creature in the loch that continue to this day. There was
apparently always something eerie about the loch, however:
tales of something in the water stretch back to the time of St

Columba, in the sixth century, who supposedly witnessed a man who was being attacked by a large 'water creature' in the River Ness.

In more recent times the canny locals of the loch have done their very best to use the story to attract the lucrative tourist dollar. A trip to Scotland would not be complete without a visit to Loch Ness. It's something that appeals to the whole family. Dad can be a monster-hunter, Mum can enjoy the scenery and the kids can get a cheap thrill worrying that they might be eaten by this modern-day celebrity dinosaur.

Truth be told, though, the idea of travelling to Scotland after my recent adventures – and as opposed to searching for the Chupacabra in Puerto Rico or the Wild Man of Borneo – was not that appealing. I was a monster-hunter and wanted to hack through jungles and climb mountains, not drive up the M1. Also, on this trip I'd be travelling with my wife and two kids. Don't get me wrong. I adore my family but it's just that when I'm 'working' I like to travel alone. This isn't because I don't miss my family when I'm gone (I do, terribly) but is because, in my opinion, to write a proper book you need to be on your own. This allows you to people-watch, eavesdrop, explore and get into trouble.

I occasionally write for the *Sunday Times* and they had provided me with a brand-new Mercedes 'family wagon' to review. They suggested that I go off on a trip with my family to somewhere in the UK to test out the vehicle. It was half term and the kids were bored. Everything was pointing in one direction. We were going to Loch Ness to monster-hunt en famille. God help us all.

The Mercedes turned up. It was a lovely, posh new yuppie-mobile and it had been brought over from Germany especially for this story. *No pressure* . . . I thought to myself as I climbed in. I got in the wrong side. It was a left-hand drive with

German number-plates. The kids loved it, playing with all the buttons in the back that turned your seat into a Jacuzzi or some such nonsense.

I punched 'Inverness' into the complicated sat-nav system and it announced in a German/English accent that the trip was about 500 miles. It was also claiming that it would take me eight and a half hours. This was crazy. I thought that Germans had no speed limits on their autobahns? It seemed the moment it got over here it was getting all Little Englander with me.

'How long until we get there, Dad?' The kids were restless and we were still parked outside the house.

'About three hours,' I said.

'Dad is lying. It's about nine hours, kids,' said Stacey.

'*Nine hours!* OMG! What the hell are we going to do for nine hours?' cried my little monsters.

'We could play I Spy?' I suggested, hoping they'd say no.

'Why did you tell them it was nine hours?' I whispered to Stacey.

'Because that's how long it is,' she replied.

'Now they're pissed off already,' I whispered back.

'Why are you whispering?' asked Stacey.

'Forget it,' I said, trying to find the button that turned the engine on.

'I spy with my little eyes something beginning with L . . . !' cried the back seat.

'It's L for Long Time – too long to be in a car!' They all laughed and for a moment forgot they were unhappy . . . But only for a moment.

I found the button and pressed it. The engine came on but was so 'eco' I had to get out of the car to check, as I couldn't hear anything. I got back in and drove out through the gates. We were off, monsters hunting monsters.

The drive was pretty much as I'd imagined it would be. The

kids bickered most of the way up. Someone hit someone; someone denied hitting someone; someone hit someone back.

'Shut up.'

'No, you shut up.'

'Dad, Parker hit me.'

'Mum, the little brat kicked me . . .'

As the soap opera developed in the back seat, things weren't much better up front. Because we were in a left-hand drive, Stacey – who was in the 'exposed' passenger seat – was convinced that every oncoming car was going to hit her. Every single time a car went past us she would flinch and scream: 'You're in the wrong fucking lane, you big bonehead! Aaaaaaaaaarrrghghgh!'

By Burford, just twelve miles away from home, I was fantasizing about murdering her. We had eight hours and forty-five minutes to go and I realized that I was on my very own *National Lampoon's Vacation*.

Suddenly a car pulled out in front of me without looking. I slammed on the brakes and just managed to avoid hitting him. I was about to remonstrate with the single-cell organism in the clapped-out Ford when he beat me to it.

'Fucking German bastard. Learn to fucking drive, you Nazi arsehole!'

He sped off, giving the finger to both the entire German nation and me. Stacey and I looked at each other and had to laugh.

Although we were after the Loch Ness Monster, we were not going to be staying beside Loch Ness. Experience has taught me that if a hotel doesn't have a swimming pool, or at the very least a hot tub, then kid trouble lies ahead. I'd found a hotel with a pool in Inverness so the idea was to hang out there and make investigative forays to the nearby loch.

I must have been high on hallucinogens when I agreed to this idea. By the time we eventually rolled into Inverness, ten hours later, nobody was talking to anybody. We simply communicated via a series of sharp elbows and seat kicks.

All I wanted to do was hit the bar, have a drink and get something to eat, but the kids had got the overpowering stench of chlorine in the lobby into their noses and wanted to swim. Reluctantly I got them into swimsuits, found towels and wandered down to the pool.

To my delight there was a hot tub right next to the pool. Unfortunately there was also an enormous tattooed Geordie sitting bang in the middle of it. Without much choice I slipped into the bubbly soothing waters. I tried to look away from the tattooed Geordie but he just sat and stared at me as though I'd spilt his pint. He appeared to be struggling to say something and it took a while but it eventually came out.

'Are youse him off the telly?'

I didn't want to talk to him. I didn't want to talk to anyone. I just wanted to sit there, relax and get over my ten-hour drive from hell. If I did this, though, he would tell everyone he knew in prison that I was a wanker who was 'up' himself and needed a 'good kicking'.

I turned and smiled and looked bashful and said, 'Yes, I'm afraid so.'

He looked at me for a while before speaking again: 'No you're not him. Are youse mocking me?'

I didn't know what to say to this without getting a smack.

'No, no, it's me. I'm Dom Joly from the telly. How you doing?' I tried to sound relaxed and friendly.

'I thought you were that fella from the comedy-house show, wasssiisname?' His red face looked like it was about to explode with exertion.

'I don't know. I really don't know. Sorry, I'm really tired and just want to chill out.' I leant back and closed my eyes and hoped he'd go away.

'Do you think youse better than me?'

I didn't wait for any more. I got up, got out of the hot tub, grabbed the kids out of the pool and started marching them towards the changing rooms. They started protesting and trying to get back into the pool.

The tattooed Geordie shouted, 'Are those your kids?'

I ignored him and we got into the changing rooms to find a man standing naked, with one leg up on the bench, blow-drying his pubic hair. We left straight away and headed for the room.

'Hey, that was quick – how was it?' asked Stacey.

'Fine,' I said, looking for the mini-bar.

After half an hour or so we went downstairs to get something to eat, only to find that the hotel restaurant closed at eight p.m.

We went next door to a 'posh' Italian restaurant. It was 'posh' enough to have nothing for the kids to eat, but 'shit' enough to leave us all very unsatisfied and with a huge bill.

As we walked back to the hotel I had to try to explain to the kids why a man was drunkenly punching another man in the face while a woman hit the same man with a handbag.

'Alcohol and weak genes,' I said.

I didn't know whether they understood and I didn't care. I just wanted to go to bed.

The next morning we woke up and everyone seemed to be in better moods. The sun was shining and Inverness looked rather lovely in the dappled morning sunlight.

To get everyone in the mood and get them up to speed on the basic legend, I showed them the *Arthur C. Clarke's Mysterious World* episode on 'Lake Monsters'. I was a little bit worried that it might freak them out and that they wouldn't want to go to the loch, but they spent the whole time howling with laughter at what people wore in 1980.

Stacey and I laughed along, remembering some of our own eighties faux pas. There was me with my crimped hair and make-up, and her with the Princess Di flick and then the perm, oh God, the perm . . .

Down we went to breakfast for the usual joyless UK-hotel experience. Having passed on the heart-attack buffet, I asked for a cappuccino and was stared at as though I'd just demanded moon rock. Surely we all know about coffee now, even up here? The fifteen-year-old boy in charge of breakfast eventually agreed to go next door to the bar and ask. He was soon back, however.

'The manager says it's impossible.'

I gave up and sat down to nibble on a tough croissant. Parker trapped Jackson's leg between their chairs and gave it a little squeeze. Jackson started screaming. Everyone in the room looked up from their troughs and started staring.

'Is that the guy from *I'm a Celeb* . . . ?' asked a scrawny mother of four potential burglars on the next-door table, as though I wasn't there.

'No,' replied the multi-earringed father out on a rare bout of parole. 'What would he be doing staying here?' I had to admit that he had a point. Even in the Congo I'd managed to get a cappuccino.

A double-decker bus drove past the window. It had a huge advert for *Celebrity Big Brother* on Five. This would have been an encouraging sign of modernity had the show not ended five weeks previously . . .

We drove towards Loch Ness. We were on our way monster-hunting and I didn't have the foggiest notion of what we were going to do. We stopped at a place that had a statue of Nessie outside it. We got a couple of photographs and the kids wanted to know whether we were done now we'd found it.

They insisted on going into the shop that was like a Scottish mega-mart. Anything was Nessied up and for sale. There were Nessie hats, Nessie humps, Nessie shirts, Nessie fridge magnets, Nessie posters and . . . Nessie everything. There was also everything Scottish you would never want. The kids went mental and bought silly tartan hats, stickers, stuffed toys. I tried to appeal to Stacey but she had gone all misty-eyed and Scottish and reminded me that both sides of her Canadian family – the MacDougalls and the Johnstones – were from here. She started buying books called things like *Your Clan Guide* and wanted tartan from each side. I was going to be bankrupted in seconds by monsters and ancestry.

My phone beeped indicating that I had a text. It was the features editor at the *Sun*, Caroline. She'd read a Tweet that I'd posted asking anyone for help in finding people to talk to about Nessie. She had sent me a list of every nutter – sorry, 'specialist' – in the area. I looked down the list.

The first one was a guy called Steve. He was the man who had jacked in his job as a burglar-alarm installer and now lived on the shores of the loch in a former mobile library. He earned his living making little figurines of Nessie while keeping a permanent watch on the loch for the 'beastie'. I felt a little guilty when I saw his name.

About twelve years ago, just before we started filming *Trigger Happy TV*, Sam Cadman and I made a recce trip up to Loch Ness. We were looking into doing some filming in the area and were driving around thinking of ideas. We heard about this guy in his little mobile home and, after a rather long session in the local pub, came up with a plan. Using driftwood, we made the shapes of an enormous pair of clawed feet. We attached these to two poles and then we waited for the lights in the beach hut to go out. When they did we approached stealthily and wandered all around the thing making 'Nessie prints'. We never hung around to see the excitement the next morning, but I'd always felt a little guilty. I rang the number and a relaxed voice said 'Hello' after about ten rings.

'Hi, is that Steve?' I asked.

'Yes, it is. Who's wanting to know?' asked the relaxed voice.

'Hi, my name is Dom and I'm writing a book on monsters. I'm currently up in the Loch Ness area and was wondering if I could pop by and have a chat with you?' I tried to sound like a friendly, non-judgemental type of guy.

'Well, that would have been great but there's just one little problem. I'm currently lying on a beach in Thailand.'

This was a turn up for the books. It seemed that there was decent money to be made in Nessie-figurine making. I thanked Steve and neglected to mention our earlier half-meeting in the shape of fake footprints.

I rang the next name on the list. It was a man called Tony Harmsworth. He answered straight away.

'Hello.'

'Hi, is that Tony Harmsworth?'

'It is he. Who are you?'

'My name is Dom and I'm writing a book about monsters and I was given your name by a journalist as someone I should talk to about Nessie.'

'Ah, well, yes, I'm definitely someone you should talk to. Unfortunately I'm currently laid up in bed with a bad back. How long are you up here for?'

'Not long I'm afraid.'

'Then it's not going to be possible as I'm totally immobile at the moment.'

Things were not going well with my investigations. Then Tony had a suggestion.

'You should go and see Adrian Shriner at the Loch Ness Exhibition in Drumnadrochit.' I thanked Tony and hung up because the family had just come out of the shop laden down with their Scottish booty. We tried to cram it all into the Mercedes' boot before heading off down the loch to Drumnadrochit.

The Loch Ness Centre & Exhibition was not hard to miss. We parked up next to a pond containing another mock-up statue of Nessie and wandered inside past a small yellow submarine that looked like it was straight out of the adventures of Tintin. Tintin did in fact come to Scotland, although not to Loch Ness. He headed up to the 'Black Island', where he ended up discovering that the Bigfoot-type animal that so terrified locals was a gorilla used by counterfeiters to keep nosey people away.

We entered the exhibition: six rooms featuring slideshows, video clips and exhibits, all lit in quite a slick manner. It's pretty professional. The problem was that I had come here for some monster stories. Although the whole place is sold on 'Nessie', the entire exhibition does its very best to deconstruct the myth and leave you at the exit wondering why you bothered to come to Loch Ness. It seemed that Adrian Shriner was not a believer – not any more, anyhow.

I met him in the vast shop through which you're channelled to get back to your car. He certainly looked the part – a crazy long beard and sporting the full tweed. He was the epitome of a mad professor.

I'd left my 'Dom Joly Monster Hunter' card at the entrance and it seemed to have done the trick. He was happy to tell me about how he got started.

'Essentially I'm a lazy man and I saw monster-hunting as a quick path to glory. People might feel that going down into the depths of the loch in a tiny submarine was brave, but it's a lot easier than hiking to the North Pole.' I liked Adrian. He had a twinkle in his eye and was clearly a smart guy. When he'd first come to Loch Ness, in the late sixties, the world had pretty much been explored and explained. Monster-hunting was a way to have an adventure while also cocking a snook at established science.

He admitted that he had started off as a very keen Nessie enthusiast but was now more interested in working out what the famous sightings actually were. He had become a sceptic.

'Age is a great rationalizer,' he said, chuckling.

Looking around the shop, however, it was clear that he was making a great living from Nessie, whether or not it existed.

The family was getting restless again and complaining that they were hungry. I sighed and said goodbye to Adrian before getting back into the family wagon. We drove past Urquhart Castle, a beautiful ruin that sits on the shores of the loch. This was the setting of the famous 'humps' photo taken by Peter MacNab in 1955. I'd read a book called *The Loch Ness Story*, written – surprisingly – by BBC reporter and Nessie enthusiast Nicholas Witchell. He's probably best known for remarks Prince Charles made about him, having forgotten he had a microphone on: 'I can't bear that man. I mean, he's so awful, he really is . . .'

Witchell was and is firmly convinced of Nessie's existence. He had MacNab's account of the moment the photo was taken.

I was returning from a holiday in the north with my son and pulled the car up on the road just above Urquhart Castle. It was a calm, warm, hazy afternoon. I was all ready to take a shot of Urquhart Castle when my attention was held by a movement in the calm water over to the left. Naturally I thought of the 'Monster' and hurriedly changed over the standard lens of my Exacta (127) camera to a six-inch telephoto.

As I was doing so a quick glance showed that some black or dark enormous water creature was cruising on the surface. Without a tripod and in a great hurry I took the shot. I also took a very quick shot with another camera, a fixed-focus Kodak, before the creature submerged.

I remembered seeing that photograph when I was a kid. I tried to tell my kids about it but they needed food and were not in the slightest bit interested. We continued on until we reached the end of the loch at Fort Augustus. We parked up and went to the Bothy for lunch. I ordered haggis and felt like a bit of a tourist but I didn't care. I genuinely love haggis and have it as often as I can. My kids asked me what was in it and I started to try to explain but they looked properly ill so I stopped. Do Scots really eat haggis? From what I saw in Inverness, the national diet seems to be chips and curry sauce washed down with a deep-fried Mars Bar and a fag. (This is the moment when, if you're Scottish, you get all angry and put the book down to Tweet some abuse at me – but why do you guys do this? If someone abuses the English, we just laugh it off or invade you . . .)

We left Fort Augustus and drove back to Inverness. The kids were annoyed that we hadn't seen Nessie and wanted to hit the pool. I took a quick look to check that the tattooed Geordie wasn't in the hot tub. It was all clear. I got the kids ready again and took them down. The smell of chlorine was particularly strong but at least there was nobody about. I hopped into the hot tub only to find that it had become a cold tub overnight. Meanwhile the kids jumped into the pool but then got out quickly rubbing their eyes in pain and crying. Somebody had just dumped a vat of chlorine in the water and it was completely un-swimmable. We retreated to our room, giving the brain-dead mullet behind the poolside front desk an evil look that didn't even register.

I tried to book us a restaurant for supper but everywhere was full. I just couldn't understand it: surely Inverness isn't *that* popular? Then I found out that it was Valentine's Day. I was slightly mortified and considered bluffing my way through, as Stacey appeared not to know either. In the end I came clean. Fortunately neither of us are really Valentine's obsessives so it wasn't too much of a disaster. We did, however, have to eat downstairs, alone in the bar. I munched on my distinctly unro-mantic carb fest of chicken balti (mostly potato) with chips and rice. Stuffed, we staggered up to our twin beds that the hotel had so kindly provided for our romantic evening. We ended our Valentine's night propped up in separate beds playing Scrabble together on iPads.

When we'd been driving about I'd spotted a sign advertising

'Nessie Cruises' on the loch, and I'd booked us a passage for the following day. The kids were a little bit worried that Nessie might attack us but everyone eventually agreed to the trip.

The next morning we left Inverness again and headed off towards the loch. On the way Parker asked Siri, the 'brainbox' who lives in my iPhone, whether Nessie exists. Siri was pretty adamant: 'No. The Loch Ness Monster is a mixture of misidentification and hoaxes.'

We caught the eleven o'clock cruise. We'd had two alternatives – a two-hour trip that included a stop-off at Urquhart Castle, or the one-hour 'basic'. We opted for the two-hour version. I was astonished to find that the boat was packed. It was low season but there were maybe a hundred people paying twelve pounds a pop, and there were five trips a day. Somebody was making a hell of a lot of money out of something that probably didn't exist. I looked around us – there were Italians, Russians, Indians, Cockneys, Martians . . .

The cruise kicked off with some God-awful Scottish 'folk' music.

I presumed that this had to be the 'magic' of Bruce Macgregor, as his CD was for sale to anybody suffering from a spot of tone-deafitis. When Bruce had finished, on came a rather unexcited recorded commentary. I wanted to hear all about Nessie and where various sighting had taken place. This, after all, was the only reason people were here. Nobody in Japan woke up in the morning and planned their dream trip to Loch Lomond . . . Well, maybe they did, because they like their whiskey, but you get my point. Everyone round the world has heard of the Loch Ness Monster and this is why they were here.

While the actor hired to read the script told us about what birds we could see on the loch, I drifted off and looked at the boat's depth finder. The water was currently 727 feet deep: that's seriously deep. Parts of Loch Ness are deeper than the North

Sea. I drifted back into consciousness in time to hear the actor get scientific and start telling us about the 'Great Glen', the geological fault that tore right across Scotland. Loch Ness, like the Okanagan, was a glacial trough. Then Bruce Macgregor came back on and several people on board looked close to suicide as they realized that they would be stuck on this hell boat for some time longer.

We went up top on to the open roof, where we listened to the actor, clearly struggling with the dullness of the text, tell us that badgers could be found in the surroundings. Parker and I looked around for lifeboats. Just as it couldn't get any worse, it did. Rod Stewart's 'Sailing' came on.

The only real mention of the monster that had brought us to this loch in the first place was in a series of 'monster toys' available to purchase on board. These monsters, however, were known as 'Jessy' not 'Nessie'. I presumed that someone had bought the copyright to Nessie, but Jessy was not the best alternative. Essentially everybody on board was there looking for a 'Big Jessy'.

As we approached the castle the boat went past it before swinging round to starboard to dock. I looked out of the window and spotted the wake: a curious corkscrew-type affair that looked just like the 'humps' in the Peter MacNab photograph. Curiously it was in almost exactly the same position as it had been in the photo. The rest of the loch was flat calm and our wake did make a very effective set of humps. There was no boat in the Peter MacNab photo but maybe it had disappeared behind the castle, as ours had done? Like almost everything else in the world of monsters . . . I hadn't the foggiest.

We docked at Urquhart Castle and the foreign hordes, who'd never managed its conquest when it was a 'working' castle, offloaded and swamped the place.

I spoke to a man who looked like he was a monster-hunter. I judged this by the fact that he was alone, clearly felt personal hygiene was for scientists and was wearing a T-shirt proclaiming that 'Nessie Exists!'

He told me that that there was an enormous underwater cave under the rock shelf supporting the castle. This, he told me, was where the creatures lived and how they avoided the extensive sonar scans that had raked the loch. Ogopogo was also supposed to live in a cave, under Rattlesnake Island. I told my new friend about this and he whipped out a notebook and started asking me a series of questions. He was writing down my answers in a fairly unintelligible scrawl, his tongue hanging out of his mouth in concentration. He told me that he had several photographs of Nessie that 'nobody has seen'. I asked him why he hadn't shown them to anybody. He told me that he wasn't ready: he was getting all his facts and putting them together into a damning exposé that would blow the story wide open.

'Did you know that, after the first photograph was taken in 1933, the police were ordered by the government to make sure that they stopped anyone attacking the creature?' He looked me straight in the eyes. I admitted that I had not been aware of this fact.

The man smiled. 'I've got lots of facts, I have.'

I asked him if I could have his email to ask him some further questions. He stopped smiling and looked petrified.

'Email? You don't want to use that . . . Ever.' He looked around the boat suspiciously.

'Why ever not?' I asked.

'They track everything I do. They came to my house once and broke in. I fought a man off with a stick. They were from the government.' He was whispering now, clearly concerned that the small Japanese man sitting next to him was one of MI5's top agents. I thanked him for the chat and backed away to the mental safety of my family and we spent the rest of the cruise looking for badgers.

In the car I looked down my list of Nessie contacts. There was one for a guy called Miko who was supposedly the head of the 'Nessie Fan Club'. Not expecting too much from this one, I rang the number and spoke to him. He was very chipper and suggested that we should meet up in the car park of Drumnadrochit.

My family had tired of monster-hunting and wanted to go to the cinema. I dropped them off in Inverness and then drove back to the loch for my meeting with Miko.

I sat in the car park waiting for my contact like some curious Cold War contact. A couple of locals wandered past and stared at me hard, trying to work out if I was a German dogger. Finally a blue car with a Finnish flag on the back pulled in and circled the car park before parking up alongside me. I lowered my window, as did the driver of the blue car. There were two people inside, a man and an elderly woman. The elderly woman looked at me and then asked me if I was Dom. She sounded like Arnold Schwarzenegger's grandmother.

'You var Dum?'

I nodded to indicate that I was indeed 'Dum'.

'Vollow uss please.' The window closed and the blue car slid out of the car park and turned right. I followed and we left the village and then turned right again on to a tiny track that wound its way up the hill that rose above Urquhart Castle. After five minutes or so we came to a stop beside a little white cottage with a fabulous view over the castle and the loch. Miko jumped out of the car and introduced himself. He was Finnish and Arnie's granny was, in fact, his mother. They were both extreme Nessie enthusiasts and happy to talk about anything. A woman called Terry, who was originally from South Carolina, owned the cottage that we were outside. Miko used her place as a location for a couple of webcams that some company in America had provided him with.

The idea was that anyone in the world could control the cameras and scan the loch at any time, creating a non-stop, international team of monster watchers. Unfortunately, despite the webcams having been blessed by a pair of white witches, it seemed that not everybody was as diligent as they should be. Terry had two rather fine-looking sheep that grazed in the field in front of her cottage. These sheep had become something of an online hit with hundreds of people going on the website to watch them do very little. Some people emailed to ask questions about the sheep, while one couple had come all the way over from Germany to meet them.

Miko told me that there was intense rivalry between the different groups of monster-hunters around the loch. Adrian Shriner, the mad professor I'd met earlier, was considered to be the don of the Loch Ness mafia. Shriner's first exhibition was originally called the 'Official Exhibition' and then became 'Loch Ness 2000' before becoming the current 'Loch Ness Experience'. Meanwhile a guy called Donald Skinner opened up another attraction just next door, called the 'Original Monster Exhibition'. This was now called 'Nessieland' after legal threats had been issued for 'passing himself off'.

A monster-hunter who lived on the other side of the Loch had rowed over and daubed 'Shriner is a madman' in orange paint on Urquhart Castle. There had also been incidents of padlocks being put on people's gates and boats being burnt.

'It was a bit of a closed shop when I first got here,' said Miko, looking down dolefully towards Drumnadrochit. He'd actually worked at Shriner's place for a while before breaking off to go solo. I asked him whether they'd ever got any famous Loch Ness enthusiasts while he worked at the exhibition.

'We had Kylie Minogue . . . And the President of Botswana.' Sadly these visits weren't at the same time and history did not record Kylie's views on the monster story.

I drove away from the cottage, having made loose plans to organize some sort of boat hunt during the following couple of days. There was talk of sonar equipment and it all sounded rather exciting. Sadly, when I returned to the hotel it was to find my whole family in full mutiny. They had had their fill of Inverness and wanted to head back south and go home. This put a serious dent in the time I'd wanted to spend around the loch. It was a valuable lesson. Monster-hunting is a lonely business and not the sort of thing you do with a young family. I told them that I would think about their request while I had a relaxing soak in the hot tub.

I had it to myself for about five minutes and was just starting to enjoy it when a young guy and his very fat girlfriend got in. They must have been about seventeen and they totally ignored me; they had eyes only for each other. They sat close together with expressionless faces and it was only after two minutes or so that I noticed that she appeared to be giving him a hand job under the bubbles. That was it. Enough was enough. Nessie would have to wait for another day. It was time to hang up my monster-hunting boots for a while.

Epilogue

The one thing everyone asks me on hearing about my monster-hunting activities is: 'So, do they exist?' The answer, I'm afraid, is still a rather disappointing 'I don't know'. I suppose that this is better than definite proof that they don't?

I think that there is definitely something of quite some size in Lake Okanagan. I know this because I think I saw it with my own eyes. Whether it is Ogopogo or some sort of sturgeon, I know not. The fact that the sightings there go back so far and have been recorded by so many people makes me feel that there must be something 'unknown' in the murky depths. My only hope is that someone will get a photo or some footage while using a decent camera and not suffering from Parkinson's disease. Just thinking about the amount of shaky footage I have viewed online in the last year makes me rather sick.

The Hibagon was always going to be the most 'dodgy' of my hunts and I rather think that this was probably some escaped monkey who happened to be seen at a time coinciding with sightings of creatures like the Yeti and Bigfoot around the world. For some reason 1965–1975 seems to have been an extraordinarily productive time for monster sightings. Maybe it was fashionable? Maybe people had Super 8 cameras for the first time? Who knows? But I am not that convinced about the Hibagon. I was so thrilled, however, to be able to visit Hiroshima and Nagasaki. Before I went to Japan, whenever I thought about these places I pictured scenes of massive destruction and horror. Now I think of them as bustling cities full of life and friendliness, a true testament to the human spirit of survival.

The Congo was the most difficult place that I have ever travelled in, and there is certainly no question that if the Mokèlé-mbèmbé exists then it has chosen one of the most remote and unvisited areas of the world to do it in. The real problem in Africa is to distinguish between reality and mysticism. Tribes talk about things in the spiritual world in exactly the same way as they would something real and earthbound. I think it is likely that something unknown to science exists in these vast wetlands but think it highly unlikely that it is a dinosaur. It seems to me that the creature might be more like a manatee, a sort of hybrid hippo/rhino thing. Who knows what lies in Lake Tele and the surrounding wetlands? Certainly not me after my disastrous trip there. But I hope that someone else makes the trip and can tell me more about it. One piece of advice: don't make a schedule; just go with the flow . . .

I also believe that there is some sort of creature roaming the thick woods of Pacific Coast America. There have been sightings from way back, but what really convinced me was the fact that so many of the people who have seen things are not keen to talk to anyone about them. I'm still not sure about the Patterson/Gimlin film. If it's authentic, then it's the most convincing and astounding piece of footage in cryptozoology. There's something fishy about it, however. Before my trip I hadn't realized that Patterson was an avid Bigfoot hunter. I just thought he was someone who'd stumbled on the creature and happened to have a camera. It just seems too lucky. On the other hand, the location was very remote and you wouldn't have needed to go that far to fake some footage. Sometimes I look at the film and spot a zip down the back. Other times I'm convinced. You'll have to decide for yourselves. I still think about those footprints Richard and I saw, though . . . What made them?

I think the Yeti is possibly the most believable of all the 'monsters' I looked into. The type of people who have reported sightings of footprints or the actual creature tend to be credible, serious types – adventurers and climbers who have no real gain in allowing people to think that they are crazy. I met so many Sherpas who all had the same belief in this creature and expressed zero surprise in regularly hearing the cries or having yaks killed by one. The mundane way in which Mingmar's brother showed me the photos he'd recently taken of footprints was compelling in itself. There's also the sheer inaccessibility of parts of the Himalayas, which makes it very possible, in my view, that something unknown lives there. The skull at the monastery in Khumjung is a puzzle. I have no way of ascertaining whether or not it's real but it certainly looked the part and I like to think that I got within a pane of glass from touching a Yeti.

And, finally, the Loch Ness Monster. Sadly, I don't believe that there is anything in there. I think the loch is too small and has been host to too much proper investigation for something to have remained unrevealed were it there. I'm not just saying this so that I don't have to go back there, promise.

It's been fun being a monster-hunter. I adore travelling anyway but to travel with a sense of purpose, however spurious, is so much more exhilarating. I've met some wonderful people and been to some amazing places. I've also met some real creeps and been to a couple of places I won't ever return to.

Whatever, life is short and the world is wide. Just get out there and go have your own adventures. Me, I fancy a bit of a lie down by a pool somewhere hot with a good book. I wonder what Borneo is like at this time of year . . .